Doing action research in early childhood studies

Doing action research in early childhood studies

A step by step guide

Glenda Mac Naughton and Patrick Hughes

McGraw Hill

Open University Press

Open University Press
McGraw-Hill Education
McGraw-Hill House
Shoppenhangers Road
Maidenhead
Berkshire
England
SL6 2QL

email: enquiries@openup.co.uk
world wide web: www.openup.co.uk

and Two Penn Plaza, New York, NY 10121-2289, USA

First published 2009

A catalogue record of this book is available from the British Library

ISBN13   978 0 335 22862 1 (pb)
         978 0 335 22861 4 (hb)
ISBN10   0 335 22862 3 (pb)
         0 335 22861 5 (hb)

Library of Congress Cataloging-in-Publication Data
CIP data applied for

Typeset by RefineCatch Limited, Bungay, Suffolk
Printed and bound by CPI Group (UK) Ltd, Croydon, CR0 4YY

Fictitious names of companies, products, people, characters and/or data that may
be used herein (in case studies or in examples) are not intended to represent any
real individual, company, product or event.

Contents

PHASE THREE   CREATING CHANGE

Preface

This book aims to encourage, enable and inspire people in the early childhood field to use action research to create professional and social changes in their field. Over the past ten years, Glenda Mac Naughton has worked with several hundred early childhood action researchers, most of whom were new to action research. Patrick Hughes has been involved in several of these projects and he has taught research methods to diverse groups of graduate and undergraduate researchers.

Our experiences of working both with new and with experienced action researchers led us to write this book. We saw the need for a 'how-to' book that addressed the specific issues and challenges that people face when doing action research in the early childhood field. We believe that *Doing Action Research in Early Childhood Studies* meets that need. It uses numerous illustrations and case studies from practice to show how possible, positive and powerful it can be to do action research in early childhood settings. We also felt that this should be more than just a 'how-to' book. We have seen in our work with early childhood professionals that when you offer practical strategies to challenge their thinking and their practice, they grasp them readily as a way to create changes. Further, we have seen that when they grasp the disparate and sometimes difficult ideas that underpin action research, their work grows in rigour, depth and quality and the professional and social changes they create grow in significance.

Doing Action Research in Early Childhood Studies explores some difficult issues associated with action research, including equity, ethics, rigour and validity. It shows that 'truth' can be a tricky idea in research and it shows that there is more than one 'right' way to perform an action research project. We hope the book helps people who seek changes in the early childhood field, whether those are changes in individuals' professional practice or social changes that create greater equity and social justice for all in the early childhood field, including staff, parents and carers, educators and trainers and, of course, young children themselves.

Acknowledgements

This book would not have been possible without the early childhood action researchers whose experiences we draw on throughout the book. We would like to thank them for their efforts to create change in the field and for their generosity in sharing their action research journeys with others through this book. We have met them in action research projects conducted by members and postgraduate students of the Centre for Equity and Innovation in Early Childhood (CEIEC), which is situated in the University of Melbourne's Graduate School of Education. Glenda Mac Naughton is the Director of the CEIEC and Patrick Hughes is a Research Fellow of the CEIEC. We have referred to those action researchers only by pseudonyms in this book, unless they have requested otherwise, in line with the University of Melbourne's Human Research Ethics Committee protocols.

A summary of major projects on which this book draws follows. More detail on the projects can be found on the CEIEC website (http://www.edfac.unimelb.edu.au).

1 *Student engagement: starting with the child, 2005/06 (South Australia)*
   This 18-month project explored what student engagement means in early childhood education and care and how best to enhance it. Participants undertook action research in their services and presented their learning to their local cluster at the end of the project.
2 *Creating and Sustaining Critical Reflection and Innovation in Early Childhood (referred to in this book as the Trembarth Project), 2002/03 (South Australia and Tasmania)*
   This was a retrospective and prospective qualitative study of how teachers working in early childhood programmes take pedagogical decisions. As part of this project, ten early childhood professionals participated in an action research project for six months.
3 *Critical Reflection and Innovation in work with Under Threes (CRIUT), 2001 (Melbourne, Victoria)*
   This project studied how 12 teachers working in programmes with children under three took pedagogical decisions. The project was conducted using an action research model over three months.
4 *Research into Action, 2004 (Tasmania)*
   This report details the learning from three action research projects conducted between 2000 and 2002 in Tasmania. *Partnerships in Literacy*

focused on parent participation in early literacy; *Literacy Journey* mapped children's literacy acquisition; and *Assessing Emerging Literacy* trialled a Literacy Journey map. The Initiatives Based in Schools programme (IBIS) funded all three projects.

5 *RESPECT: Researching Equitable Staff Parent Relations in Early Childhood Today, 2005/06 (Victoria)*
This small-scale Australian investigation explored staff–parent relations in culturally diverse early childhood communities. The City of Melbourne funded the project. Twelve participants undertook small-scale centre-based action research projects over a 12-week period, supported by CEIEC researchers.

6 *Children's Voices and Diversity in Early Childhood Curricula, 2005/06 (Victoria)*
This action research project enabled early childhood educators to build their capacity to listen to and engage children in decision-making, to enact children's rights and to increase their commitment to issues of social justice and equity in early childhood.

7 *Children who Challenge, 2003/4 (Victoria)*
This is a published case study of action research exploring ways to work in early childhood settings with children whom adults found challenging.

The book also draws on action research projects conducted by masters and doctoral students that Glenda Mac Naughton has supervised. We would like to thank Louise Taylor, Millie Olcay, Karina Davis, Kylie Smith and Sheralyn Campbell for their careful, thoughtful and inspiring journeys into action research. Each of them pushed the boundaries of what it means to do action research in early childhood conceptually and practically. If you are looking for inspiration as an action researcher, any one of them is a good starting point. We have drawn on their original studies, as follows:

- Campbell, S. (2001) The description and definition of a justice disposition in young children. Unpublished PhD thesis, the University of Melbourne.
- Davis, K. (2004) Approaches to teaching young children about indigenous Australians. Unpublished PhD thesis, the University of Melbourne.
- Olcay, M. (2007) Exploring the issues and challenges facing educators in honouring children's voices in early childhood curricula. Unpublished Masters thesis, the University of Melbourne.
- Smith, K. (2004) Reconceptualising observation in early childhood settings. Unpublished PhD thesis, the University of Melbourne.

- Taylor, L. (2007) Rethinking professional learning in early childhood. Unpublished PhD thesis, the University of Melbourne.

We would also like to thank the members of the CEIEC team who understood what it meant to be up against the deadlines that this book brought us. The commitment among the team to action research for social change provided a supportive and hopeful intellectual home within which to write a book such as this. A special thanks to Kate Alexander, who is part of the CEIEC team and who did some critical literature searching for us just when we felt that the book would never be finished.

Introduction
The action research cycle

This book is written for students, early childhood practitioners, curriculum advisors, policy officers and managers who are just starting action research. If you are undertaking an action research project as part of a postgraduate qualification, you should find the book helpful, but you will need to consider several issues in greater depth than this book does. For this reason, we have suggested readings and resources for 'Going deeper' at the end of each chapter especially for you.

Introducing action research

Action research is a cyclical process of 'think – do – think' to research and create change. We think about what we do at present, then we do something to create change, then we think again about what we've done and its effects. Our thinking informs our practice; and our practice informs our further thinking. Action researchers call this cyclical process of 'think – do – think' the action research cycle (sometimes referred to as the action research spiral).

Different action researchers differ in detail about the action research cycle, but they all agree broadly that it involves several phases of thinking and doing to create change. Sometimes the phases of the action research cycle may overlap. For example, as you *reflect* to decide what you want to change, you may well start to *plan* how to create that change; and sometimes, you may start your action research in the middle of a phase. Nonetheless, the cycle is still a useful way to summarize the process of change that is action research. Action research that creates meaningful change generally goes through several cycles.

This book takes you step by step through the four phases of the action research cycle. *Figure 1.1 The action research cycle* outlines each phase and its steps. The steps in each phase form the content of the remainder of this book.

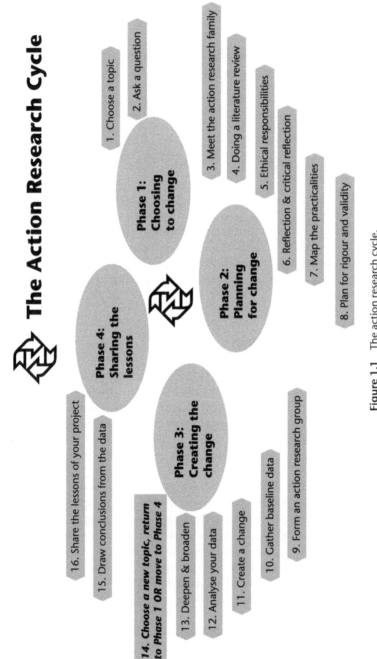

Figure 1.1 The action research cycle.

You'll see differences in the number of steps you need to take when first embarking on action research (your first cycle). Once you are through your first cycle, the steps involved in each cycle reduce and often blur as your change process gains momentum.

PHASE ONE
Choosing to Change

> Somehow the image of bungee jumping seemed to capture the exhilaration,
> excitement and danger we found in action research!
>
> (Campbell et al. 1999: 4)

Action research begins with hopes, dreams and desires. An action researcher
hopes that they can create a change for the better, *dreams* of a better world and
desires to make a difference. Sometimes action research goes just as we planned
it, but sometimes it doesn't. This can excite and inspire us, but it can also
unsettle and scare us.

Sheralyn Campbell used the metaphor of bungee jumping to describe her
first experiences with action research as a doctoral student; and in terms of
that metaphor, she'd just jumped off the platform!

> Action research was a challenge which I initially felt I understood. I
> was asking and investigating a question about how fairness worked
> for children in my theory and practice, and looking for answers or
> confirmation. In terms of 'bungee jumping', it seemed a bit like climb-
> ing that 'bungee ladder' and standing on the platform at the top –
> hoping to see further. After twenty years of working in the early
> childhood field, I felt secure and sure of the knowledge I had – and the
> way I put that knowledge into practice. I guess I thought as a research
> student that the platform at the top of the ladder was what I was
> striving for – answers which provided a nice, certain, safe structure.
> However, what I found was scary! I began to see the contradictory
> effects of my knowledge and practice for children and families. This
> new way of seeing meant that if I was to continue my work for equity,
> I had to rethink everything I knew. At this point, I realised that I had
> to actually jump off that nice, safe, secure bungee platform and begin
> to try to do my praxis differently. However, it was the leap into the
> void that was so exhilarating and heart-stopping. This is why I think

the image of bungee jumping captures the experience, because it was not simply flying or free-falling. My 'jump' was constantly (interrupted) by the flexible cord (which I think of as my past knowledge) that kept pulling me up and stopping me in ways and moments that were unexpected, frustrating and often disheartening. However, it was these necessary pauses that were pivotal in initiating another cycle of critical reflection, which made it possible for me to remember the thrills and pleasure and want to jump again!

(Campbell et al. 1999: 6)

Despite the risk and uncertainty involved in action research, many early childhood professionals choose it because they have hopes, dreams and desires to improve the lives of the children, parents and colleagues with whom they work. Some hope to change their daily practices, some – like Sheralyn – dream of fairer outcomes for the children with whom they work, some may desire to change a policy that isn't working well. Whatever their particular hopes, dreams and desires, action researchers work to improve what they do normally. This brings 'thrills and pleasure' but it can also be 'unexpected, frustrating and often disheartening'. Knowing the 'ups and downs' of action research helps you to understand that – like all social research – action research is not a precise or predictable endeavour because it involves people.

Step 1 gets you ready for the pleasures, thrills and uncertainties of creating change through research done with others. It will help you to plan an action research project that is achievable in your specific circumstances and will guide you through your first cycle of action research. Remember, there are more steps in this cycle than in future cycles as the planning and learning are greater at this point. Most action researchers are keen to start making changes and it's hard to be patient at this point in a project. However, good solid planning provides a more secure foundation for making your first 'jump'.

Step 1 Choose a social practice to change or improve

Page 1

Hey Journal . . . I'm so confused! I have no idea where to start! . . . Research? What? There are so many things to focus on. . . . Where do I start? . . . Do I have a group? . . . What observations do I make? . . . What will my research be used for? . . . And this Journal – is it my personal property or the group's? . . . Who do I turn to during the project? . . . What impact will this research make on the wider community?

(Kari, Transcript from her *Action Research Journal*)

As you start your first action research project you may face many uncertainties, as Kari did. This is not unusual – after all, you are embarking on something you have never done before. Nonetheless, you need to find some certainty in order to take Step 1 in your action research project – choosing a topic to research. As the excerpt from Kari's Journal illustrates, a research topic doesn't necessarily just jump at you. Thus – like Kari – your first step is to find a topic and judge whether it will lend itself to the particular approaches of action research.

Unlike Kari, Lydia embarked on her action research project with a clear idea of what she wanted to investigate and some idea of what action research involves. Consequently, in her first step, Lydia concentrated on refining her research topic:

> I hoped that this project would support me to start to unpack some of the thoughts and issues that I have and provide many opportunities to reflect upon and start to change some of my practices . . . within the classroom in order to create a more genuine space for all stakeholders' voices to be woven throughout the early childhood curriculum.

Before you start to read about Step 1, we advise you to create an *Action Research Journal*. As we take you step by step through the process of doing your action research project, you should note in your Journal your responses to the ideas that you meet and to the tasks that we ask you to perform. (Your Journal could be in whatever form suits you best – a paper notebook, an audio recorder or an electronic journal.)

What you'll need to take Step 1:

Time
- to read this step, to reflect on its content and to complete its two Thinking Boxes;
- to talk with those who will be involved in your project.

Knowledge
- How much choice will you have about the topic of your project?
- Who will be involved and who should be involved in your project?

Other resources
- an *Action Research Journal* in which to record and track your reflections and decisions.

Preparing to take Step 1

In Step 1 of the action research process, you find a topic for your project (action), assess its suitability as an action research topic (reflection) and decide whether you will research it (action). This section of this step guides you through that process. It identifies four characteristics of action research and examines each one in turn. You need to know these characteristics to assess the suitability of your topic as an action research topic. The four characteristics are: (1) an action researcher intends to improve and change their circumstances; (2) improving social practice/s; (3) creating new knowledge about those social practices; and (4) staying relevant to their specific locality.

Improving and changing your circumstances

Each of us tries to make sense of our world by studying it in order to decide how to act in it. We observe our surroundings, think about our observations, act accordingly and then observe whether and to what extent our actions had the effect we intended. By studying and acting in the world in this way, we can understand our place in it and our ability to change it; and this frees us from religious, superstitious or ideological accounts. Studying our world changes our relations with it because it increases our ability to change it. Action researchers study things in order to improve them, so the first step towards becoming an action researcher is to decide what you want to improve. This is the topic of your action research project.

There is no limit to the range of topics you might choose as a starting point for your action research adventure. In early childhood settings, action research can change what you do with children, colleagues, parents and the wider community; it can change how you do it; and it can change how you think about it. For example, you could use action research to improve your relationships with parents by changing how you relate to them day-to-day and how you think about them; or you could use action research to improve gender fairness in children's play with each other by changing what you do around their play and how you think about it. Here's just a small range of topics that the action researchers you'll meet in this book have studied:

- Gender equity
- Anti-bias curriculum
- Student engagement in learning
- Children's voice in the curriculum
- Literacy strategies in the classroom
- Parent and staff relationships
- Documenting children's learning
- Curriculum planning.

Some simple brainstorming yourself or with others is a simple way to find your topic or to make it more specific. For instance, Lillith and Sandy (*Student engagement: starting with the child* project) were interested in how to improve boys' engagement in learning in their preschool setting. They had each noticed how boys were using two new – higher – tables that the centre had just bought. They were curious about 'why the construction sets have been so popular at these tables' and they 'brainstormed' possible answers. This was the result of their brainstorming:

> The tables were attractive and colourful – bright yellow and red (all the other tables in the centre are light blue, green and white).
> Children looked comfortable (at them).
> They were new.
> It was different having construction on a table and perhaps more inviting – at their eye level.
> One had the feeling that they were surrounded by the equipment due to the indents* in the table.
> The shape – enabled children easier reach, gave them a space (or designated area) that others seemed to respect. (Sometimes when on the floor, other walked into that space and it was easier to knock another child's creation down.)
>
> * The new tables were circular, with areas cut out of the perimeter for a child to sit *in*.

From this brainstorming, they decided to refine their focus on boys' engagement by researching how changing specific aspects of the physical environment influenced boys' engagement in learning. Sarah Henroid and her colleagues also used brainstorming to refine the focus of their action research on parent participation:

> Collectively (teachers and research associate), we identified an issue that we felt was significantly important. We discussed how parental participation looks in our centre and described processes we were engaging in to promote it. We then reflected on our current practices, and brainstormed ideas on how we could present more opportunities for parent participation and involvement in the programme.
>
> (Sarah Henroid, in Meade, Ryder and Henroid 2004: online)

Improving social practice/s

Action researchers improve their practice (what they do) both by changing their practice *and* by finding new ways to think about it. In this way, action research increases our understanding of what we do and why we do it (McTaggart, 1992). Against that background, the topic of your action research project should allow you to improve social practices by changing them and to create new knowledge about those social practices.

Social practices are actions whose meaning depends not just on our intentions ('This is what I intend this action to mean'), but also on how other people understand them ('This is what I think your action means'). There are different sorts of social practices, but they have some things in common, as you'll see in the three instances that follow.

Rituals

A ritual is a social practice because it is an action (or a set of actions) that we perform repeatedly *according to an established formula*. Its meaning or significance depends partly on our intention in performing it, but also – and more importantly – it depends on other people knowing the formula underlying it. A wedding, starting school and the opening of parliament are rituals: we all know the formula underlying each one, we expect it to be followed and any deviation from that formula takes away the meaning of the ritual. (Is a wedding still a wedding if only one person is getting married? Can someone start school at 98? Would we be watching the opening of parliament if MPs were dancing and wearing fancy dress?) Early years rituals vary from one context to another. In some early years settings there may be rituals (established formulae) about starting and ending the day, coming together for a story or singing, eating, sleeping, gardening or going on visits.

Customs

A custom is a social practice because it is an action (or a set of actions) that we perform repeatedly *at a specific time or on a specific occasion*. Its meaning or significance depends partly on our intention in performing it, but also – and more importantly – it depends on other people recognizing that we are doing so at a specific time or on a specific occasion. For example, marking birthdays by giving presents, marking specific festivals with specific meals and awarding degrees in graduation ceremonies are customs: we all recognize that each one is happening at a specific time and we expect certain actions to follow. We would probably regard any other, unexpected actions performed at that time as 'wrong' or meaningless. (Would a gift still be a birthday present if we gave it six months early? Would a party mark someone's coming-of-age if it happened two years earlier? Would a student graduate if they were awarded their degree a year before they finished their course?) In early years settings, customs (things we perform repeatedly at a specific time or on a specific occasion) also vary from setting to setting but it is likely that annual customs will develop around celebrations such as birthdays, outings and specific festivals.

Conventions

A convention is a social practice because it is an action (or a set of actions) that we perform repeatedly *to conform to particular rules or regulations of conduct*. Its meaning or significance depends partly on our intention in performing it, but also – and more importantly – it depends on other people recognizing that we are doing so to conform to a rule or regulation of conduct. For example, announcing bad news without smiling, taking turns in a conversation and working hard to succeed are conventions: we all know the rule or regulation of conduct underlying each one and we expect it to be followed. We regard any-one who behaves otherwise as . . . well . . . unconventional. There are many rules of conduct that appear in early childhood settings. Rules may exist about the use of equipment, children's use of toys from home, sharing, what hap-pens when some is hurt or crying, talking at group time or how to behave in a particular area (e.g. not throwing sand in the sandpit).

The rituals, customs and conventions through which we relate to young children, to their parents and to our colleagues are all social practices, i.e. their meaning depends just as much on how children, parents and colleagues understand them as they do on our intentions in performing them. That inter-action between our intentions and others' understandings of our actions means that an individual can't change the meaning of their behaviour uni-laterally by saying, 'It means this now.' Instead, the meaning of an action changes only if and when there is general agreement to it. However, we *can* change the meaning of a social practice – we can choose to break our habits, customs and conventions and to do them differently. Action research is a way to change social practices. For Elsie, the conventions associated with the 'babies' room' were causing problems for her. She wrote in her *Action Research Journal* (*Critical Reflection and Innovation in work with Under Threes (CRIUT)* project):

> At the moment the babies' room is so busy that I feel I do not get a chance to spend <u>time</u> with the children. . . . It is all routines – 10 different ones each day and no time (to) extend their learning. We do extend their learning with routines, etc. but not the way I feel I want to, e.g. extend on their play. Children learn from routines as well, but I want to sit down with each one – at least for five minutes with each child, not only with routines.

Elsie's problems with the conventions in the babies' room became the social practices that she chose to change through an action research project.

Creating new knowledge

Action research can change our knowledge about what we research because it can make us question what we know and do at present and, indeed, it can shake our faith in what we know and/or in what we do. Action research can also change how we think about things because it generally raises more questions than it answers. This means it helps us to think differently. New knowledge is created when we come to understand the world differently from how we understood it before.

From the start of her project, Elsie wanted to create new knowledge. She was part of an action research project entitled, 'Pedagogical problem-solving and innovation in programmes for children under three'; and for her, 'innovation' in how she thought about what she did was as important as changing things in practice. Action research was a way for 'seeing different views, opening new doors; being flexible, trying new ideas'.

Staying relevant to your specific locality

It's important that the topic you choose for your action research project is relevant to your locality. It has to meet not only your needs and interests but also the needs and interests of others in your context. Depending on your specific locality, this may include your project supervisor or critical friend, your colleagues, your co-researchers, the children and families you work with or your employing and/or funding organization. You should talk to those involved in your project *before* you decide your final project. They may have reservations and/or suggestions that will help you to ensure that your topic is suitable for the locality in which you are conducting your research and that it achieves the purposes you intend it to.

If your project is being assessed as part of a formal course of study, it is especially important to talk to your supervisor or advisor early in the process to ensure that your topic is appropriate and acceptable to the course in which you are enrolled.

In summary: you will be more or less free to choose your topic, depending on your specific circumstances. To illustrate this, consider the circumstances of Lynne, Terry and Sabena. Each of them is more or less free to choose their topic, because each occupies a specific position in the early childhood field.

- *Lynne is an undergraduate student researcher.* She is studying for a degree in early childhood studies and has just begun a new subject – 'Children as social learners'. This subject requires her to do an action research project to improve her capacity to support children's skills in solving social problems.
- *Terry is an early childhood practitioner researcher.* He has just been to a conference on children's rights with two of his colleagues. The conference inspired them to rethink children's participation in decisions about curriculum. They have decided to do an action research project on this topic as part of their professional growth and learning.
- *Sabena is a school curriculum leader researcher.* She has just been asked to lead an action research project – funded by central government – in her school district to improve indigenous children's literacy. Sabena can't change the research topic but participants in the project can choose specific questions about the topic that catch their interest.

'Niggles, norms and nevers'

Brainstorming – by yourself or with others – can help you to find your research topic. This process works whether you are free to choose your topic for yourself or have a topic imposed on you. Glenda has helped people to choose a research topic by using a four-part brainstorming process she calls 'Niggles, norms and nevers'.

- *Part One.* Identify the social practices (rituals, customs or conventions) that *niggle* you (in your current work or in the research topic you have been given) that you know something about but you'd like to know more.
- *Part Two.* Identify what you do *normally* about this niggling social practice and what you would like to be different.
- *Part Three.* Identify what you would *never* do about your 'niggle' and what you would like to change.
- *Part Four.* Identify the most interesting and meaningful way to resolve your 'niggle' through an action research project and suggest a research topic.

At the end of this process, you should be able to complete *Thinking Box 1.1 Finding a topic: my niggles, norms and nevers*. Note the results in your *Action Research Journal*.

Thinking Box 1.1 Finding a topic: my niggles, norms and nevers	
Social practices (broad or specific) that niggle me	
1 2 3 etc. Which one is the most important to me?	
What *niggles* me about this practice is	I would like to know more about . . . .
What I *normally* do about this 'niggle' is	What I hope, dream and desire could be different is . . . .
What I *never* do about this 'niggle' is	What I would like to change is . . . .
The most interesting and meaningful way to resolve my 'niggle' through an action research project would be	My action research topic will be . . . .

One instance of how to use 'Niggles, norms and nevers' to decide a research topic focus comes from a collaborative action research project about staff–parent relationships in Victoria, Australia (*RESPECT: Researching Equitable Staff Parent Relations in Early Childhood Today* project). Ainslie was a member of this project. In deciding on her specific topic, Ainslie reflected on what she *normally* does with parents, what she *never* does with parents and what *niggles* arise from this. She wrote about her struggles in her *Action Research Journal*, from which these excerpts are taken:

> (Norms) Always acknowledge them when they enter the room or the centre – ask for any messages and/or changes in routines. Be interested in them, as well as in their children. Document or acknow-

ledge concerns. Invite parents to be involved in planning for their child.

(Nevers) Never suffocate or rush the parent or the child; always suggest, 'When you are ready to leave, I will take your child'. . . . Never rude, although you may not agree. . . . Never discuss my personal life (but share some life experiences). . . . Never offer unwelcome advice.

(Niggles) When I am busy and a parent just wants to talk. . . . When a parent repeats the 'same same' and being patient to listen to the same thing over and over. . . . (They) don't want their child to get wet or dirty, but they don't offer a change of clothes. . . . Parents just want to hear good things (about their child).

Reflecting on those niggles, norms and nevers, Ainslie decided to improve staff–parent communication through her action research project.

Assessing your topic's suitability as an action research topic

You have identified a topic for your project, but are you sure that it is suitable for an *action research* project? It may well be more appropriate for a different kind of research and you don't want to realize this once you've started. Remember: an action researcher intends to improve and change their circumstances by improving social practice/s, creating new knowledge about those social practices and staying relevant to their specific locality. *Thinking Box 1.2 Assessing the suitability of my research topic* helps you to assess the suitability of your research topic. You might like to complete this by yourself or with your co-researchers or project advisors. Note the results in your *Action Research Journal*.

Thinking Box 1.2 Assessing the suitability of my research topic			
In my early years work, I would like to improve the following:			
This is associated with these rituals, customs or conventions:			
My proposed research topic is:			
My proposed research topic is suitable for action research because its foci are:			
Improving and changing my circumstances	It can improve . . . (list)	It can change . . . (list)	

Improving social practices	It will focus on these rituals:	It will focus on these customs:	It will focus on these conventions:
Creating new knowledge	It will create new knowledge about . . . (list)		
Relevant to my locality	My supervisor and/or critical friend agrees with my topic	My co-researchers (e.g. colleagues, children, parents) agree with my topic	People and organizations(s) involved (e.g. colleagues, children, parents, school, local government, centre) agree with my topic

Taking Step 1: a case from practice

Sharon was an early childhood literacy advisor in South Eastern Australia. She joined a research project exploring how early childhood professionals create and sustain critical reflection in their work (the *Trembarth* project). Each participant in this project was asked to develop their own mini-action research project. Sharon came to the first meeting of the group with no idea what the focus of her project would be. However, when she was asked, 'What niggles you in your current work?', Sharon found her focus quickly! She wrote about this process in her *Action Research Journal*:

> What niggles?
> That teachers in their developing understandings about critical literacy or role of a text analyst see it as being a separate part of the literacy curriculum or a special unit of work.
> That many teachers view children's interests in popular culture as being not appropriate texts for students to engage in.
> That teachers view literacy as the development of knowledge and skills, rather than empowerment of students to interact with a wide range of texts in different settings.
> That teachers feel that they don't have confidence to deal with social justice issues for fear of offending someone.
> I find critical reflection difficult to do well on my own → unless I have a framework or series of questions to use to guide my reflection.

Sharon combined her niggles about critical reflection, social justice and literacy to create what she called her 'focus area'. She wrote about this in her *Action Research Journal*:

> I would like to be able to develop a framework to support teachers in engaging in critical reflection in relation to their literacy programmes and the issues of equity, gender and race.
>
> . . . I haven't got a clear notion of my question yet, more a focus area.

At that time Sharon didn't have access to *Thinking Box 1.2* to help her to assess the suitability of her topic for action research. However, with Sharon's permission we have drawn on her research journal and field notes from the project to complete it so that we illustrate it in action.

Sharon's' Thinking Box 1.2   Assessing the suitability of my research topic on literacy

In my early years work, I would like to improve the following: *How teachers critically reflect on social justice issues in their literacy programmes.*

This is associated with these rituals, customs or conventions: *Conventions of how literacy is taught, the issues that should be included in a literacy programme and the texts that are considered appropriate to use.*

My proposed research topic is: *Teacher reflection on social justice issues in literacy programmes.*

My proposed research topic is suitable for action research because its foci are:

Improving and changing my circumstances	It can improve *how social justice issues are addressed and understood in early literacy teaching*	It can change *the ways in which teachers think about their literacy texts.* *How I work with teachers on literacy in the district.* *How I understand my role as a literacy advisor.* *My own knowledge of critical reflection.*	

Improving social practices	It will focus on these rituals:	It will focus on these customs:	It will focus on these conventions:
Creating new knowledge	It will create new knowledge about *how teachers can improve the relevance of their literacy practices for boys and for indigenous students.*		*Conventional texts in early childhood literacy. Conventional ideas about what literacy is. Conventional ideas about the place of social justice issues in literacy teaching.*
Relevant to my locality *It links directly to my role at present and to what I have seen in the field as an issue that needs to be addressed to improve the relevance of literacy teaching for marginalized groups in the area.*	My supervisor and/or critical friend agrees with my topic *I have shared this topic in the research group and checked its focus is relevant to the project.*	My co-researchers (e.g. colleagues, children, parents) agree with my topic *I have not yet talked with the teachers I am working with, but I will need to do this.*	People and organizations(s) involved (e.g. colleagues, children, parents, school, local government, centre) agree with my topic. *I will need to share and agree my topic with the schools that I am conducting literacy Professional Development for.*

Taking your first step: your actions and reflections

If you have completed *Thinking Boxes* 1.1 and 1.2 in this step, you should now be in a position to decide what your topic is and to note it in your journal. If you are still uncertain about your topic, visit the 'Going deeper' resources (below) and then complete the *Thinking Boxes* again. Note your decision in your *Action Research Journal*.

Further resources: going deeper

In print

Crosser, S. (2005) *What Do We Know about Early Childhood Education?: Research Based Practice*. Thompson Delmar Publishing Clifton Park, NY.

Online

Classroom Action Research is a free access site provided by the Madison Metropolitan School District in the USA. It houses over 500 teacher action research abstracts and papers and its searchable database of classroom action research reports shows the diverse range of topics that by teachers in the district have explored. Available at: http://www.madison.k12.wi.us/sod/car/search.cgi

Meade, A., Ryder, D. and Henroid, S. (2004) Promoting dialogue in early childhood education centres of innovation, Keynote Address to New Zealand Action Research Network Conference, 8/9 July, Christchurch, NZ. Available at: http://www.minedu.govt.nz/index.cfm?layout=document&documentid=9850

Step 2 Ask a question about your chosen social practice

How ~~might~~ ^{do} I ~~rethink~~ ^{revise} my practices regarding giving children a voice, ~~to involve them in the curriculum~~ ~~more~~/to encourage their engagement in the curriculum more?

How do we ~~rethink~~ ^{re-examine} encouraging children's participation, to allow for ~~further~~ ^{increased} engagement in the curriculum?

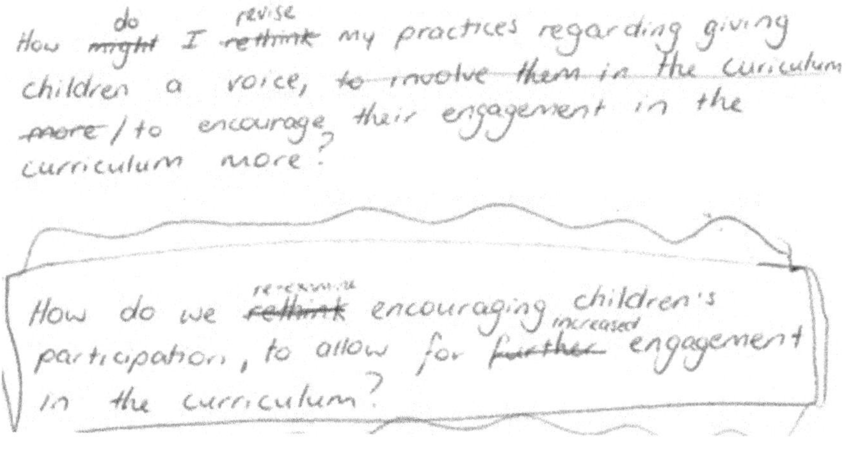

Figure 2.1   Rose's Action Research Journal: 3.

Step 2 in your action research project is to turn your research topic – your chosen social practice – into a research question. This might sound straight-forward – just put 'How do?', 'Is it?' or 'Does it?' in front of your topic! How-ever, as page 3 of Rose's *Action Research Journal* (*Student Engagement – Starting with the Child* project) shows, creating a workable action research question can often be demanding. It can be a struggle to find the right words for your question and to phrase your question in a way that makes sense to you. Indeed, Rose tried six times before she formulated a question with which she was satisfied: 'How do we re-examine encouraging children's participation, to allow for increased engagement in the curriculum?'. After your first action research cycle your question may change and you may need to revisit this Step to ensure your new question(s) are sound action research questions.

What you'll need to take Step 2:

Time
- to read this step, to reflect on its content and to complete its three *Thinking Boxes*;
- to talk with those who will be involved in your project;
- to talk to colleagues and friends about your key terms.

Knowledge
- What resources will you have to answer your action research question?
- Will you have the information you need to answer your action research question?

Preparing to take Step 2

In Step 2 of the action research process, you turn your research topic – your chosen social practice – into an action research question (action), assess its suitability as an action research question (reflection) and decide whether you will make it the focus of your action research project (action).

Asking an action research question

Your action research question should concern change. Action researchers create changes in practice and in how we think about practice; and then they (you!) share that new knowledge with a wider community. A good and practicable action research question directs what you do and reminds you what you intended to do.

Asking an action research question is both a skill and an art. When you first develop a question you need to ask yourself, 'Will answering *this* question about my research topic tell me what I want to know about it, or should I ask a different question about it?' This might seem obvious: 'Of course I know what my question is. That's why I want to do the research!' Finding a practicable action research question can be a frustrating struggle, but the time required to find one is time well spent.

To start to find your question, ask yourself what you would like to be different about your current social practices. Indeed, you have begun this already, when you found your research topic. Recall your hopes, dreams and desires and use them to ask 'What could be different?' and 'How could it be different?' Bring your hopes, dreams and desires to life by asking, 'What if . . .?'. To help with this, try to complete each sentence in *Thinking Box 2.1 Generating research questions.*

Thinking Box 2.1 Generating research questions		
The social practice that I wish to improve	The questions associated with my chosen social practice	My ranking of these questions in order of importance to me
	'What if . . .?'	
	'What else could happen . . .?'	
	'Why can't we . . .?'	
	'How could X be different?'	
	Other/s	

What is a good action research question?

Good action research questions are:

- change-oriented
- inquiry-friendly
- knowledge-generating
- ethical
- manageable.

Change-oriented questions

Here are some examples of general, change-oriented research questions:

- What else is possible in this situation?
- What should be done differently in this situation?
- What are the gaps between where we are now and where we want to be?

(Cherry 1999)

Here are some examples of change-oriented research questions that are specific to early childhood settings:

- How can we share information about children between services differently?
- How can we reform our assessment of children's learning so that we can share our knowledge with other services?
- How can we expand our ways of sharing knowledge about children?

- How can we learn more about each others' approaches to learning and assessment?

Inquiry-friendly questions

A good action research question leads you to inquire and to think openly. To decide whether your research question will lead you to do this, ask yourself:

- Will my research question shake my faith in what I know and/or in what I can do?
- Will it make me feel that I don't know it all?
- Will it help me to challenge my existing knowledge and practices?
- Will it raise more questions than it answers?
- Will it encourage me to keep exploring?
- Will it encourage me to collect evidence about what is happening?
- Will it inspire me to keep learning and to inquire further?

Knowledge-generating questions

Action research creates not just change in current practices, but also new knowledge about those practices. If you are doing action research as part of an academic programme of study, your question should generate new theoretical and/or methodological knowledge, together with new knowledge about practice. To decide whether your research question will generate new knowledge, ask yourself:

- Will my research question lead me to discover something really new?
- Will it help others to learn something new about teaching and learning?

Ethical questions

Action research questions, like all research questions, should be ethical. They should not involve secrecy or subterfuge and they should not undermine people's rights. In Step 5, you will learn more about the ethical issues associated with action research, so for now, to decide whether your research question is ethically sound, ask yourself:

- Would I be comfortable discussing my research question with people who are implicated in it or who are likely to be affected by it (e.g. children, colleagues, parents)?
- Does my question allow people who are affected by it to have a say in what happens to them?

Manageable questions

Action research questions, like all research questions, should be ones that you can manage to explore, given your resources and constraints. To decide whether your research question is manageable, ask yourself:

- Will my research question maintain my current interest in it over time?
- Can I manage to address it with my current resources (including time)?
- Can I find the information I will need to address it in my daily work?

Here is an example from an early childhood setting of a good action research question.

Earlier, you saw Rose refining the focus of her research question until she felt that she had a good one: 'How do we re-examine encouraging children's participation, to allow for increased engagement in the curriculum?' Do you think that Rose's question is a good action research question?

How can I form a good action research question?

Action researchers ask all sorts of research questions, of course, so there is no formula with which to form a good research question. However, here are a few devices that have helped other action researchers.

- Brainstorm with key terms.
- Use 're-' words to keep your focus on inquiry and change.
- Use 'if' and 'how' to raise possibilities and address practicalities.
- Use 'p's to generate knowledge.
- Check that your question is manageable.
- Check that your question is practicable.
- Check that your question is meaningful.

Brainstorm with key terms

As you prepare to formulate your action research question, list all the 'key terms' (sometimes called – incorrectly – 'keywords') that you can associate with your research topic – your chosen social practice. Key terms are 'key' in two ways: they are essential to any definition of your research topic; and they are the words that are generally used in 'professional conversations' about your research topic. To help you to list your key terms, you might ask colleagues and friends what terms come to their mind when they hear your research topic.

To create research questions, combine each of your key terms with, 'Who?', 'What?', 'When?', 'Where?', 'Why?' and 'How?'. Keep a note in your *Action*

Research Journal of the questions you create, then work your way through our tips (below) and note your responses to them, too. *Thinking Box 2.2 Brainstorming with key terms – an example* shows how this could work in a project concerning parents' participation in planning and evaluating a programme; you can, of course, replace the key terms with your own.

Thinking Box 2.2 Brainstorming with key terms – an example				
	KEY TERMS			
	Parents	Participation	Programme	(Etc.)
Who?				
What?				
When?				
Where?				
Why?				
How?				

The Tasmanian government ran a collaborative action research project called, 'Assessing Emerging Literacy'. Participants brainstormed with their key terms (as in *Thinking Box 2.2*) and generated these questions:

- How can we reconceptualize our understanding of what children know and can do in early literacy?
- In which contexts do children demonstrate literacy?
- How can we find out more about what children know and can do?
- What new forms of assessing reveal most about what children know?
- What can teachers, carers and parents do to enhance literacy learning?
  (Department of Education 2004: 18)

Use 're-' words to keep your focus on inquiry and change
The prefix 're' means to do something again or anew, so use 're' words in your question to keep your focus on inquiry and change. Avoid questions that just describe what exists. Once you have used a 're' word in your question, check whether it addresses the issue that you want to change and, if it doesn't, refine it until it does.

- Some suitable 're' words: re-examine, reinvent, rethink, reconceptualize, re-imagine, refine, refresh, reform, rebuild, reconstruct, revise, remodel, regenerate, revisit.

- Some examples of 're' questions:
  - How could we *reconstruct* our reports on children's learning so that they are meaningful to other services?
  - How could we *reinvent* our programme to give children greater continuity of learning between the child care and preschool sectors?

Use 'if' and 'how' to raise possibilities and address practicalities

'If . . .' raises possibilities and 'How' addresses the practicalities. The combination can be a great help in structuring your question, as Riel explains:

> Good questions often arise from visions of improved practice and (from) emerging theories about the change that will move the researcher closer to the ideal state of working practices. When stated in an if/then format, they can take the shape of a research hypothesis. If I [insert the action to be taken], how will it affect [describe one or more possible consequences of the action]?
>
> (Riel 2007: online)

- Some examples of 'if' questions:
  - *If* we opened thirty minutes later, who would benefit and who would be disadvantaged?
  - *If* we allowed children to do as they pleased, would they become more or less respectful of each other?

Use 'p's to generate knowledge

Questions that generate new knowledge are ones to which you don't already know the answer; and they rarely have simple 'yes' or 'no' answers. They are questions that ask you to think about the relationships between four 'p's: people, problems, phenomena and programmes. Thus:

- *People* are those with whom you work, including children, colleagues and parents.
- *Problems* are the things you want to change (your 'niggles'), together with your hopes, dreams and desires to resolve them in particular ways.
- *Phenomena* are the facts, relationships and experiences that make up your practice or other people's practice.
- *Programmes* are your plans to achieve something in your work with children and their families, together with the specific resources (e.g. tools, rituals, routines and curriculum) with which you implement your plans.

A good knowledge-generating action research question will explore relationships between at least two of the 'p's. For example, 'How can I reconceptualize play outdoors to increase girls' safety when they play in the sandpit?' explores relationships between all four 'p's:

> How can *I* (people) reconceptualize *play outdoors* (programme) to improve *girls' safety* (problem) when they *play in the sandpit* (phenomenon)?

Check that your question is manageable

Every researcher has to balance what they *want* to research against what they *can* research. That's not always an easy balance to strike. You may think that if your research topic genuinely interests you and if you work hard enough in researching it, then success is guaranteed. However, before you decide to embark on your action research adventure, consider these two questions carefully and be realistic in answering them:

- Will I have sufficient time to complete all the work required?
- Will I have *sufficient* access to the *appropriate* research data (in whatever form) that I will need?

Check that your question is practicable

It is easier to decide if your research question is manageable if you can be sure that it is practicable. Often, draft research questions are too broad, too narrow, too vague or too complex.

- Too broad? You need to be sure that you ask a question that is within your reach. Do you have the resources required to answer your question?

  This is too broad:

  > *How can I improve outcomes for children from ethnic minority families?*
  > Can you – acting alone – improve outcomes for *all* children in *every* ethnic minority . . . in the country? In the world? Do you *know* their current outcomes? Can you improve *all* outcomes – educational, social, economic, etc.?

  This is better:

  > *Does my current practice disadvantage the children from ethnic minorities who attend this centre?*

- Too narrow? Action researchers generally ask questions about their local circumstances and they are very cautious about applying the results of their project in other circumstances. Nonetheless, try to ask a question that is sufficiently broad to resonate with other early childhood practitioners, even though their experiences will be different to a degree from yours.
  This is too narrow:

    How can I get Billy to participate more in outdoor play?
    Does Billy have characteristics in common with any other children? Is participation in outdoor play an issue for any other children besides Billy?

  This is better:

    What factors affect children's participation in outdoor play at our centre?

- Too vague? Your question needs to state as clearly as possible just what you intend to investigate, how you will investigate it and who will be involved. You shouldn't have to ask further questions to clarify the meaning of your research question!
  This is too vague:

    How do administrative structures affect a child's self-image?
    What are 'administrative structures'? Are they the same as organizational structures, or administrative routines, or administrative procedures? Who is 'a child'? Are you referring to *every* child? How do you discover a child's self-image?

  This is better:

    How can we gather background information about children and their family in ways that make them feel they are part of a bigger family here at this centre?

- Too complex? The more complex your question, the harder it will be to answer – or even to know if you've answered it. Of course, life in an early childhood setting is complex; but if you focus too closely on the complexities, you risk losing sight of the 'big picture' that is the context of those complexities.

This is too complex:

> *How does a parent's age, gender, occupation and home location affect the nature and extent of their involvement in our centre; and how can we take each factor into account in planning our parent involvement programmes?* Where to start?! Answering this question will require you to conduct intensive (intrusive?) interviews with each parent at your centre, track their involvement in the centre, match each parent's involvement with each of your four factors, analyse the results, then use those results as the basis for a new – and very complex – parent involvement programme!

This is better:

> *What factors determine whether and to what extent a parent becomes involved with our centre?*

Here's an example of an action researcher refining her question ruthlessly to ensure that it is practicable. You'll see that Sue's first draft isn't even a question – it's an ambition. Her second draft, however, is much more to the point:

> First draft: 'To reconceptualize the style, type and variety of display options available to (our programme) through actively engaging the children, staff, and parents to regenerate (our programme) into the school/local community area through displays.'

> Second draft: 'How can the inclusion of children's voices help us reconceptualize our programme?

Check that your question is meaningful

This is a little more complex than it appears. It's important that your question and how you frame it make sense to you. To ensure this, use a reputable dictionary (or even two) to define the key terms in your question. Then use a thesaurus to compare and contrast the different meanings of a word. Only when you have done this should you decide that your question makes sense to you *and* that you can explain it to other people who may not have given it as much thought. *Thinking Box 2.3 Checking meanings* will help you to do this.

Thinking Box 2.3 Checking meanings	
Questions	Answers
What are the key terms in my research question?	1 . . . . 2 . . . . 3 . . . . Etc.
What does each of my key terms mean?	1 . . . . 2 . . . . 3 . . . . Etc.

Some action research questions to avoid

Try to avoid questions that merely recreate existing knowledge, rather than generating new knowledge. (Riel 2007) identified three types of questions to avoid in action research projects because they don't generate new knowledge.

1   *Questions to which the answer is known.* Try to avoid questions to which the answer is known, but the aim is to demonstrate it to others. For example, if you have been holding 'family maths nights' for years and have seen that they increase parent participation, avoid asking 'Do "family maths nights" increase parent participation?' merely to demonstrate to others what you know already.

2   *Questions to which the answer is 'yes' or 'no'.* Generally, such questions will prevent you from studying the many nuances of your specific early childhood setting and the interactions that happen there. Try to transform such a question into a more fruitful one. For example: 'Will introducing project-based learning increase student engagement?' can be answered 'yes' or 'no'. In contrast, 'How will introducing project-based learning affect student engagement in my classroom?' suggests that you look for the aspect/s of project-based learning (e.g. ownership, collaboration, self-assessment) that seems to increase student engagement.

3   *Questions to which the answer is in the literature.* Questions that you can answer by reading the literature do not generate new knowledge

– they merely explore existing knowledge. For example, the answer to 'What does "community of practice" mean?' can be found readily in the literature on action research. Try to transform such a question into a more fruitful one. For example: 'How will increasing the time for teacher collaboration in grade level teams affect the development of a community of practice at our school?'

Evaluating your action research question

You should start to plan your action research project in detail ONLY when you can convince not just yourself but also someone who is more detached from the idea (e.g. your supervisor, your immediate manager) that you can confidently answer 'Yes' to each question in *Thinking Box 2.4 Evaluating your action research question*.

Thinking Box 2.4 Evaluating your action research question		
IS MY QUESTION A 'GOOD' ACTION RESEARCH QUESTION?		YES/NO
IS IT . . .	change-oriented?	
	inquiry-friendly?	
	manageable?	
	knowledge-generating?	
	ethical?	
	meaningful	
DID I USE . . .	're-' words?	
	'if' and 'how'?	
	'p's to generate knowledge?	
DID I AVOID . . .	questions to which the answer is known?	
	questions to which the answer is 'yes' or 'no'?	
	questions to which the answer is in the literature?	

A group of action researchers in South Australia was curious about whether and how gender influences children's engagement in an out-of-school-hours programme. They generated these questions:

- How does gender influence engagement in the out-of-school-hours programme?
- How do we revise/re-examine our practices regarding gender in a pre-school setting?
- How does gender influence children's engagement in the outdoor environment?
- How does gender influence engagement in the out-of-school-hours programme (in five core areas across the service)?

Choose *one* of their questions and decide whether it meets some or all of this step's criteria of a good action research question.

Taking Step 2: a case from practice

The excerpt from Rose's *Action Research Journal* at the beginning of this step showed that it can take several attempts before you formulate a satisfactory action research question. Rose worked hard to form a good action research question, as we can see in the following sequence of excerpts from her *Action Research Journal*. The excerpts include elements that Rose crossed out as she refined her research focus. On Page One, her first draft of a question begins 'Does . . .' This requires a 'Yes' or 'No', so it doesn't focus on teachers creating change. Her second draft – 'How can we . . .' directs attention to change, but it is a very broad question. By Page Three, Rose is incorporating 're' words into her 'How' questions, with the result that she begins to get a tighter focus on a specific way to improve children's engagement – changing their participation in curriculum decision-making.

> Page One
> 'Does children having choices and taking responsibility for their own learning encourage more participation in curriculum?'
> 'How can we engage children in play (their learning) more?'
>
> Page Two
> ~~'By encouraging children to make choices'~~
> 'Topic/Enquiry: Encouraging children to make choices and take ~~re~~ ownership of their learning.'
> 'By incorporating children's interests into the programming, will they participate (and be engaged)* in the curriculum more, ~~and'~~
>
>
> * Rose added the phrase in brackets later.

Page Three
'How does giving children a voice, impact on / make a difference ~~chi~~ to their engagement in the curriculum?'

'How ~~might~~ do I ~~rethink~~ revise my practices regarding giving children a voice, ~~to involve them in the curriculum more~~ / to encourage their engagement in the curriculum more?'

'How do we ~~rethink~~ re-examine encouraging children's participation, to allow for ~~further~~ increased engagement in the curriculum?'

'How do we rethink programming to better engage children in the curriculum?'

Taking your second step: your actions and reflections

If you have completed *Thinking Boxes* 2.1 to 2.4, you should be ready to settle on an action research question. You may still feel uncertain about your question, but remember that your question may be just a starting point. As you learn new things about your research topic, it is likely that you will want to refine your question. At this point, you are not seeking perfection, just a question to prompt you to act and think differently about your research topic. If your question does that, you are ready to take your next step. Note your decision in your *Action Research Journal*, together with any issues or questions associated with it.

Further resources: going deeper

In print

Coghlan, D. and Brannick, T. (2005) *Doing Action Research in Your Own Organization*, 2nd edn. Thousand Oaks, CA: Sage.
Herr, K. and Anderson, G. L. (2005) *The Action Research Dissertation: A Guide for Students and Faculty*. Thousand Oaks, CA: Sage.

Online

Riel, M. (2007) Understanding Action Research, Center for Collaborative Action Research. Available at: http://cadres.pepperdine.edu/ccar/define.html. A good discussion of what appropriate action research questions require.
The *Participatory Action Research network* offers resources, books, etc., plus opportunities for online discussion. Available at: http://www.scu.edu.au/schools/gcm/ar/arr/links.html

Dick, B. (1997) Approaching an action research thesis: an overview. Online. Available at: http://www.scu.edu.au/schools/gcm/ar/arp/phd.html

A list of action verbs. If you feel stuck with phrasing your question or choosing just the 'right' word, visit this online list of action verbs to prompt your thinking. Available at: http://www.rfp-templates.com/List-of-Action-Verbs.html/

PHASE TWO
Planning for a Change

At the first session, we were rather surprised to find that Glenda was not planning to provide us with the framework for our research, but rather to challenge us to develop our own journey. We were encouraged to trust the process and not over-focus on the outcomes.

Good research centres on having good research questions that will help us to achieve our outcomes. We need to plan the journey, not the end; look at what we know and what we might do differently. We need to question, gather information, look at other research and discover things afresh. We need to gather information in the real world and interpret that information. Action research is a cyclic process. We need to keep revisiting, collect data over time and use the combined knowledge of the group to interpret the data.

(Department of Education 2004: 11)

In Phase Two of your action research project, you decide what you need to know and what you will do, when, and with whom before you begin to answer your action research question. Phase Two can influence the shape of your project considerably, but you may find it a very 'messy' time. It can be hard to decide where to start planning your project . . . but you have to start it somewhere. We offer several possible starting points in no particular order or priority. Start with those that seem to make most sense in the specific circumstances in which you will initiate your action research project. In making your choice, you may find it helpful to reflect on Averill's comments on the early phase of community-based action research:

(Action research begins) in the middle of whatever it is you are doing . . . not with a question but with the muddle of daily work, with the moments that stand out from the general flow. . . . The activities attached to this phase are not linear, in fact, all research-related actions proceed in more of a circular fashion.

(Averill 2006: 2–3, 4–5)

The 'muddle and . . . the moments that stand out from the general flow' often create 'niggles' which, for the action researcher, spark their questions and their research to answer them.

Like any research, good action research rests on good preparation and planning. It is important to understand what action research is, what others have said about your research topic, your ethical responsibilities as a researcher and how best to approach your data collection and interpretation. Phase Two of your first action research cycle requires you to understand these responsibilities and tasks and to ensure that you work through them systematically. Many of the steps in Phase Two you will only need to take in your first action research cycle.

Step 3 Learn more about the action research family

> The parents really wanted to be involved. They wanted to be kept informed as to what was happening. The community wherever you are working will have a lot to contribute to any research project.
>
> (Early Childhood Action Researcher, Department of Education 2004: 27)

If a collaborative action research project is to have any integrity, everyone with a stake or interest in it should have a say in it. For example, parents should have a say in each phase of a collaborative action research project exploring their role in young children's emerging literacy. However, not all action research is collaborative action research. Action researchers are part of a research 'family', whose members have different views and values about collaboration and about the sorts of changes that action researchers should aim to create.

What you'll need to take Step 3:

Time
- to read this step, to reflect on its content and to complete its *Thinking Box*;
- to talk about the action research family with those who will be involved in your project.

Knowledge
- Which branch of the action research family would it be most appropriate to apply in your circumstances?
- Has any form of action research been conducted already in your circumstances?

Other resources
- Access to a library if you wish to learn more about specific members of the action research family.

Preparing to take Step 3

In Step 3 of the action research process, you learn about the two major branches and distant cousins of the action research family (i.e. you take action); decide which branch is most appropriate for your particular project (i.e. you reflect on your action); and decide whether and how it will influence your research (i.e. you take further action). This first section introduces the action research family's heritage and describes the similarities and differences between the family's two major branches, together with some 'distant cousins'.

Meet the action research family

It is quite easy to describe the action research cycle in broad terms – we did so in this book's Introduction. However, when you describe the cycle in more detail, you find that there are several versions of it, reflecting the several different – yet related – approaches to action research. As a result, you need to choose – early in this second phase ('Planning for a change') of the action research cycle – which approach to action research will guide your specific research project.

We use the term 'the action research family' as a way to visualize relationships between the different – yet related – approaches to action research. Adherents to the various approaches to action research agree in broad terms about what action research means. For example, they agree in broad terms about the structure and operation of the action research cycle. However, they can differ significantly about the detailed practicalities of an action research project. As this step will show, you can't evaluate each member of the action research family in terms of whether it is better or worse than the rest; and you certainly can't say that one member is the 'right' way to do action research. Instead, you face a real choice when you start to design your action research project – which member of the family is likely to be the best guide to your project, bearing in mind your specific topic, circumstances and locality?

Different approaches to action research have developed in different places and at different times, resulting in a collection of approaches that we call 'the action research family'. As in any family, there are disputes between the branches of the action research family and between the members within each branch. There are disputes about family values and disputes over who is 'really' a member of the family. More specifically, there are disputes about:

- aims and intentions
- focus of change
- principles and processes

- theoretical foundations
- appropriateness to specific types of projects and/or settings (for example, its use in early childhood settings).

Figure 3.1 The action research family is a map of the action research family, showing its two branches and the members of each branch.

The disputes between and within the branches of the action research family reflect a broader dispute concerning 'appropriate' links between research and social change. The earliest promoters of action research (including Kurt Lewin) saw it as a way to create social change. Their view took root in different forms at different places and at different times, which is why the contemporary action research family is so diverse and houses so many debates. As you read this short family history, remember that all the different approaches to action research share an interest in creating strategic (or planned) change, but that each approach has a specific target for change.

Early days: Academics in the USA take action research to classrooms

Alice Meil, Stephen Corey and their colleagues at Columbia University in the USA first took Lewin's approach to action research into schools and school

	BRANCH ONE Action research for professional change	BRANCH TWO Action research for social change
Key values	Wise practice through professional innovation	Emancipation through social action
Family members	• Individual Practitioner Action Research* • Teacher Action Research* • Collaborative Action Research** • Whole-site Action Research** • School-based Action Research**	• Critical Action Research • Transformative Action Research • Participative Action Research • Emancipatory Action Research • Fourth-Generation Action Research • Feminist Action Research • Reconceptualist Action Research
	* Performed by an individual ** Performed by a group	Emphasizes research in groups, but a research project may start with an individual researcher.

Figure 3.1   The action research family.

districts in the 1940s and 1950s (Schmuck 2006). Like Lewin, they saw action research as a way to create social change, but their links with social change movements decreased as McCarthyite concerns about the influence of Marxism and communism in the USA increased. Kemmis explains:

> Thus, the version of action research that began to attract adherents in education in the '50s was shifting from one which connected easily with the progressive ideals of the first half of the century towards one which was more self-consciously 'scientific' – as this was understood in terms of the positivist aspirations of the social and educational science of that time.
>
> (Kemmis 1993: online at http://epaa.asu.edu/epaa/v1n1.html)

Action researchers began to present their research as 'scientific' or positivist to avoid any McCarthyite charges that they were trying to undermine the status quo. Positivists believe that their (scientific) research is value-free because it merely discovers objective facts about the world, rather than seeking to change it. They deny that their research is based on any values or beliefs other than the value of objective truth and the belief that the researcher's job is to discover it. More specifically, they deny that their research has any relationship (positive or negative) with the status quo, because it seeks merely to discover the truth about it.

Phase Two: Teachers in the UK do action research by and for themselves

Action research first appeared in the UK education system via the 'teacher as researcher' movement of the 1960s and 1970s. Led by teachers and supported by academics (Lawrence Stenhouse and John Elliot), the movement sought to democratize research by enabling and encouraging teachers to do research for themselves, rather than leaving researchers to do research about teachers. The movement generated the Collaborative Action Research Network (CARN) and the journal, *Educational Action Research* (Zeichner 2001).

Phase Three: Activists and academics in Australia use action research for indigenous emancipation

Action research took hold in Australia's education system via the Participatory Action Research movement in the 1980s. The movement emerged to challenge indigenous oppression in schools and beyond and it consisted of activist teachers, together with academics (especially Stephen Kemmis, Robyn McTaggart and Shirley Grundy). The primary aim of Participatory Action Research is to create positive and progressive social change; and its distinguishing feature is that the people who are directly affected by such change are involved in the research process.

Kemmis and McTaggart developed Participatory Action Research (PAR) into a theory and practice of Emancipatory Action Research, through which equity and social justice became a major focus for action research in education. While Emancipatory Action Research emerged from Participatory Action Research, it also had roots in strong critical social theory and in the practices of the UK 'teacher as researcher' movement.

Cutting across Phases One to Three: Oppressed groups use action research to create change

While action research was taking hold – in different forms – in the education systems of the USA, the UK and Australia, Participatory Action Research movements emerged in parts of Africa, Asia and Central and South America. There, researchers used action research to promote social justice and equity in and through education systems; but they also linked with oppressed groups outside of the education system – in society at large – and used action research in local community action. At about the same time, feminists in Australia began to point to the lack of a feminist standpoint in action research literature and worked to re-conceptualize action research as a tool for feminist change.

New teacher researcher movements grow in the USA

Since the 1990s, a new teacher researcher movement has grown in the USA. Led by teachers and supported by academic partners and facilitators, it tends to be more focused on individual teacher change than action research for social change (Zeichner 2001).

Bailey (2004) offers a good illustration of this form of action research in early childhood. Bailey was a support teacher to classroom teachers with children with disabilities in their classrooms. The broad focus of her project was to explore the effect of using e-mail to communicate with staff about her work with visually impaired children in their classrooms. Her action research question was: 'What happens if I rely primarily on e-mail as a means of communication?' She documented e-mail messages between herself and 15 case managers in nine schools and then analysed them for information about how effectively she was meeting student and teacher needs by using e-mail as her primary form of communication. She used what she learnt to plan changes to how she communicated with them for the following year. You can view a number of examples of this form of teacher research on the *Classroom Action Research* site listed in the 'going deeper' section of this step.

Grouping family members into one of two 'branches'

The action research family has a 60-year history to date. In that time, the family has grown in size, while family members have developed diverse identities and practices in their work at local and national educational sites. The resulting array of different-yet-similar titles and practices can sometimes be confusing, but each one rests on one of three very broad strands of thinking about social and educational change:

- The 'technicians' see educational change as a technical, 'can do' process of solving specific problems in the classroom. Researchers seek one or more techniques to improve classroom practice; and educational change happens as teachers use these techniques to do things in new ways.
- The 'ethicists' see educational change as an ethical and moral process of creating wise teachers. Researchers explore the ethics, morals and effects for others of teachers' existing practice; and educational change happens as teachers understand how and why to act wisely in their specific circumstances.
- The 'activists' see educational change as a process of political critique and action. Researchers explore how power dynamics and ideas constrain and enable teacher practice and change; and educational change happens as teachers learn new ways to be, to think and to act that promote social justice.

When Kemmis (1993: online) identified these three strands, he noted the 'sharp differences' between them. We agree, but to avoid confusing readers further, we have reduced those three approaches to educational change to two: action research for *professional* change and action research for *social* change. Action research for *professional* change describes the work of both the 'technicians' and the 'ethicists'; action research for *social* change describes the work of the 'activists'. The 'technicians' create educational change through new techniques; the 'ethicists' create educational change through new wisdom. Despite their significantly different *means* of creating change, both the 'technicians' and the 'ethicists' have the same *target* for change – individual teachers and their practices in the classroom. In contrast, the 'activists' have as their target the education system, which they seek to improve through improving shared social practices, their meanings and their institutional contexts. It is possible to improve a teacher's educational techniques without changing the education system in which they work; and it is possible to improve the ethics and morals of a teacher's practice without changing the education system in which they work. It is impossible to change an education system without changing teachers' techniques and the ethics and morals of their practice.

The action research family's two branches: differences and similarities

Figure 3.2 The action research family's two branches: differences and similarities gives an overview of the two branches of the family. You should review this before reading about the family in more detail.

	BRANCH ONE Action research for *professional* change	BRANCH TWO Action research for *social* change
	AIMS AND INTENTIONS	
	1. To generate innovation by changing early childhood practitioners' social practices. 2. To generate wiser practice by generating new and deeper thinking about it.	1. To challenge how individuals and/or groups link their practices with existing power relations. 2. To promote emancipation by generating new and deeper thinking about the effects of current practices.
	FOCI FOR CHANGE	
	The everyday problems, issues, dilemmas, questions, concerns or practices of individuals, teams, or groups of early childhood practitioners.	Early childhood practitioners' attitudes to the place of social justice, equity, diversity and difference in their everyday practices.
	KEY PRINCIPLES AND PROCESSES	
Research site	Researchers' local early childhood settings.	Researchers' local early childhood settings.
Research topic	Concerns of interest and importance to individual early childhood practitioners and/or to their team, professional network or funding agency.	Questions of justice and fairness identified by individuals or by a team, a professional network or a funding organization.
Research process	Researchers change their practice (how they think and act) through the action research cycle.	Researchers change their practice (how they think and act) through the action research cycle.

Figure 3.2 The action research family's two branches: differences and similarities.

(*Continued overleaf*)

Figure 3.2 continued

Working with others	Researchers may work alone or with others; or collaborate through a research group or a community of learners. An external research facilitator may support their research.	Researchers may work alone initially, but they try to work with others for social change, especially with those affected most directly by unfair practices. An external research facilitator may support their research.
Sharing with others	Researchers who receive funds to do their work may have to report their findings to the funding source and, perhaps, more widely.	Researchers who receive funds to do their work may have to report their findings to the funding source and, perhaps, more widely.
USES IN EDUCATION (INCLUDING EARLY CHILDHOOD SETTINGS)		
Individual action research	Promoting professional growth and learning in individuals who can initiate change around an issue.	Promoting professional growth and learning in individuals who can initiate change to create more just and equitable policy, praxis and/or relationships.
Collaborative action research	Promoting professional growth and learning in individuals and teams who can initiate change around an issue; and/or driving site-wide or system-wide change.	Promoting professional growth and learning in individuals and teams who can initiate social change around an issue; and/or driving site-wide or system-wide change for greater equity and justice in policy, praxis and relationships.
THEORETICAL FOUNDATIONS		
	• Inform professional practice with practical knowledge. • Improve professional practice by starting from practitioners' concerns. • Ensure that practitioners 'own' and manage change.	• Improve social practices through critical reflection and social critique that include individual reflection. • Create social change through embodying and enacting participatory and democratic principles.

The family's first branch: action research for <u>professional</u> change

Aims or intentions
- To generate innovation by unsettling, informing, changing, improving and renewing the social practices of individual and/or groups of early childhood practitioners.
- To generate wiser practices by deliberately and systematically exploring early childhood practitioners' practice and generating new and deeper thinking about it.

Key foci for change
- The everyday problems, issues, dilemmas, questions, concerns or practices of individuals, teams, or groups in early childhood settings.

Key principles and processes
- Research site. Researchers' local early childhood settings.
- Research topic. Concerns of interest and importance to individual early childhood practitioners and/or to their team, professional network or funding agency.
- Research process. Researchers change their practice (how they think and act) through the action research cycle.
- Working with others. Researchers may work alone; or link with other researchers in their locality for support; or collaborate more formally through a research group or a community of learners. An external research facilitator may work with individuals or groups to support their research. Generally this occurs only when there are funds to pay the facilitator.
- Sharing with others. When researchers – individuals or groups – receive funds to do their work (e.g. in site-based or school-based projects), they may be required to report their findings formally to the funding source and, perhaps, more widely (e.g. through publications). When researchers are not funded for the research project, the choice to share or not to share is theirs.
- Sometimes a funding organization, policy group, auspicing agency, government department or professional network will initiate the research and determine its broad foci. Individual practitioners are then invited or required to participate in the research and given more or less control over its foci. For instance, in a school-based action research project to improve literacy outcomes in the school, all the teachers in that school may be required to participate and are given more or less control over which specific aspects of their practices around literacy they will research.

Theoretical foundations

Action research for *professional* change has its roots in three key ideas about relationships between knowledge, action and change.

1   Professional practice can and should be informed by praxis (practical knowledge). Praxis is knowledge for a purpose. It is the practical knowledge that we acquire and use as a basis for action. Praxis informs our practice which, in turn, informs our ideas. In contrast, theoretical knowledge is 'knowledge for its own sake'. It is the knowledge that we acquire and use because it is the truth about something. As O'Brien (2001: 11) put it: 'That knowledge is derived from practice, and practice informed by knowledge, in an ongoing process, is a cornerstone of action research.'

2   You can improve professional practice by starting with practitioners' concerns. This idea has its roots in a now classic text on changing professional praxis by Argyris and Schön (1974: 612–13) in which they wrote: '(Action research should take) its cues – its questions, puzzles and problems – from the perceptions of practitioners within particular, local practice contexts.'

3   Educational change is most effective when practitioners own and manage change. The literature on professional change continually features the argument that teachers should be involved in educational change and problem solving because it is they who will have to make changes work in the classroom. This idea originated with the US educationalist and philosopher John Dewey.

In educational settings – including early childhood settings – action research for professional change has taken two forms: individual and collaborative.

Individual *action research for professional change*

This is generally used to:

- promote professional growth and learning in individuals;
- inform the individual and sometimes their immediate colleagues, parents and/or the children with whom they work. What is learnt generally has meaning locally, and has what Newmann (1992, cited in King and Lonnquist 1992: 3) called a 'subjective generalizability' for other practitioners.

Individual action research for professional change is appropriate when:

- individuals have questions, puzzles or problems that they want to explore in their locality;
- individuals believe that something in their practice can be changed and improved;
- individual researchers can control the issue or concern that they wish to change. Examples of such concerns include:
  - relationships in the classroom or setting;
  - teaching methods or strategies that are not mandated by the next level of management or administration;
  - curriculum content, resource usage or learning areas that are not mandated by the next level of management or administration;
  - evaluation tools and strategies that are not mandated by the next level of management or administration.

A good example of individual action research for change is Bailey's (2004) study of the effectiveness of e-mail as a primary means of communication.

Collaborative *action research for professional change*
This is generally used to:

- promote professional growth and learning in individuals and teams;
- inform the individual, their immediate colleagues, parents and/or the children with whom they work;
- drive site-wide or system-wide change.

Collaborative action research for professional change is appropriate when:

- individuals share with others some questions, puzzles or problems that they want to explore in their locality;
- colleagues share a belief that something in their practice can be changed and improved;
- a system-wide or network-wide question or issue is identified and teams or groups are supported to explore it within their local context. This can extend the range of issues that it is possible for researchers to focus on. However, they should aim to change only those practices that they can control.

A good example of collaborative action research for professional change is the study by Diebling, Mackman and Myers (2006), in which three teachers in the USA collaborated to explore the effects of three specific programmes designed to improve students' relationships with their school. The programmes were: a 'student buddy' programme, a blood donation drive within the school (responding to child with a blood disease in the kindergarten) and an 'Open Mic' talent quest and quiz. Each teacher implemented the three programmes with diverse students and studied what happened. Their question was: 'Will implementing specific programmes affect students' relationships with their school?'

The family's second branch: action research for <u>social</u> change

Aims or intentions
- To unsettle, inform, change and improve how individual and/or groups of early childhood practitioners see links between their practices and existing (fair and unfair) power relations.
- To promote emancipation through exploring current practices deliberately, systematically and critically, generating new and deeper thinking about their effects on themselves and on others (including children).

Foci for change
- The everyday problems, dilemmas and questions of early childhood practitioners (individuals, teams, or groups) about the fairness and justice of their current practices.
- The attitudes of early childhood practitioners (individuals, teams, or groups) to the place of social justice, equity, diversity and difference in their practices.

Key principles and processes
- Research site. Researchers' local early childhood settings.
- Research topic. Questions of justice and fairness identified by individuals or by a team, a professional network or a funding organization.
- Research process. Researchers change their practice (how they think and act) through the action research cycle.
- Working with others. Researchers may work alone initially, but they try to work with others for social change, especially with those affected most directly by unfair practices. An external research facilitator may work with individuals or groups to support their research. This is most likely when the research is funded externally.
- Sharing with others. When researchers – individuals or groups – receive funds to do their work (e.g. in site-based or school-based projects), they may be required to report their findings formally to the funding source and, perhaps, more widely (e.g. through publications). When there are no funds to support the research, the decision to share or not to share is then the decision of those involved.

Theoretical foundations

Action research for *social* change has its roots in two key ideas about relationships between knowledge, action and change.

1 Critical reflection and social critique (including self-reflection) are crucial to any attempt to improve the rationality and justice of social circumstances and practices; and critical reflection must examine knowledge, contexts and action. Fay (1987: 49) defined critical reflection as the ability to 'evaluate one's own desires and beliefs on the basis of some such criterion as whether they are justified by the evidence, whether they are mutually consistent, whether they are in accord with some ideals'.

   Critical reflection is 'critical' in that it is questioning, it is explicitly and deliberately political and it aims to create structural change, not just personal change. In educational settings – including early childhood settings – critical reflection is an outcome of debate about the nature of the educational decisions taken in a particular setting, the ends to which these decisions are directed and the means by which they are achievable. Carr and Kemmis express this forcefully:

   > Social structure, as well as being the product of the meanings and actions of individuals, itself produces particular meanings, ensures their continuing existence, and thereby limits the kind of actions that it is reasonable for an individual to perform ... (therefore researchers need to) ... examine not only the meanings of particular forms of social actions, but also the social factors that engender and sustain them.
   >
   > (Carr and Kemmis 1986: 95)

2 People affected directly by a social practice must be involved in its improvement and their involvement must embody democratic principles. As Kemmis (1993: online) put it: 'It aims to help people understand themselves as the agents, as well as the products, of history. In my view, action research is also committed to spreading involvement and participation in the research process.'

Action research for social change is especially appropriate when researchers aim to improve children's and adults' educational experiences through reducing inequality.

The action research family's 'distant cousins'

Action research is similar to and different from three other forms of inquiry into practice that are used in early childhood settings – action learning, teacher research and inquiry-based learning. All three share some similarities and differences with action research.

Action learning

Action learning is a form of work-based professional learning. Staff identify an issue, task or problem that affects them and they learn new ways to think and act as they collaborate in a group to explore their shared issue, task or problem. Action learning originated in the work of Reg Revans on group problem-solving in the UK coal industry during the 1940s. From this work, Revans developed a formula for learning:

L (Learning) = P (Programmed content) + Q (Insightful questions).

Revans (1982: 69) described action learning as, 'a social process . . . [in which] . . . a lot of people start to learn from each other, and a learning community comes into being'. He believed that: 'Action learning particularly obliges subjects to become aware of their own value systems, by demanding that the real problems tackled carry some risk of personal failure' (International Foundation for Action Learning, no date).

Action learning differs from action research in four ways:

- It does not start with a research question.
- It does not use the action research cycle to create change in practice and thinking.
- It does not always seek to create change.
- It is not always oriented to social change.

Teacher research

Teacher research is 'systematic, intentional inquiry by teachers' (Cochrane-Smith and Lytle 1993: 7) that starts with a research question about teachers' current practice. It refers to a variety of ways in which teachers gather and analyse data about their classroom practices in order to understand them better; and so its roots lie in various projects, not all of which use action research. Teacher research differs from action research because it does not always and necessarily seek to create change.

Inquiry-based learning

'Inquiry-based learning' is an umbrella term that refers to various forms of teacher-driven inquiry into their own practices, issues and understandings. An individual teacher initiates their inquiry-based learning by asking a research question about their current practice. They ask questions and gather information about it, creating new ideas, making choices and sharing conclusions.

The roots of inquiry-based learning lie in John Dewey's problem-posing approach to learning in education; and in constructivist and socio-constructivist theories of learning that emphasize our capacity to construct our own knowledge about the world and to make new meanings about it. Inquiry-based learning differs from action research because it does not always seek to change practices. However, it resembles action research in two ways. First, it seeks to create new ways of thinking. Second, its five-step cyclic inquiry model (Bruce 2007: online) – ask a question, collect information, create new ideas, discuss your new ideas with others, reflect on what you've learnt (and then ask again) – resembles the action research cycle.

The role of collaboration in action research

Some action researchers insist that action research – by definition – must be collaborative, because it entails working with others. Kemmis and McTaggart (1988: 5–6) are clear on this point: 'The approach is only action research when it is collaborative, though it is important to realise that action research of the group is achieved through the critically examined action of individual group members.'

Other action researchers argue that action research must be collaborative because left by themselves, individuals tend to merely reinforce what they think already, rather than generate new thinking. Borrowing from Lewin (1946), we can say that our habits of thinking can be obstacles to change. For example, when Bartlett and Burton (2006) studied teacher action research in the UK, they found that teacher researchers often used their research results to reinforce their existing beliefs and practices, rather than to change them. This is why some action researchers (in one of those 'family disputes') believe that forms of action research conducted solely by individuals – such as practitioner action research and teacher action research – aren't 'real' members of the action research family.

Taking Step 3: a case from practice

Most first-time action researchers do not make an active choice between the two branches of the action research family. In our experience, they are familiar with only one branch, because their facilitators or supervisors tend to favour one branch of the family over another. Thus, this case from practice shows how to make such an active choice. In it, Glenda explains why she actively chose action research for social change as the means to investigate gender praxis in early childhood:

I decided to focus on action research for social change for three reasons. Firstly, using an explicitly feminist agenda in the analysis of gendering, as I did, leads theoretically and practically to a position of arguing for a need to reconstitute gendering within the early childhood setting. Feminists challenge patriarchy. The paucity of feminist practice and theory in early childhood education and the evidence that many children are being actively constituted by, and constituting, patriarchal gendering within early childhood education suggested the need for research that could help teachers develop strategies for reconstituting gender to empower both adults and children. Research that explored gendering in early childhood education without actively trying to reconstitute patriarchal practices and discourses via the research would implicitly contribute to patriarchy's maintenance. It would run the risk of becoming ethically and politically disengaged from the project's feminist concerns and intents.

Secondly, discourses and practices become transparent/visible when they are held up for rethinking. Through establishing moments where this occurs, the intricate discursive networks implicated in feminist pedagogies should be brought into sharper relief. By focusing on teachers' practices at the local level as they work for change, moments of critical awareness and questioning could highlight internal contradictions in the different pedagogical discourses within the field.

Thirdly, a focus on changing praxis could pin-point how particular pedagogical discourses are deconstructed and reconstructed for gender equity. It would also enable identification of some of the gaps, resistances and sites of contradiction within early childhood pedagogies. By highlighting these moments, the system of differentiations concerning gendering in the early childhood curriculum could be illuminated and thus open to deconstruction.

For these reasons, I decided to undertake a social change action research project in which I could gather empirical information about specific aspects of pedagogical change in relation to gender.

(adapted from Mac Naughton 2000)

Taking your third step: your actions and reflections

Use *Thinking Box 3.1 Which branch of the action research family is right for me?* to decide which branch of the action research family is most appropriate in your research project, then note your decision in your *Action Research Journal*.

Thinking Box 3.1 Which branch of the action research family is right for me?		
	BRANCH ONE: Action research for *professional* change	BRANCH TWO: Action research for *social* change
My research question aims to:	• generate innovation by changing early childhood practitioners' social practices. • generate wiser practice by generating new and deeper thinking about it.	• challenge how individuals and/or groups link their practices and existing power relations. • promote emancipation by generating new and deeper thinking about the effects of current practices.
My foci for change are:	• the everyday problems, issues, dilemmas, questions, concerns or practices of individuals, teams, or groups of early childhood practitioners.	• early childhood practitioners' attitudes to the place of social justice, equity, diversity and difference in their everyday practices.
My research question addresses:	• concerns of interest and importance to individual early childhood practitioners and/or to their team, professional network or funding agency.	• questions of justice and fairness identified by individuals or by a team, a professional network or a funding organization.

Further resources: going deeper

In print: General

Reason, P. and Bradbury, H. (eds) (2001) *Handbook of Action Research: Participative Inquiry and Practice*, Thousand Oaks, CA: Sage.

Online: General

Au, Y.S. (2004) Raising teachers' competence in action research, downloaded from http://content.edu.tw/primary/society/ks_ck/nine/n4.htm on 25 August 2004.

In print: On teacher action research

Burnaford, G., Fischer, J. and Hobson, D. (2001) *Teachers Doing Research: The Power of Action Through Inquiry*, Hillsdale, NJ: Lawrence Erlbaum Associates.

Online: On teacher action research

A teacher action research site. http://www.lupinworks.com/ar/change.html

In print: On participatory action research

Carr, W. and Kemmis, S. (1986) *Becoming Critical: Education, Knowledge and Action Research*. London: Falmer Press.
Action Research Journal. Sage Publications. ISSN 1741–2617.
Participatory Learning and Action series. Peer-reviewed informal journal.

Online: On participatory action research

Participatory Action Research Network (PARNet) (not active as of Feb. 2007).
Center for Collaborative Action Research (CCAR) at Pepperdine University.

Step 4 Learn more about your topic from the literature

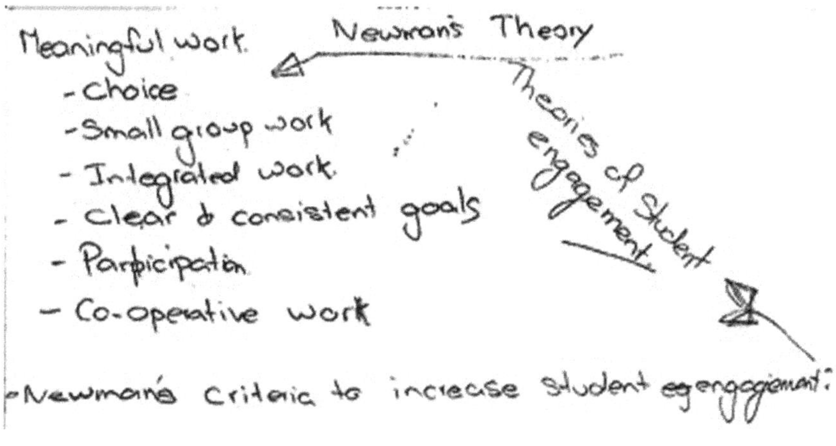

Figure 4.1 Julia, *Action Research Journal*: 5.

Julia wanted to improve student engagement in her early childhood setting (*Student engagement: Starting with the Child* project) and she read what other people had written about her topic. On Page 5 of her *Action Research Journal* (see above), she summarized key ideas from the theory of student engagement that had most interested her at the time. She used her notes on this theory to reflect with her colleagues on the extent to which meaningful work practices existed in their setting. On the basis of their reflections, the group planned their first change to improve student engagement.

Step 4 in your action research project is to find out more about your research topic by reviewing the published literature (academic and other) about it, so that your first action to create change is well informed. By reviewing the published literature, you can learn about whether and how other researchers have explored your research topic; and you can gather ideas about how best to explore your topic and some good ways to improve your practice in your specific circumstances. As your research progresses through new cycles, you should return regularly to the literature. It will help you to make sense of what you are learning (perhaps by building theories about it) and it will help you to plan your next steps in the action research cycle. New readings can spark new directions in all phases of your project as this preschool teacher found:

> The [Project Officer] gave me an article today called 'Meanings of Readiness and the Kindergarten Experience', by Elizabeth Graue. Reading it was like having a light switched on. She talks about readiness for school as being contextual and depending more on the social context and beliefs and ideas of parents and professional staff than being a measurable characteristic of children. This really opened my eyes. What are we getting children 'ready' for? What characteristics are valued? How much does it really matter where children are really 'at' when they enter school? So what is 'school readiness' in my context? How do I know where each child is at? What is my responsibility as an educator of 3½–5 year old children who are functioning in a society obsessed with school readiness?
>
> (Preschool Director, Critical Teaching Project, in
> Mac Naughton et al. 2001)

What you'll need to take Step 4:

Time
- to read this step, to reflect on its content and to complete its *Thinking Box*;
- to discuss the contents of this step with those who will be involved in your project;
- to familiarize yourself with any libraries that might be sources of literature relevant to your research topic and to discuss your search strategy with a librarian;
- to find literature relevant to your project, to read it and to summarize it.

Knowledge
- Where am I most likely to find literature relevant to my topic?
- How can I best search for literature relevant to my topic?
- How can I best read and summarize the relevant literature (e.g. in print, downloaded from online sources, on-screen)?
- How can I best retain any items of literature for possible use in future?

Other resources
- a literature search diary (print or a computer file);
- access to a current literature search software package;
- an indexable means (paper or computer folder) of organizing and storing the results of your literature search.

What is a literature review?

A literature review is an organized, systematic process in which you find literature about your research topic, read it, then summarize it in written form, such as an essay, an informal think-piece, an issues paper, or a step in a report or a thesis. As you review the relevant literature, you learn more about your research topic by asking yourself questions such as:

- What do I know now about my research topic?
- What more do I need to know about it?
- How do I find out more about it?
- What are my most important questions about my research topic?
- How can I use the results of my literature review to create change (alone or with others) through my action research project?

You review the relevant literature to discover what other people have thought, done and said about your topic already. They may have published their own research, their own reviews of the literature, their own theoretical discussions and expositions and their own reports. Reviewing the literature helps you join a wider professional conversation between other researchers about your topic. (See http://csumb.edu/academic/graduate/education/thesis/LitReview.html)

Review the literature in an organized, systematic way and record what you find in a similar fashion, even if you don't create a formal, written document (e.g. an essay or a report). This will make it easier for you to use the results in planning your research project. It will also enable you to draw a mental map of different approaches to your topic, which is the first step towards 'thinking openly' about it. 'Thinking openly' about your topic helps you to become better informed about it and to understand whether and how your research might add to the existing knowledge about your topic. Further aspects of 'thinking openly' are:

- learning what others have struggled with and found in their research on your topic;
- learning what others think are the questions that have/haven't been answered about your topic;

- becoming familiar with the big ideas and theories about your topic;
- reviewing your research question;
- considering whether other researchers' approaches might be useful in your project;
- thinking about how to design your action research project in light of what you've read.

A literature review to meet your need

Your review of the literature will be more or less formal and comprehensive, depending on when in your research project you do it and on whether you are required to report formally on your project and to whom. You *will not* normally be required to produce a formal literature review if you are undertaking a small-scale project as part of an undergraduate unit of studies or as an informal, individual process of developing your practice at work. You *will* normally be required to produce a formal literature review if your project is:

- part of a formal course of study accredited by a professional body;
- part (or all) of a structured process of professional development that is part of your job;
- part of an externally-funded research project.

The rest of this section of this step introduces various types or levels of literature review; they are summarized in *Thinking Box 4.1 Choosing the appropriate type or level of literature review*. To choose which type or level of literature meets your need, look at *Thinking Box 4.1* and then go to the relevant section of this step.

Whichever type or level of literature review you choose, it will be easier and more satisfying if you get to know a librarian at your local (or your employer's) library. Librarians have expert knowledge and skills in finding and retrieving information. Don't be afraid to ask for help! Ask your librarian for the library's *latest* guide to searching the Internet.

As you start your literature review, bear in mind these two key questions about it:

- How do I find and review literature that is relevant to my research topic?
- How do I use my literature review in designing my action research project?

Thinking Box 4.1 Choosing the appropriate type or level of literature review		
TYPE OF ACTION RESEARCHER		TYPE OR LEVEL OF LITERATURE REVIEW
Student action researcher	*Writing a proposal for a small, short-term research project*	A quick overview of the literature
	Beginning a small, short-term research project	A selective, in-depth literature review
	Beginning a large, long-term project (e.g. for a PhD)	A formal and comprehensive literature review, updated as the project progresses.
Action researchers in informal, unfunded projects		A comprehensive literature review
Action researchers in formal, funded projects		A formal and comprehensive literature review, updated as the project progresses

A quick overview of the literature

A quick overview of the relevant literature can help you to focus your thinking by giving you a sense of what is and isn't known about your topic. Hart (2001) suggested that a quick overview of the literature involves five stages:

- Get to know the library you'll be using. Ask a librarian for a map of the library or make your own; then ask the librarian where to find books and journals on your topic and note their location on your map.
- Define your topic as clearly as you can, then use a thesaurus to create a list of key terms and their synonyms.
- Use the library's reference section (e.g. handbooks and encyclopaedias) to discover the major ideas, issues and information around your topic.
- Search for relevant books and articles in the library.
- Search the Internet for relevant articles, etc.

A selective, in-depth literature review

Once you have started your action research project, you might want to learn more about how other people have approached your research topic. You can extend the scope and scale of your quick overview of the literature by conducting a further search that retrieves more information, but from selected sources only. (However you limit your further search, ensure that each item you retrieve is relevant to your project and is readily accessible.) You can limit this further literature search in one or more of these ways:

- Limit the time of publication. For example, only look for research published in the past two years.
- Limit the type of literature. For example, only look for original research articles accessible from online sources.
- Limit the type of studies. For example, only look for action research studies, or only look for studies which involve children of a particular age, or which involve teachers.
- Limit the theoretical perspectives. For example, only look for studies based on critical social theory; or only studies based on a feminist perspective on gender.

A comprehensive literature review

You will need a comprehensive review of the literature when you are passionate about your project – whether it is part of formal studies, funded research or something you want to do with others or for yourself. If you are doing action research because you personally want to create change (professional or social), then your literature review might never stop. When you are passionately interested in something, literature becomes a friend to you in your search for knowing more, knowing more wisely and knowing more justly.

A formal and comprehensive literature review

You will probably need to conduct a formal and comprehensive literature review if you are conducting your action research project as a student undertaking formal tertiary studies or if an organization is funding your project. If you are a student, your college or university will specify how comprehensive your literature review should be. (This normally depends on the level of your studies and the length of your course. Clearly, a literature review for a single semester undergraduate project will be different in scale and scope to a literature review for a doctorate.) If an organization (e.g. your employer or a government department) is funding your project, ensure that you agree with them how comprehensive your literature review should be.

The outcome of a formal and comprehensive literature review should be a highly-structured essay or a chapter in a report or a thesis. It should document the facts it presents and the sources on which it draws; and it should summarize and analyse the research literature associated with a particular topic, issue, problem, debate, etc. The more comprehensive the literature review, the more diverse its sources will be.

As well as evaluating the published literature concerning your topic, a formal and comprehensive literature review has these four specific functions:

1 It demonstrates your familiarity with the tradition (or traditions) of research and commentary on your research topic and with specific contemporary expressions of that tradition. This is important for formal studies and for externally-funded projects.

2 It analyses and (where appropriate) categorizes the literature according to common issues and/or approaches. The *substantive* aspect of the review categorizes different ways to think about your research topic; and the *methodological* aspect of the review categorizes the different ways in which researchers have investigated the topic to date.

3 It presents your conclusions about the state of knowledge about your research topic, highlighting what is present in the literature and what is absent from it. The following questions may help you to draw your conclusions:
   • What does/doesn't the literature say about your research topic?
   • What research has/hasn't been done on your research topic?
   • Which paradigms have/haven't governed research on your topic?
   • Which research methods have/haven't been used in research on your topic?
   • Which aspects of research on your topic have/haven't been contentious?

4 It presents your judgments about the state of knowledge about the area and its significance for your proposed research project. The following questions may help you to make your judgments:
   • What is the present state of knowledge about your research topic?
   • How relevant and/or significant to your proposed action research project is the existing knowledge about your topic?
   • Is your proposed research similar/different to the present knowledge about your topic? How?
   • In what way/s will your proposed action research project contribute to our knowledge about your research topic?

When you start your action research project, your literature review brings you up to date with the 'professional conversation' around your topic. However, as your project progresses, so does that 'professional conversation', so you need to keep up to date with what's being said:

Once you have focused your keywords and developed a successful search approach that has resulted in finding the information you want, it is a good idea to put in place some strategies to ensure that you are staying up to date with the literature that becomes available after your original search has been completed. There are several ways to do this such as saving searches, e-mail alerts, table of contents alerts or new journal issue alerts.

(Alexander 2007: 3)

A good way to join professional conversations in early childhood is to sign up for e-mail alerts from your preferred early childhood journals and associations. For instance, *Early Childhood Australia* has a free e-mail newsletter (*ECA WebWatch*) that includes a section on emerging research. *Early Childhood Research Quarterly* (the journal of the National Association of Early Childhood Education in the USA) has a free journal alert service, as do journals such as *Contemporary Issues in Early Childhood*. Most large commercial publishers also have a book alert service.

Starting your literature review

You will save time when you do your literature review if you prepare thoroughly by:

- choosing your topic and the key terms that describe it;
- deciding what you want your literature review to achieve;
- planning the order of your literature search;
- choosing the best tools for your literature search;
- planning how to organize and store the results of your literature search;
- learning how to use a current literature search software package;
- creating a literature search diary.

Choose your topic and the key terms that describe it

When you have chosen the topic of your literature review, you need to choose 'key terms' (sometimes called – incorrectly – 'keywords') to drive it. Key terms are important for two reasons: (1) they are essential to any definition of your topic; and (2) they are generally used in 'professional conversations' about your topic. For example, if you were searching the literature for research that is relevant to early childhood settings, your key terms should probably include the following:

- Child care
- Child minding

- Early childhood education – activity programmes
- Early childhood education – curricula
- Early childhood services
- Early childhood teachers
- Early childhood classrooms
- Early years
- Education, preschool
- Education, kindergarten
- Family day care
- Home-based care
- Long day care
- Nurseries
- Nursery schools
- Preschool playgroups
- Preschool teachers.

Many libraries have specialist software packages that search literature. These packages enable you to find variations of your key terms automatically. For example, if you wish to find variations of 'education', add an asterisk ('*') to the word-stem 'educat' to get 'educat*' and you will find any items containing it, such as educate, educated, education, educational, educator.

To find all the items containing your key terms, you may need to link two or more of your key terms with 'AND'. For example, to learn about services for children in a specific context, you may need to link some key terms such as: 'nursery schools AND preschools AND playgroups'. If the number of items you find in your literature search overwhelms you, limit or restrict your search by doing one or more of the following:

- add one or more key terms (e.g. preschool AND early childhood AND curriculum);
- specify publications (e.g. early childhood journals, education journals);
- specify locations (e.g. Australia, Laos);
- specify dates (e.g. 1995–2000).

To get a sense of the key terms used to describe issues in early childhood, look at appropriate dictionaries, encyclopaedias and handbooks, such as:

- *Encyclopedia of Early Childhood Education;*
- *International Handbook of Early Childhood Education.*

As you choose your key terms, bear in mind that users of the same language in different countries may spell a particular word differently. For example, a particular word in English may be spelt in at least two different ways in the UK, the USA, Canada, New Zealand and Australia.

Alexander provides very sound advice on using key terms to make your literature search efficient and effective:

> To search effectively, you need a set of keywords related to the topic you wish to research. Some databases have a dictionary or thesaurus function that you can use to find further keywords related to your topic. This is especially useful when searching international databases, where reference terms and keywords may differ slightly from your own. For example, when you type 'gender' into the ERIC database thesaurus, it suggests that you use 'sex' instead. Similarly, typing 'gender bias' generates 'sex bias', 'sex prejudice' and 'sexism' as alternatives. Once you have defined your set of keywords, you can use search operators such as 'and', 'or' and 'not' to broaden or narrow your search. You can also use search fields such as author, title, publication date or type to limit your searches.
>
> (2007: 4)

Decide what you want your literature review to achieve

The aim of a literature search is, generally, to discover the key ideas, authors, books and articles relevant to your action research topic. You should identify any 'landmark' studies that have influenced how people think about your topic. You should also identify the most recent studies and see whether they say anything new. This may require you to learn specialist or technical terms. Starting your own 'dictionary' of the key terms, ideas and theories that you find in the literature can help you to appreciate how people are thinking about your topic – including how to create change around it.

Plan the order of your literature search: strategies

What will you search for first? Reviewing the strategies below for searching the literature will help you to decide this.

A library catalogue enables you to find various kinds of resources about specific topics through various means.

Gateways to online resources
Most library catalogues are becoming gateways to online resources, including full text electronic books, journals and websites.

Searching by subject, key terms and references
Searching by subject headings can be challenging, as you may not know exact headings or the best search terms to use. Start by searching for key terms, note

the subject headings that emerge and use these to search further. NB: bibliographies and reference lists are good sources of additional material on a topic.

Other library catalogues

If you need an item that you can't find in your library catalogue, use the 'Google Scholar' search engine (see below) to look for it elsewhere.

Sources of information

Print (books, book chapters, journals and reports) is a major medium of information and electronic (online) information is rapidly achieving equivalent significance to researchers. However, an action researcher does more than just 'collect information' – s/he decides what information s/he needs, when s/he needs it and where to go to get it.

The latest research findings, reviews of the literature and scholarly debates are published as journal articles, conference papers and reports – in print or on the Internet. Although the Internet provides access to a vast and ever increasing amount of information from around the globe, researchers still need to visit libraries. A library generally requires proof of identity and some form of membership.

Charles (1998) provides some useful tips (Figure 4.2).

In a research library, you can find information about your research topic in:	
Primary sources, such as: Journal articles Conference papers Dissertations Monographs Scholarly books Technical reports Government reports	**Directories**, such as: ERIC Descriptors Dissertation Abstracts Education Index Resources in Education Psychological Abstracts Books in Print
Secondary sources, such as: Encyclopedia Yearbooks Digests and reviews of research Handbooks of research Scholarly books Magazine articles Newspaper articles	**Electronic databases**, such as: ERIC databases UnCover Periodical abstracts Newspaper abstracts

Figure 4.2 Sources of information in a research library.

Source: After Charles (1998: 76).

Journals
Look for research findings in academic journals, not popular magazines. Each academic journal has a panel of experts ('peers') that decides whether an article submitted to the journal is acceptable for publication. A journal will usually state on its inside cover whether or not its contents are peer-reviewed.

Theses or dissertations
Several publications list theses, but exclude Honours and postgraduate coursework material.

Sources of specialized information

Specialized information is available in the 'Reference' section of a library, which can provide a great deal of information quickly on various topics.

- *Dictionaries* are useful for defining terms and clarifying concepts. They can be particularly useful for definitions of specialized and subject-specific terminology.
- *Subject-specific encyclopaedias* provide concise information, a list of references and maybe some further reading.
- *Subject bibliographies and guides to the literature* list material (books, journal articles, government reports, etc.) published on a particular topic.
- *Biographies* usually provide details about people, often including their career, qualifications, awards, achievements and publications.
- *Directories* for example, telephone directories list names and contact details for individuals or groups.
- *Government publications* deal with an extremely wide range of subjects. Some government documents are located in the library's book collection and are listed individually in the library catalogue.
- *Published statistics*. There will be a central repository for statistics in many countries. For instance, the Australian Bureau of Statistics and the UK's Central Statistics Library. An online search for statistics about your specific circumstances will generally find your relevant central repository.

The Internet

Researchers can use the Internet in various ways.

Library subject guides
Your local library may produce subject guides to books, journals, databases and

Internet sites in an area. Each subject guide includes key print and electronic resources that the library owns or subscribes to, as well as those on the Internet.

Databases

When you want to locate journal articles, conference papers or newspaper stories on a topic, but don't have a particular journal or title to look for, try searching the online databases. They enable you to search the contents of journals electronically. We list some databases relevant to early childhood below; your local library may subscribe to at least some of them.

- ERIC (CSA): Info www.eric.ed.gov/ERICWebPortal/Home.portal. It houses a specialist early childhood collection;
- Education (Informit);
- Educational Research Abstracts (Taylor & Francis);
- Web of Science (ISI);
- Education Complete (Proquest). Many international educational journals are indexed and abstracted and most provided in full text;
- Education Research Complete (EBSCO);
- Expanded Academic ASAP (Gale).

Searching the web

The Internet contains a wealth of resources but, unlike a library, doesn't have a central index or mechanism to organize its contents systematically. In an attempt to improve the ease and speed of locating information, different searching tools or finding aids have been developed. These tools include subject gateways, directories and search engines. No one tool will always suit your needs exactly.

Search engines

A search engine is a tool with which to scan the Internet for details of sites and pages. This data is then stored in searchable indexes or databases that can be searched by typing keywords on the search engine's home page. There are dozens of search engines, each with particular capabilities and ways of working. Choose a search engine that is flexible and allows you to search using very specific key terms. The broader your search terms, the more sites the search engine will visit, only a few of which may be relevant to your topic.

You may need to try several search engines before deciding which meet your needs best, but one of the most popular and efficient is *Google* (www.google.com). Increasingly, researchers are using search engines such as *Google Scholar* (www.scholar.google.com) and *Google Books* (www.books. google.com) to see what has been published in their area. However, you will need access to a library that subscribes to full-text versions of a search result.

Online directories

Online directories organize Internet resources by subject (e.g. key organizations). They give a sense of the field, rather than access to scholarly articles. Two online early childhood directories are:

- *Google Directory: Early Childhood* includes many early childhood sites and it has its own easy search function. www.google.com/Top/Reference/Education/Early_Childhood/Subjects/
- *Yahoo Education Directory: Early Childhood* is dominated by US and commercial sites. http://dir.yahoo.com/Education/Early_Childhood_Education/

Choose the best tools for your literature search

Review the tools for finding literature above and then write down the tools you will use in your literature search and their location. If you are using tools online, bookmark them as you visit each resource. You can then organize your bookmarks into readily accessed folders.

Plan how to organize and store the results of your literature search

You can store the results of your literature search physically (in folders or binders) and/or electronically (in computer files). Either way, you will need to devise an index so that you can retrieve items easily. N.B. If you store the results of your literature search electronically (in computer files), create 'back-up' files and store them in a different physical location to your originals.

Learn how to use a current literature search software package

You can create an electronic bibliography by using software packages such as *EndNote, Procite* and *Citation*, each of which is used widely in academic circles. Once you've installed such a package on your computer, you can use it to create your own database of references either manually (typing them in) or electronically (downloading them from library catalogues or online databases). Once an entry is in your database, you can insert it in a document (e.g. Microsoft Word or WordPerfect) as a citation and include it in the document's bibliography without typing a single word! The software also enables you to manipulate, edit, format and reformat your references into more than 500 different styles. This feature is especially valuable if you intend to publish the results of your project, because different publications require authors to list their references in different styles.

Create a literature search diary

Record each relevant item that you find meticulously in a 'search diary' (e.g. a notebook, a computer file). This makes it easier to find an idea, or technique later and it also prevents any confusion over the precise details of a reference. *Figure 4.3 An example of a literature search record* could be used as it is, or (more likely) you could amend it to suit your specific needs.

In your search diary you can record where you searched (e.g. a particular library, a particular online database, a particular CD-ROM database), when you searched, what key terms you used and what you found. This can help you to write a formal literature review.

Term, idea or theory	Definition (a quote or a précis)	Location/s (full reference details)	My comments	My problems or questions

Figure 4.3   An example of a literature search record.

Ensure that you cite each item appropriately

When you join in professional and research conversations on your chosen topic, it's important to acknowledge other people's ideas when you use them to help your own thinking. Others have worked hard to do thinking and research on the topic and to share it with others. If someone's thinking or research has influenced your thinking, then you should acknowledge that fact by citing their work. This honours what others have contributed to the conversation and makes it clear that they have influenced you. It is also a way to clarify just what you are contributing to the conversation – how your thinking and research is moving it forward or helping it to change direction.

There are several academic referencing or citation styles and conventions. It is important to be consistent and accurate and to use a standard format for your bibliography and footnotes. Different universities, schools and faculties have different preferences for referencing style, as do government organizations and other groups that publish material. Find out your organization's preferred style of referencing before you begin your literature search, because this will save you time in the long run. If your organization has no preferred style, then agree early on which style you will use.

Analysing the results of your literature review

The most obvious (but often overlooked) reason to review the literature about your topic is to discover whether anyone has addressed your research question as you intend to answer it. There are four possible links between your proposed research and earlier research:

- Has someone attempted *successfully* to answer your research question as you intend to answer it?
- Has someone attempted *unsuccessfully* to answer your research question as you intend to answer it?
- Has someone has used *a different approach* to answer your research question?
- Has someone has answered *a different question* using your intended approach?

Has someone attempted <u>successfully</u> to answer your research question as you intend to answer it?

For example, imagine that you want to investigate whether there are links between class, race and student engagement. When you review the appropriate literature, you discover that a researcher has successfully done precisely what you propose to do! In these circumstances, ask yourself:

- Are my circumstances sufficiently different from the earlier researcher's to make it worthwhile for me to repeat the exercise or should I formulate a different research question?
- Since that earlier research, has anyone offered a new perspective on links between class, race and student engagement?
- If nothing has changed since the earlier research, won't I just repeat it?

Has someone attempted <u>unsuccessfully</u> to answer your research question as you intend to answer it?

For example, imagine that you want to investigate whether children make sense of children's television programmes from Australia and from the USA in different ways. When you review the appropriate literature, you discover that a researcher has asked this question already, but the children's responses were so diverse that there were no consistent patterns in the results. In these circumstances, ask yourself:

- Can I modify my research plan to avoid the problems that the earlier researcher encountered?

- Did the earlier research share my approach to the topic? If not, would my approach reduce the diversity of responses in the earlier research?
- Are children's television programmes from Australia and from the USA so different that they preclude categorization?
- Should I investigate Australian and US versions of another product designed for children?

If you can suggest a different research method and/or a different research focus, then it's worth continuing with your original research proposal. Indeed, you may be able to show that its amended form improves on earlier research.

Has someone used <u>a different approach</u> to answer your research question?

For example, imagine that you want to interview your colleagues to discover whether 'political' cartoons in newspapers prompt them to take some form of political action. When you review the appropriate literature, you discover that a researcher has already asked that question of a random sample of the population using a postal questionnaire. The two projects share a research question (they resemble each other substantively), but use different methods to answer it (they differ from each other methodologically), so in these circumstances, ask yourself:

- What can I learn from an interview that I can't from a postal questionnaire and vice versa?
- Are my colleagues a random sample of the population or do they share characteristics that differentiate them from the rest of the population?
- Are those differentiating characteristics likely to differentiate my colleagues' responses from those of the rest of the population?
- Can I use the results of the previous research project, together with the answers to my earlier questions, to reconsider my proposed research and either confirm it or amend it?

Has someone has answered <u>a different question</u> using your intended approach?

For example, imagine that you want to investigate whether and how direct intervention by staff can promote gender equity among children. When you review the appropriate literature, you discover that a researcher has already investigated whether and how direct intervention by staff in their early childhood setting promoted racial equality among the children. Why does this matter to you?

- That earlier piece of research illustrates how your proposed research method works in practice – what it can and can't achieve. Reconsider your proposed method in this light and either keep it or change it.
- Reading this earlier piece of research enables you to have more confidence in your chosen method than if you hadn't read it.

Sharing the results of your literature review

You can use the results of your literature review to create change by summarizing them and then sharing them with others. Here are some ways to summarize your results:

- *An annotated table of results*, to give an overview of the thinking about your research topic.
- *Thinking pieces*. Pull together two or three major questions or big ideas from the literature review into short 'thinking pieces' and then distribute them among a group to prompt discussion about their own ideas on the research topic.
- *Issues papers*. Write a short paper about a key issue that has emerged, then distribute it to prompt critical thinking about that issue. Headings could include: key findings, common debates, common concerns, questions this raises, some ways to respond, resources, references, further reading.
- *Specialist annotated bibliographies* – it may be helpful to share short summaries from key pieces of research from the literature to focus attention on key learning from it. They can also offer a way into the literature for people who have not been able to participate more fully in the literature review.
- *'Big ideas' concept map* – concept maps are a way to show what you consider to be the relationships between different concepts or ideas. You can use these to visually present some of the big idea findings of your literature review to others as a tool to support critical reflection in the group on what they currently think about your topic. We have provided some suggested resources at the end of the chapter that introduce you to different types of concept mapping and link you to software tools that can help with this.

You can produce each of these ways to share your results in various formats, such as a printed document, overhead slides or a PowerPoint™ presentation.

Glenda was the facilitator for a group of early childhood professionals who were researching student engagement in early childhood settings. The group was unsure how to define and to measure student engagement, so Glenda did a comprehensive review of the literature on student engagement. She shared the results as follows:

- She summarized the ideas and topics that she had found in the literature and created resource sheets about them, including 'Definitions of engagement', which categorized different ways to think about engagement and different levels of engagement.
- She provided the group with copies of key research articles in which researchers had defined student engagement in ways that enabled them to measure it.
- She shared a research article in which the researchers had engaged critically with traditional methods of measuring engagement.

The research group used the articles and resource sheets to reflect on these questions:

- How would you define student engagement?
- Whose conception of engagement is most worthwhile from your perspective? Why?
- What are the challenges for you in defining and measuring student engagement?

Taking Step 4: a case from practice

A review of literature can play different roles at different times in a project. Researchers in each of the two cases that follow used research literature differently to inform the early phases of their action research work.

Refining your action research focus

A team of early childhood practitioners working in the Berth Out of School Hours services (*Student Engagement: Starting with the Child* project) were curious about whether and how gender influenced the choices of children of different ages in their programme. They used a search engine to do a quick overview of the literature to help them gain a focus and to generate a research question around which to collect their 'baseline' data.

BOS Action Research Journal entries

20/5
We have decided to collate as much past research as possible on

the topic to present to the research team at our next meeting. Thought: do a journal search on the HOST search engage. See what I can dig up.

23/5/05
Borrowed an interesting book from the library today: *Gender in Early Childhood*, and it's a written recently book. I will start reading, skimming through. (Yelland, N. (Ed.) (1998) *Gender in Early Childhood*. Routledge, London.)

Our question – Initial thoughts:
Do all staff provide mixed gender activities for all children to engage in throughout the day?

Deepening and broadening the focus of change

Staff at the Undervale preschool were also curious about gender. Entries in their *Action Research Journal* (*Student Engagement: Starting with the Child* project) show how one specific piece of research literature on boys in preschools prompted them to start planning their first change. Their journal entries also showed that after they created their first change, they returned to the literature to deepen and broaden their change strategies. They used what they had found in the research literature to develop an extensive list of specific changes that staff could make to their teaching to enhance boys' engagement in their preschool programme.

.Entries in Undervale Action Research Journal

Staff decided initially to experiment with the fact that recent research has shown – boys prefer to stand when completing table top activities/may be more likely to engage in a table top activity with stand room only (Ian Lillicoe).

Our initial idea was to introduce a taller table activity in order to encourage the boys to engage more successfully in table top activities that require the use of fine-motor skills. This had very positive outcomes for all the children, especially boys. Where/what to next?

- After completing some readings/research on boys, the staff has brainstormed ideas for further changes to enhance boys' engagement in preschool.

Taking your fourth step: your actions and reflections

- What type of literature review should you do and what – if any – are the formal requirements for your literature review?
- What do you know already about your topic and what do you hope to find in the literature?
- What referencing or citation system does your organization use?

It's now time to do the search. Use *Thinking Box 4.2 Which is my best search strategy?* to decide how best to approach your literature review and note your decisions in your *Action Research Journal*. Remember: you'll probably visit the literature at several points in your project and, as the focus of your action research project shifts, you may want to broaden your sources of information.

Thinking Box 4.2 Which is my best search strategy?		
What information do I want to collect? What are my key terms? What do I want to learn?	Where can I find this literature? (Circle those most relevant for you.)	Where will I start? What will be the order of my search?
	Primary sources, such as: • Journal articles • Conference papers • Dissertations • Monographs • Scholarly books • Technical reports • Government reports **Directories**, such as: • ERIC Descriptors • Dissertation Abstracts • Education Index • Resources in education • Psychological Abstracts • Books in Print **Electronic databases**, such as: • ERIC databases	

| | • UnCover
• Periodical abstracts
• Newspaper abstracts

Secondary sources, such as:
• Encyclopedia
• Yearbooks
• Digests and reviews on research
• Handbooks of research
• Scholarly books
• Magazine articles
• Newspaper articles | |

Further resources: going deeper

In print: literature search strategies

Hart, C. (2001) *Doing a Literature Search: A Comprehensive Guide for the Social Sciences.* Buckingham: Open University Press.

Mac Naughton, G. and Rolfe, S. (2001) The research process. In G. Mac Naughton, S. Rolfe and I. Siraj-Blatchford (eds), *Doing Early Childhood Research*, Buckingham: Open University Press, pp. 12–30.

Online: literature search strategies

Alexander, K. (2007) Searching for equity: how databases can work for you, CEIEC Member's Briefing paper 6.1 Melbourne: The University of Melbourne. Available at: education-ceiec@unimelb.edu.au

Raszewski, M. (2006) Smart searching: Planning and building your search. Available at: http://dydo.infodiv.unimelb.edu.au/index.php?view=pdf;docid=2938 (accessed 20 September 2006).

Vickers, K. (2005) Searching the early childhood literature online. Available at: http://dydo.infodiv.unimelb (accessed 20 September 2006).

Online: concept-mapping resources

Concept mapping. Offers different ways to map ideas. Available at: http://www.graphic.org/concept.html

Concept mapping resource guide. Specific focus on concept mapping in research. Available at: http://www.socialresearchmethods.net/mapping/mapping.htm

For further resources, visit the CEIEC website, 'Dimensions of Action Research for Equity'. Available at: http://www.edfac.edu.au\CEIEC\DARE

Step 5 Learn more about your ethical responsibilities

The ethical demand of Action Research is about the power relationships inherent in the social sciences. Because the social sciences can make a difference in people's lives, power and responsibility are unavoidable issues.

(Hilson, 2006: 32)

Permissions slips
. . . There are two lots of permission slips required
CEIEC/University of Melbourne
  • teachers need to sign – teacher form
  • parents need to sign – child form
Remember the parents of the children you are choosing to study need to give permission – for some of you this is only the three you identified earlier in the year and gave each child a pseudonym.

DECS
  • teachers need to sign – educator form (see attachment)
  • parents need to sign – child talent release form (see attachment)
Educator form is needed for all staff at your centre who are contributing to the work.
Parent form is for any child whose picture or work you are using/giving DECS.

(E-mail communication to participants from the DECS Project Officer, Learning Engagement – *Starting with the Child* project, October 2006)

At this stage in your project, you need to consider conceptual and practical ethical issues. Conceptually, you need to learn what research ethics are and as Hilson (2006) suggested (see above), you need to learn about the specific ethical issues associated with action research. Practically, you need to organize yourself to gather and complete whatever formal paperwork concerning ethics your project requires. As the DECS e-mail communication (see above) suggests, you will need to gain participants' consent if you researching in large organizations and/or with university researchers.

What you'll need to take Step 5:

Time
- to read this step, to reflect on its content and to complete its *Thinking Box*;
- to discuss potential ethical issues with those who will be involved in your project;
- to familiarize yourself with the ethical processes and timelines of your project;
- to draft, submit and revise your ethics proposal;
- to gain informed consent from participants in your project.

Knowledge
- Where will I find out about the ethics requirements?
- Who can help me with preparing my ethics proposal?
- How can I decide what is an ethics issue?

Other resources
- Access to a computer to prepare your ethics proposal.

Introducing ethics

Groups, institutions and societies often believe that there are right and moral ways to behave; and they sometimes collect these statements into what are called codes of ethics. These groups, institutions and societies often talk about ethical behaviour as if it is universal, i.e. as if it is behaviour that every right-thinking person in any society at any time would regard as the proper way for any human being to behave. Indeed, unless ethics are universal, a researcher could dismiss them as merely a collection of arbitrary, culture-bound and historically-dated statements. (Not a good defence if a researcher is caught behaving unethically!)

In contrast, Foucault (in Rabinow 1997) believed that ethical behaviour isn't universal but, instead, varies between societies and is, therefore, associated with particular times and places. He argued that ethics are always bound up with the particular relations between power and knowledge that character-ize a specific society; and that each society's particular knowledge–power rela-tions mean that some ways to behave (with others and with oneself) come to be considered right and proper . . . and others don't.

Every researcher who researches people ('human subjects') faces choices about ethical behaviour, whether they regard ethics as universal statements of right and proper behaviour, or as statements that are specific to particular times and places. Any major institution in which research happens (for example, universities and government organizations) will have a code of ethics that states how that institution expects research to be conducted. These codes usually include penalties – at least implicit if not explicit – against any transgression. Codes of ethics for researchers can vary between institutions, between professions and between countries. However, they generally include some broad ethical principles to guide research involving human subjects that insist on truth, dignity and some version of justice and fairness in research.

Researchers' *general* ethical responsibilities

Codes of ethics for researchers generally include four broad ethical principles to guide their work:

- Find and follow the specific ethical code/s appropriate to research in your specific circumstances.
- Minimize harm and maximize benefits for research subjects and keep them safe.
- Learn about 'informed consent' and include it in the design of your research.
- Maintain research subjects' privacy and prevent unauthorized access to information that they provide.

Find and follow the specific ethical code/s appropriate to research in your specific circumstances

Many organizations have a formal ethics committee or process to guide research involving human subjects. Your first step in establishing a research project is to discover whether your organization has such a formal ethics committee or process and, if so, to familiarize yourself with its requirements. For example, an organization may require researchers to gain the consent of a formal ethics group, such as a Human Research Ethics Committee or a Management Committee, before they begin their research. Gaining such consent can take time – especially if that formal ethics group meets only occasionally – so you should familiarize yourself with the procedures well before you intend to start your research project.

If your organization lacks such a group or process, there are national and international codes of ethical research that you can use to guide you. These codes are generally publicly available via the World Wide Web: the 'Further resources' at the end of this step includes examples of such codes from different countries.

Minimize harm and maximize benefits for research subjects and keep them safe

An ethical researcher aims to 'do no harm' to their research subjects and to keep them safe during the research project. More specifically, an ethical researcher ensures that in their project, the advantages and benefits of being a research subject outweigh any disadvantages or risks. Any research project needs a 'favourable risk–benefit ratio' (Khanlou and Peter 2005: 2333). To judge whether your planned research project meets this requirement, ask yourself whether you would enjoy being a research subject in your project, what advantages it would bring and what you would risk (Zeni 2005). When you have answered those questions, ensure that your research plan minimizes any risks. Finally, explain to your potential research subjects the advantages, disadvantages and risks associated with your research project *and* ensure that they have understood them thoroughly.

No matter how well a researcher plans their project, they rarely anticipate everything that happens in it and as a consequence of it. Consequently, an ethical researcher will also plan to care for their research subjects if their participation in the project harms them in any way (physically or emotionally). In preparing such a plan, they may seek the advice of other (perhaps more experienced) researchers; and their plan should include sources of appropriate advice and counselling for research subjects in the event of unforseen outcomes.

Learn about 'informed consent' and include it in the design of your research

Research with human subjects is ethically acceptable only if those human subjects give their informed consent to participate in it. Informed consent is given without any inducement (e.g. payment if consent is given) or threat (e.g. harm if consent is refused); and it is consent to be part of a research project that has been explained in plain, everyday, jargon-free language. Such an explanation consists of:

- the research project's aims and methods;
- what research subjects will be asked to do in the research project and how much time this is likely to take;
- any possible risks associated with being a research subject in the project;
- the measures that will be in place to protect research subjects' privacy and anonymity (where appropriate);
- research subjects' freedom to withdraw from the project at any time without giving a reason and with the assurance that any unanalysed data they supplied will be destroyed if they wish.

Most research institutions require researchers to gain their research subjects' informed consent in writing on a 'Consent Form' approved in advance by the institution's ethics committee. A researcher may also need to gain consent to their planned project from administrators, management committees and other regulatory or funding authorities. This requires the researcher to consult them as they plan their project and gain their consent before they start their project.

Maintain research subjects' privacy and prevent unauthorized access to information that they provide

An ethical researcher's research plan states how they will maintain their research subjects' privacy and prevent unauthorized access to the information that they provide; and in their Consent Form (see above) they tell potential research subjects about these measures. Here are some measures to maintain research subjects' privacy and anonymity and to prevent unauthorized access to research data:

- Keep details of research subjects' identities (e.g. their names, addresses, age) separate from research data gained from them in the course of the project. This prevents any unauthorized person from matching a particular research subject with particular research data.
- Give each research subject a pseudonym (or invite them to choose one for themselves) that you can use to track and share what research subjects say and do and yet maintain their privacy.
- Keep research records in a locked cupboard, cabinet or folder and, if these folders are electronic, protect them with passwords.

An example from an early childhood research project
In an action research project to increase children's participation in local government in the Victorian City of Port Phillip, Dr Kylie Smith invited children to choose a pseudonym as part of the process of gaining their informed consent to participate in the project. *Figure 5.1 Children's consent* shows a section of the informed consent form that she designed for use with children.

When we write about the ideas children share with us so that City of Port Phillip and other people know, we won't use your name. Do you have a name or word you would like us to use when we talk about your work?

Yes ⊗   No ⊗

Name to be used:

Figure 5.1   Children's consent.

Action researchers' *specific* ethical responsibilities

An action researcher has all the ethical responsibilities of any researcher. Thus, action researchers who work with others (e.g. parents, children and professional colleagues) must obtain explicit permission from the relevant ethics body to observe or collect data from them or to examine documentation relating to them. However, action research research carries with it additional ethical responsibilities. For example, it is hard to maintain anonymity in an action research project in a relatively small, enclosed organization such as an early childhood setting, because anyone who knows the people involved can link its outcomes and its participants. In these circumstances, each potential research subject (e.g. each colleague, child and parent) needs to understand clearly that they and their contributions to the project may be identified in any public record of the project (Zeni 2005). Khanlou and Peter (2005) suggest an early meeting with the potential action research participants to explain the project to them in detail, including how data will be collected; and to invite them to ask questions about the project and their involvement in it. This is especially important if the research participants do not know the researcher.

Additional ethical responsibilities arise because action research is open-ended and, sometimes, politically risky; and because some action researchers regard the formal process of gaining research subjects' informed consent as condescending. Consequently, some universities in the USA have withheld ethics permission from proposed action research projects (Brydon-Miller and Greenwood 2006; Detardo-Bora 2004). Let's examine each of those issues in turn, highlighting the ethical responsibilities it implies.

Action research is open-ended

> A good traveller has no fixed plans and is not intent on arriving.
> (Lao Tzu, 570–490 BC)

Like any researcher, an action researcher starts with a research question they wish to explore but, unlike other researchers, an action researcher cannot always be sure about where their research will take them and their research subjects. Whether a particular action research project aims to create professional change or social change (see 'Step 3'), its direction will depend on the outcome of the action research cycle of 'think, do, think' (See this book's 'Introduction'). This lack of a clear direction makes it hard for ethics groups to consent to an action research project, because they need to know its potential risks for research subjects.

There are some solutions to this tricky problem. First, Brydon-Miller and Greenwood (2006) suggest that action researchers should seek permission to do action research in a specific context rather than to do specific things within the action research. An alternative solution is for action researchers to seek permission to conduct the first stage of the action research cycle ('Choose a social practice to change or improve') and identify the general principles that will guide the subsequent stages. Action researchers can strengthen this proposal by emphasizing that subsequent stages of the project (i.e. of the action research cycle) will be collaborative ventures between researchers and research subjects; and that they are asking the ethics group for permission to collaborate with their research subjects. In such collaborative action research, all the people involved decide what will happen. Everyone involved in the project is a researcher and 'research subjects' become 'research participants'.

Action research is, sometimes, politically risky

Action research for *social* change involves collaboration with marginalized or oppressed groups in order to foreground their voices and to create greater justice and fairness for them. This sort of research can be politically risky because, as research participants relate their experiences of hostility and conflict, they challenge the society that created those experiences and yet excludes them from its stories of everyday life. This is particularly so if you are researching in areas where there is overt conflict. As Lundy and McGovern (2006: 49) explain: '[I]n situations where political violence has occurred and marginalized groups have experienced social injustice, it is ethically impossible and morally reprehensible for social researchers to remain detached and silent.'

Generally, action research for *professional* change is less politically risky because it is not necessarily geared towards changing power relationships or challenging injustice.

Some action researchers regard informed consent as condescending

Action researchers would mostly agree that in an ideal action research project, there are no distinctions of status between researcher and research subjects. Instead, 'the roles of researcher and researched are blurred' (Khanlou and Peter 2005: 2333) and everyone becomes an equal participant or co-researcher, sharing ownership and responsibility in the project. (Equality of participation still allows for different participants to have different tasks to complete.) The aim is to share power in designing and conducting a research project and in sharing its results, thus producing fairer power relationships between researcher and 'researched'. However, in this democratic ideal, whose responsibility is it to ensure that participants give their informed consent to be part of the project? Indeed, who should seek informed consent from whom and in what form?

Cornwall and Jewkes highlight these links between collaboration, respect and rights in collaborative (or what they term participatory) action research:

Ultimately, participatory research is about respecting and under-standing the people with and for whom researchers work. It is about developing a realization that local people are knowledgeable and that they, together with researchers, can work toward analyses and solu-tions. It involves recognizing the rights of those whom research concerns, enabling people to set their own agenda for research and development and so giving them ownership over the process.

(1995: 1674)

Eikeland (2006) strikes a cautionary note, arguing that institutional require-ments for informed consent recreate the distinction between researcher and research subjects; that this distinction is condescending to the people it now labels 'research subjects'; and that the distinction undermines any claims by a researcher that their project is a collaboration between equals to create shared understandings. These problems are greatest when an outsider or newcomer to a group ('the researcher') instigates an action research project and invites group members to join. There is always the risk that the instigator will be regarded as the 'real' researcher and that anyone who joins 'their' project will be regarded merely as 'novice' researchers.

Collaborative action researchers' *specific* ethical responsibilities

An action researcher who is involved in a collaborative project faces the additional ethical responsibility to share power with their co-researchers. There is no easy, simple way to do this, but here are some suggestions:

- devise clear, written protocols and procedures to guide collaboration;
- seek reciprocity;
- build participants' trust in themselves;
- plan to deal with the politics of difference;
- plan to deal with disagreements (and with agreements!).

Devise clear, written protocols and procedures

McTaggart (1992) identified several protocols and procedures to guide collaboration:

- Make your protocols and procedures binding and make them known before you start your action research project. Each person who will be involved in your project must agree to those principles before they become involved.
- Involve participants in shaping the project. Ensure that they have

understood what the project involves and what their role will be in generating research data.

- Negotiate with those affected by your project. Not everyone in the setting will want or be able to be involved in the project directly, so you should ensure that the project acknowledges their responsibilities and wishes.
- Check that your accounts of other people's points of view are accurate in *their* terms, not just in yours.
- Report progress to those affected by your project. Keep the project visible and remain open to suggestions so that you can take account of any unforeseen and unseen ramifications. For example, people whom the project affects adversely must have the opportunity (and feel comfortable) to protest to you about it.
- Conclude data-gathering sessions by debriefing participants, offering them reassurance about their contributions and offering them an opportunity to withdraw – at any stage – their contributions and/or data collected from or about them.

(adapted from McTaggart 1992)

Seek reciprocity

Reciprocity is the mutual give-and-take in a relationship – for example, a relationship between researchers and research subjects or between co-researchers – and is an important ethical component of collaborative action research (Hilson 2006). Lather's definition of reciprocity in research for social change (what she calls 'emancipatory empirical research') is used and cited often, because it links reciprocity, knowledge and power: 'Reciprocity implies give-and-take, a mutual negotiation of meaning and power. It operates at two primary points in emancipatory empirical research: the junctures between the researcher and the researched, and between data and theory' (1991: 57).

Reciprocity doesn't mean that everyone in a research project does the same things. In a reciprocal action research project, researchers or research participants distribute responsibilities and tasks according to agreed and equitable procedures, encouraging each person to share ownership, involvement and responsibility in the project. These responsibilities and tasks include not just doing the research, but also making sense of the results and building theory about them. This entails inviting everyone in the project to answer these questions:

- What are we learning and how are we learning it?
- How should we organize what we've learnt in order to share it with others?
- How should we organize the writing-up of the project?

For example, a university-based action researcher working with school principals in a professional development project involved them in theory-building by writing a paper and giving it to the principals to read and critique (Robertson 2000).

Marshall and Rossman (2006) suggested that researchers balance the desirability of reciprocity with factors that might reduce or prevent it, such as:

- *Levels of participation in the research conduct.* What will you do and what will your co-researchers or participants do? For instance, will you collaborate in data collection including observations, interviews and other techniques used the project?
- *Levels of openness.* What will you reveal about yourself to your co-researchers or participants and what will they reveal about themselves?
- *Degrees of involvement.* How intensively will you and your co-researchers or participants be involved during a day, a month, etc.?
- *Duration of involvement.* For how long will you and your co-researchers or participants be involved in the project?

Build participants' trust in themselves

Hilson believed that action researchers have an ethical responsibility to increase 'participants' ability to act on their own behalf' so that they come to 'trust their own powers of action and decision' (2006: 28); and that this is also an ethical practice of action research. This responsibility to build participants' trust in themselves is part of an ethical researcher's general responsibility to 'Minimize harm and maximize benefits for research subjects and keep them safe' (see p. 80). An ethical researcher should enable and encourage people to believe that they can create change, but should also respect people's freedom to choose whether or not to create change. This is especially important when working with groups of people who have experienced unfair treatment, been silenced and/or have lost hope in their capacity to change their world.

Plan to deal with the politics of difference

In any collaborative action research project, the politics of difference will be the arena in which you will try to build collaboration, seek reciprocity and build participants' trust in themselves. Whether and how the design and operation of your project includes or excludes gender, 'race', ethnicity, class and culture is an ethical issue. Despite your best efforts to achieve equity in what is said, done and understood through your project, all the participants may not feel equally able, confident or safe in the project, because of their experiences of oppression and discrimination. For instance, racism has been a feature of the political and social landscape in countries such as Australia and the UK for decades, so a sole black participant in an otherwise all-white group of co-researchers may find it hard to share their views and ideas and may feel that to do so is unwise or unsafe. A woman in an otherwise all-male group of researchers may have equivalent feelings. Hamelink (2000: 144) put it thus: 'Providing equal liberties to unequal partners functions in the interests of the powerful.'

Inevitably, the politics of difference in your society will affect the politics of difference within your research group. When the politics of difference interacts with the politics of knowledge, particular ideas will influence what participants in an action research project say, do, think and share. Merely 'being nice' to each other and sharing jobs cannot, in and of itself, counteract that influence. Weems (2006) urges us to take an ethically responsible view of the 'historical, social, cultural, and locally contingent discourses that enable particular knowledges and practices of representation' to influence our research, at the expense of other knowledges and practices. Making this explicit and ensuring that participants feel comfortable discussing it is a way to take responsibility for any effects it might have in your action research project.

Many ethics committees overseeing research with human subjects attach especially stringent conditions to research with groups of people whom researchers have traditionally marginalized or exploited or groups that have an unequal power relationship with the researcher. Ethics committees often call these groups 'high risk' groups, because there is a high risk that they will participate in a research project without giving informed consent in its full sense. Collaborative action researchers always have an ethical responsibility to think and act respectfully with research participants, but this responsibility is heightened when they collaborate with people in 'high risk' groups. In Australia, 'high risk' groups can include:

- children/legal minors (anyone under the age of 18 years)
- the elderly
- people from non-English-speaking backgrounds
- pensioners or welfare recipients
- a person whose capacity to provide informed consent is impaired or compromised
- a person who has a physical disability
- a patient or client of the researcher
- a person who is a prisoner or parolee
- a ward of the state
- Aboriginal and/or Torres Strait Islander people and/or communities
- other groups where a leader or council of elders may need to give consent for the group as whole before research progresses.

Plan to deal with disagreements (and with agreements!)

Collaborators do not always or necessarily agree with each other. Our choice to become involved in the same research project is no guarantee that we will make sense of the world in the same way. Indeed, it is important that collaborators in an action research project are clear about the differences between their views of the world. Our particular view of the world influences how we understand events, so sharing our understandings with each other and negotiating any differences between them is an important element of our reflections in the action research cycle.

Just as we cannot communicate in any depth with each other without some degree of commonality in our languages, so we cannot communicate in any depth with each other about the world without some degree of commonality in our view of it. For example, consider this hypothetical circumstance:

> Three people are sitting in a room without talking to each other. One person speaks only English and sees the world as an eternal battle between the forces of good and evil, of darkness and light. Another speaks only Mandarin and sees the world as an ever-changing process of natural, social and geological evolution. The third person speaks only Tamil and sees the world as a resource to be plundered by an innately superior species – humanity. It is very hard for any two of them to talk about anything in depth and an in-depth three-way conversation is almost impossible.

Despite the communication difficulties associated with different language and, more fundamentally, with different world-views, the aim of an action research project is for participants to share their different – sometimes conflicting – understandings of events, so that they can learn from each other, be challenged by each other and find new ways to understand and act in the world as individuals and as a group. This is why action researchers need to 'think openly' (see p. 57). The need for open thinking is especially pressing when unwelcome truths surface in the research and/or when difference arises between the researchers themselves or between the researchers and others in the research setting. Kemmis (2007) invoked the parrhesiastes of ancient Greece when advising action researchers how to handle 'unwelcome truths':

> The ancient Greeks described the task of bringing bad news or telling unwelcome truths as 'parrhesia' (Foucault 1985, 2001). The task required of the person doing it – the parrhesiastes – immense courage and conviction. If much action research leads to no bad news, no unwelcome truths, then it is unlikely to require of those who do

it that they display the courage and conviction of the parrhesiastes – the obligation or duty to speak with the greatest courage and conviction we can muster when the time comes to speak honestly to the tyrant, the assembly, the head of the department, or our friend.

(Kemmis 2007: online)

Action researchers who discuss differences early in their project and plan how to handle them are less likely to be surprised and flustered when differences emerge. It is highly likely that differences will emerge within an action research group or between that group and others in their research setting, especially in the light of Kemmis's point that good action research brings change through unsettling ideas and keeping critiques of practice to the fore. Therefore, action researchers should debate differences actively as part of their 'open thinking' and as part of the democratic and emancipatory project of action research for social change:

> In short, such 'truth' as we can ever find will be in communication, and we will find it only through communicative action – by being locked or engaged together in the search for intersubjective agreement, mutual understanding and consensus about what to do. . . . [Such debate] . . . requires truth-telling among co-participants in projects, with the wider communities and institutions we serve, and in our relations with government and the institutions of our professions. Inevitably, then, it requires a pluralistic outlook, a sense of one's own fallibility, and, in respect of others, civility and courtesy.
>
> (Kemmis 2007: online; following Habermas)

Action researchers' *specific* ethical responsibilities in early childhood settings

For over twenty years, researchers have debated how to engage ethically with young children in research (e.g. Davis et al. 2007; Mac Naughton and Smith 2005; Farrell 2005; Alderson and Morrow 2004). Coady explained why this issue has been so contentious:

> Children are heavily represented among victims of research, as are other socially powerless groups, such as prisoners, the mentally disabled and those living in poverty. The likelihood of being a research victim increases if one experiences more than one of those vulnerabilities.
>
> (Coady 2001: 64)

The long history of debate about how adults can forge ethical relationships with children influences whether and how adults listen to and respond to children in diverse contexts, including in research projects. Action research in early childhood settings raises some specific ethical responsibilities and challenges concerning children's involvement. A researcher's understanding of ethical action research with young children depends on how the researcher sees adult–child relationships. For example, a researcher who sees children as less knowing and less capable than adults will involve children in their research quite differently than a researcher who sees children as having knowledge and capabilities which are different from – but not necessarily inferior to – an adult's. This raises three question about action research with children:

1   Can children give informed consent?
2   Who can refuse consent for children to be involved in research?
3   Can children's involvement in a research project go beyond their informed consent?

Can children give informed consent?

Traditionally, a child's parent or guardian has been required to consent to the child's involvement in a research project. However, there is a growing belief that children can and should also consent to their involvement. This belief is linked to the belief – detailed in the United Nations Convention on the Rights of the Child (UN 1989) – that children have a right to participate in decisions affecting them:

> If we were to take (informed consent) literally, no research using children as subjects would be admissible. … According to legal definitions, children cannot give consent, but the child's legal guardian can give consent on behalf of the child. It is good practice, however, and in keeping with the United Nations Convention on the Rights of the Child, to ask the child also to give consent, or 'assent' as it is known in these circumstances.
>
> (Coady 2001: 65–6)

Such a children's rights perspective gives researchers a new ethical responsibility – to recognize children's right to participate in matters that affect them directly (Mac Naughton and Smith, 2005). This includes recognizing that children have the right to give or withhold their consent to being involved in research, ensuring that children are informed fully what this means and ensuring that they understand what they have been told. Steps to help with this are:

- Make all children with whom the action researcher is working aware of the project. When the researcher is also the early childhood educator, this gives them the opportunity to inform children and to invite them to be co-researchers.
- Give children time to consider their response to your invitation and ensure that they understand that 'No' is an acceptable response.
- Invite children to re-assert their informed consent as the project progresses and ensure that they understand that 'No' is an acceptable response at any time during the project to a request to document their ideas and/or to record their interactions.

Who has the right to refuse children's involvement in research?

In early childhood settings, there is often a dependent relationship between the adult who proposes a research project (the researcher) and the parents and children with whom s/he works. This dependent relationship is an ethical issue because it may enable the researcher to influence whether children give or withhold informed consent to be involved in the proposed research. For example, the researcher may try to persuade a child's parents or guardians to consent to their child's involvement, or the researcher may ask a child's parents or guardians to persuade their child to consent to being involved, or the researcher may use their position to 'punish' a child who withholds their consent.

Can children's involvement in a research project go beyond their informed consent?

The growing belief that children have a right to participate in decisions affecting them is leading some researchers to ask whether and how children can be involved in research projects more comprehensively than just giving informed consent. Researchers (Mac Naughton et al. 2008) have shown that children can be involved meaningfully in each stage of a research project, i.e.:

- commenting on the initial design;
- choosing their pseudonym;
- helping to choose the research tools and strategies;
- deciding what data from the research project can be shared with whom and how it should be shared;
- identifying research data about them that they do not want to share with anyone else (even if they agreed initially);
- choosing the most important things to share and deciding what has

been learnt from the project. (Researchers should ask the children whether their view of what happened or what is important coincides with the researcher's views.)
- sharing the lessons of the project with other people.

Davis, Mac Naughton and Smith (2007: 182) identified four axes of research participation for young children. Reflect on which axis is aligned most closely with your research project and why; then note your reflections in your *Action Research Journal.*

1 *Children are assigned to an adult-initiated project but are informed*
Adults decide on the research project and adults assign children to participate in it. Research protocols focus on ensuring that children understand what is required of them in the research project, that they know who decided to involve them, and why. Adults respect the young people's views by seeking them as a key part of the data gathering.

2 *Adults initiate projects and share decisions with children*
Adults have the initial research idea, but they involve children in every step of planning and implementing it. Children can volunteer to be involved or withdraw. Not only are children's views considered as research data, but also children are involved in taking the decisions about how the research project will progress.

3 *Children are consulted and informed*
The project is designed and run by adults, but the children are consulted about the shape of the project in all stages. The children are helped to understand the process fully and their opinions are taken seriously in how the research evolves.

4 *Children initiate and direct the research*
Children have the initial idea about what they would like to research and decide how the project is to be carried out. Adults are available to the children but do not take charge.

Taking step 5: a case from practice

Dr Kylie Smith recently undertook an action research project with young children in a child care centre. In the following excerpt from her action research journal, Kylie describes the ethical challenges she faced when a child refused to allow her to use data about her. Kylie called this episode, 'No. I'll tell you what I like about the room'.

No. I'll tell you what I like about the room
I had been exploring with children aged three to five years their identity construction and how Barbie influenced this. I had been working with children individually at the drawing table, documenting their ideas as they spoke. I then asked them to draw and paint the images that they had discussed. I asked children to work individually with me so that they had private space to express their ideas and understandings. Each child waited patiently for a turn throughout the morning. At lunchtime when I had to finish working with the children, Phoebe (four years of age) was waiting for her turn. She had been waiting for her turn since nine o'clock that morning. I told her that I would come back at one o'clock so that we could work together.

When I returned at one o'clock, I asked Phoebe to tell me what she liked about Barbie. She replied, 'No. I'll tell you what I like about the room.' Phoebe then proceeded to talk about the room and then draw in intricate detail all the objects in the spaces in the room. We spent an hour where I listened and Phoebe elaborately described the room and what she liked. I frantically documented the words as she wove her ideas together. I had imagined Phoebe as one of the quieter children in the room, who spent much of her time in the reflective space reading books. However, her vivid descriptions and elaborate drawings illustrated her interest and interactions in the room in a different light for me. When Phoebe was finished, I excitedly read back her dialogue and pointed out in the painting the issues she raised with me. I then asked if I could use her work to reflect on further and to share with others. She replied, 'Well, no. Actually, no – I need to take it home.' I replied, 'Oh. Oh, okay let's put it up to dry and then you can take it home.' Initially, I felt deflated. I had been so excited and enticed with the emergence of data that I was analysing it before the ink was even dry. However, on further reflection, I became really excited that Phoebe had said 'No' and that I had respected her response and treated her as a competent participant, able to articulate her own views and opinions, rather than coercing her into giving me what I wanted – her data.

When Phoebe's mother came to collect her that afternoon, I explained what had happened. Phoebe's mother asked if I would like her to try to get Phoebe to agree for me to use her work. I said 'No', because if I was to maintain my ethical integrity, Phoebe's trust and respect her right to data ownership, then I needed to step away from this piece of data.

(Mac Naughton and Smith 2005: 119)

Taking your fifth step: your actions and reflections

- What do you think it would be wrong to do as a researcher?
- Are there any types of social research in which you wouldn't participate? Why not?
- Who will choose the pseudonyms for participants in your research
  project?
- How and with whom will you share decision-making during the
  project?

You should now be in a position to choose the ethical protocols that you will
use in your project and to submit your application for approval to the
appropriate ethics body. *Thinking Box 5.1 Keeping my project ethical* is an aide-
mémoire to help you to track your decisions around ethics issues.

Thinking Box 5.1 Keeping my project ethical			
Processes	**Date**	**Date completed**	**Comments**
Ethics filing processes organized			
My ethical protocol			
Ethics proposal submission			
Ethics approval			
Formal informing of key stakeholders			
Invitation to participants			
Informed consent sought			
Informed consent gained			
Emerging ethical issues			
Ethics reporting dates			

In your *Action Research Journal*, note the date that you submit your ethics proposal, the date you receive permission and the process for storing all your forms and papers associated with ethics issues. Also, note your ethics protocols, the timing of processes for gaining informed consent and any reports about ethical issues that you are required to submit as your project progresses. It's helpful to create a special file or section in your journal where you note any ethical issues that emerge and how you have responded to them.

Further resources: going deeper

In print: Power and ethics in early childhood research

Coady, M. M. (2001) Ethics in early childhood research, in G. Mac Naughton, S. Rolfe and I. Siraj-Blatchford (eds) *Doing Early Childhood Research: International Perspectives on Theory and Practice*. Sydney: Allen & Unwin, pp. 64–72.

Grieshaber, S. (2001) Equity issues in research design, in G. MacNaughton, S. Rolfe and I. Siraj-Blatchford (eds) *Doing Early Childhood Research: International Perspectives on Theory and Practice*. Sydney: Allen & Unwin, pp. 136–46.

In print: Research ethics in organizations

Coghlan, D. and Brannick, D. (2005) *Doing Action Research in Your Own Organization*, 2nd edn. London: Sage.

Zeni, J. (2001) The IRB, the HSR – and the ethics of insider research. *Networks: An Online Journal for Teacher Research*. Available at: www.oise.utoronto.ca/%7Ectd/networks/journal/Vol%204%281%29.2001may/note.html

Online

For further ethics resources, visit the CEIEC website, Dimensions of Action Research for Equity (http://www.edfac.unimelb.edu.au/CEIEC/DARE). Links to:

- case studies of presenting action research to ethics committees;
- national and international Human Research Ethics (HRE) guidelines;
- a sample letter inviting participation in an action research project;
- ethics and cultural relativism: are ethics a white, male invention?

Step 6 Learn about reflection, critical reflection and practice

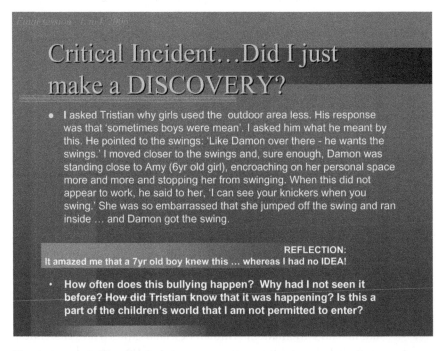

Final session Evie Felton

Critical Incident...Did I just make a DISCOVERY?

- I asked Tristian why girls used the outdoor area less. His response was that 'sometimes boys were mean'. I asked him what he meant by this. He pointed to the swings: 'Like Damon over there - he wants the swings.' I moved closer to the swings and, sure enough, Damon was standing close to Amy (6yr old girl), encroaching on her personal space more and more and stopping her from swinging. When this did not appear to work, he said to her, 'I can see your knickers when you swing.' She was so embarrassed that she jumped off the swing and ran inside ... and Damon got the swing.

REFLECTION:
It amazed me that a 7yr old boy knew this ... whereas I had no IDEA!

- **How often does this bullying happen? Why had I not seen it before? How did Tristian know that it was happening? Is this a part of the children's world that I am not permitted to enter?**

Figure 6.1   Melanie's reflections.

Researchers make discoveries by reflecting on their data and action researchers are no different. Some action researchers' discoveries happen in the moment of creating change, as Melanie's did. Melanie and her colleagues wanted to improve girls' engagement in her service's outside programme (*Student Engagement: Starting with the Child* project) and they had decided to involve the children in this work. It was in this context that she asked Tristian why girls used the outdoor area less than boys, leading to her 'DISCOVERY'.

Other discoveries happen outside of the moment, when you take time to step back from your actions and reflect on them. Reflection and critical reflection 'in action' (in the moment) and 'on action' (after the moment) are core drivers of change in action research.

Step 6 in your action research project is to learn about reflection, critical reflection and practice and how each relates to the others. Reflection is an ongoing step throughout each phase and all cycles of your action research process. You may find it helpful to return to this step and refresh your understandings at several points in your project.

What you'll need to take Step 6:

Time
- to read this chapter and to reflect on its content;
- to talk with those who will be involved in your project about the issues this chapter raises;
- to talk with supportive colleagues to find alternative ways to think about and practise your current work.

Knowledge
- Where will I find out about reflection?
- Who can help me with the difference between reflection and critical reflection?
- How can I decide if I am being reflective?

Other resources
- Access to colleagues and co-researchers who will act as critical friends.

Reflection and reflective practice

At its simplest, to reflect on something is to think about it, but we tend to reflect more on something that is surprising, puzzling or unexpected than on something that is just routine. We often reflect 'in the moment' about things we see or do. We can't always explain our reflections 'in the moment' and we don't always remember them but, nonetheless, they often lead us to change what we do or to try to do something different. In contrast, when we do something that surprises or puzzles us, we sometimes 'mull it over' for a while to make sense of it. We may wonder why we did it, whether we'd like to do it again, what might happen if we did, or whether we'd rather not do it again.

Mulling over is certainly a form of reflection, but if we also ask questions about an event or an idea we can deepen our thinking about it. We may ask why sometimes our actions and thoughts differ from other people's and come to realize that it is because particular ideas and beliefs 'frame' what we do and how we think about it and that particular 'frames' cause people to behave in particular ways (Peters, 1999). This realization can be a foundation on which to build theories about why things happen as they do. For example, 'I think that Fred acted that way because he "frames" children as merely incomplete adults; and I think that Anne acted differently because she "frames" children as beings in their own right.'

'Open thinking'

Our particular 'frames' (ideas and beliefs) shape how we act and think, but they also prevent us from acting and thinking differently. Therefore, reflecting on our particular 'frames' can be a first step towards deciding whether we are happy with them or whether would like to explore other frames that might offer alternative ways to act and think. Such reflection on our 'frames' is an instance of 'open thinking'. Open thinking requires you to do two things. First, keep up to date with new ideas and developments in your area, because these may offer you new 'frames' within which to reflect on your practice and plan improvements to it. Second, discuss your reflections with sympathetic colleagues and consider whether and how their ideas could help you to expand your range of 'frames' and theories (Kay 2004). Melanie reflected on Tristian's answer to her question by thinking openly, i.e. by opening herself to the children's perspectives to expand how she understood daily practices in her programme.

Reflective practice

To reflect on our practice is to be curious about what we're doing, why we're doing it and what its effects are; and it also involves trying to think openly about our past and present practices in order to improve on them. Action researchers reflect on their practice because they are curious about it and want to improve it. They think about what they are doing, why they are doing it and what its effects are as a prelude to change. As Killion and Todnem (1991: 15) put it: 'Reflection, then, is a process that encompasses ... past, present and future simultaneously. ... While examining our past actions and our present actions, we generate knowledge that will inform our future actions.' However, reflective practice doesn't just happen spontaneously. It takes time, as Sommers et al. (2005: 9) emphasized: 'Reflective practice requires a *pause*. Sometimes the pause is intentional – a purposeful slowing down to create a space in which presence and openness can emerge. Sometimes the pause happens unexpectedly in response to a crisis or dilemma.'

For example, at the start of an action research project to review her current practice, Mindy noted in her *Action Research Journal* that there just wasn't sufficient time to think through any innovations, with the result that many failed:

> As a staff team there is such limited time to really pull ideas apart / explore options. [There is a] tendency to rush into things and then abandon [them] as they haven't been effective. For ideas to be effective, all staff, parents and children need to be on board.

Critical thinking and critically reflective practice

Reflection is a specific form of thinking that is the foundation of reflective practice and we reflect on our practice as a prelude to changing or improving it. Critical reflection is another specific form of thinking. It is the foundation of critically reflective practice and we reflect on our practice critically in order to challenge any social habits or customs that prevent us from changing it. In common usage, to be critical is to make unfavourable or negative judgements. However, action researchers use 'critical' in its original sense, derived from the Greek word 'kritikos', which means to question, to analyse or to make sense (Kopp 2005). Thus, to think critically is to question and analyse our circumstances in order to understand them better. Action researchers regard critical reflection as a combination of reflecting and thinking critically; and they reflect critically on their practices as the first step in changing how and what they know about them (Yost et al. 2000).

For example, Mindy (whom we just met) was introduced early in her action research project to the idea of reflective practice. In her *Action Research Journal*, she wrote about it thus:

> Project has encouraged reflection on good/best practice. Not necessarily a new thunderbolt! Am constantly challenged by my own current practice in relation to teaching young children and what is really important.
>
> Creeping pressures, like portfolios, summative reports, large group sizes (and) parent expectation/culture have posed many questions.
>
> Am really confronted by current practice and my inability to find the answers. Any changes need to be whole centre, not just one person giving it a try, letting go, etc.

There are two broad approaches to critical reflection: one has its roots in interpretivism, the other in critical theory. Each approach expresses a different understanding of what we need to question and analyse in order to understand our world. Action researchers for *professional* change generally use critical reflection that draws on interpretivism; action researchers for *social* change generally use critical reflection that draws on critical theory.

Critical reflection and interpretivism

Interpretivists are interested in whether our current way to think about what we know and do is the most effective way; and they believe that what they call 'sound thinking' is the most effective form of thinking. Sound thinking involves:

- thinking logically, clearly, precisely and accurately;
- becoming aware of other ways of thinking;
- being consistent, relevant and fair in our thinking;
- using sound evidence and sound reasoning in our thinking.

(Scriven and Paul online: www.criticalthinking.org/
university/univclass/Defining.html)

Interpretivists use 'sound thinking' to reflect critically. To increase their understanding about how we think and act, an interpretivist reflects critically. In an early childhood setting, an interpretivist would ask questions such as:

- What purpose, problem or question in my work with children and their families do I want to explore?
- How do others (e.g. colleagues, parents, children) think about, engage with and talk about my chosen purpose, problem or question; and what assumptions do they make about it?
- Are there alternative ways to think about, engage with and talk about my chosen purpose, problem or question; and what assumptions do these alternative approaches make?
- What are the implications and consequences of each of these alternative approaches for: (a) my current practice; (b) my colleagues' current practices; and (c) my organization's policies?

Thus, to reflect critically on a specific topic or issue, an interpretivist needs broad and deep knowledge of alternative approaches to it and of the assumptions underlying those alternative approaches. They draw on that broad and deep knowledge to answer their questions (such as the four listed above) and then they make clear, accurate, precise, logical, relevant, reasonable and fair judgements about how best to think and talk about that topic or issue and how best to act on it.

Interpretivism has its origins in hermeneutics – a term that referred originally to the scholarly interpretation of the Bible, but which has been expanded to mean the interpretation of the social world through the experiences, ideas and thoughts of those involved in it. Interpretivists assume that each of us is free to think about things as we wish; and they also assume that an 'insider' can understand their part of the social world better than an 'outsider' – even if the 'outsider' is an experienced researcher (Crotty 1998: 66, 67). Consequently, interpretivist researchers regard people's interpretations of their circumstances as 'sound knowledge' and take this as their prime data; and they believe that the individual can transform what they know through sound thinking. In the early childhood field, there is an element of this belief in much professional development: transmit 'sound thinking' about an issue (e.g. staff–parent relationships) to people and they will use it to transform their thinking about that issue.

Hermeneutic reasoning

Hermeneutic reasoning (sometimes called practical reasoning) is a form of open thinking, in that it evaluates competing ways to understand our world. However, hermeneutic reasoning adds an ethical dimension to open thinking. Hermeneutic reasoning consists of two steps:

Step 1 Examine how we think and act. This involves asking question such as:

- How can we interpret the meaning and significance of this action?
- What rules usually guide action in this situation?
- What are the origins of those rules?
- Are those rules the only guide in this situation? Are they the best guide?

Step 2 Form morally wise judgements about how to act. This involves asking questions such as:

- How could I act differently in this situation?
- Which is the most morally wise way to act in this situation?
- Who will benefit from my action? Who should benefit from my action?

Interpretivists believe that we increase what we know gradually and incrementally through hermeneutic reasoning. They assume that when we think about something, we come to know it differently, that this different way of knowing it will influence us the next time we think about it and so on, in a cycle of hermeneutic reasoning (sometimes called the hermeneutic circle). Further, they believe that the more that we reflect on the meanings of our daily actions and examine the best rules to guide them, the more likely we are to find morally wise ways to act. For example, an early childhood practitioner could use hermeneutic reasoning to evaluate competing ways to understand how children learn and then form morally wise judgements about their place in children's learning.

An interpretivist is critical of 'unsound thinking', i.e. thinking that is based on faulty logic and/or on poor evidence and that lacks awareness of other ways to think about a topic. They are not critical of society as a whole, nor of what a society regards as fair or unfair. This is what distinguishes interpretivism from critical theory.

Critical reflection and critical theory

Critical theorists reflect critically on what we know and do in order to create social change. There are different traditions of critical theory, but they share a desire for social change and they share three linked foci:

- the dynamics of power, i.e. how ideas, institutions and the distribution of resources benefit some people more than others;
- the politics of identity, i.e. how identities such as gender, 'race', class, ability, sexuality and religion affect people's well-being;
- the institutions of injustice, i.e. how the dynamics of power and the politics of identity interact in a society to create inequities.

One major strand of critical theory draws on conflict theories of society, such as Marxism. Critical theorists within this strand define critical reflection as the collective examination of the social and political factors that produce knowledge and practices, in order to critique ideology and, thereby, create socially progressive change. (For instances of this strand, see Carr and Kemmis 1986; Giroux 1991; Friere 1996; MacIsaac 1996.) The German social theorist Jürgen Habermas is a prominent proponent of this strand of critical theory. Habermas believes that what he calls 'critical knowledge' is the truth; and that social and political emancipation depends on reaching the truth by exposing ideologies. Smith and Lovat (1990: 69) summarized Habermas's position as follows: 'For Habermas, it is only when we have reached . . . [critical knowledge] . . . that we are guaranteed true knowledge, because true knowledge demands that we be free.'

Like interpretivists, critical theorists value 'sound thinking' because it can point to better ways to think about what we know and do. Indeed, hermeneutic reasoning can become critical reflection for social change if we place our understandings of the world alongside that of others. McTaggart and Singh (quoted in Grundy 1987: 124) put it as follows: 'Critical reflection involves more than knowledge of one's values and understanding of one's practice. It involves a dialectical criticism of one's own values in a social and historical context in which the values of others are also crucial.'

Unlike interpretivists, however, critical theorists ask questions about difference, justice, fairness, power, domination and emancipation. In an early childhood setting, a critical theorist would ask questions such as:

- Who benefits from my current thinking and practices about (for example) young children and their families?
- What do I know about equity around gender, 'race', culture and class? What assumptions about each one underpin my work with (for example) young children and their families? Do I attend to those issues in my work? Should I?
- How (if at all) do my colleagues understand and respond to gender, 'race', culture and class in their work? Are their understandings and responses different to mine? Are these differences significant and, if so, to whom?
- How (if at all) do the children and parents with whom I work understand and respond to gender, 'race', culture and class? Are their understandings and responses different to mine? Are these differences significant and, if so, to whom? Do I take account of their understandings and responses in my work?
- Do my understandings and practices around gender, 'race', culture and class advantage any particular social or cultural group? If they do, am I happy with that?
- Do my understandings and practices around gender, 'race', culture and class prevent me from increasing equity around them? If so, are there alternative understandings and practices that could I use to increase equity?
- What are the implications and consequences of each alternative understanding and practice around gender, 'race', culture and class for the colleagues, children and families with whom I work?

When we have answered such questions, we can then weigh up the evidence and make clear, accurate, precise, logical, relevant, reasonable and fair judgements about how to disrupt unfair power relations – and the resulting politics of difference – within early childhood settings. This process resembles the interpretivists' 'sound thinking', but critical reflection differs from 'sound thinking' in that it requires us to think openly about how interactions between identity and power create injustices and inequities between people – an issue that an interpretivist would not address.

A 'will to truth' or a 'will to know'?

To be effective (and reflective) researchers, we should constantly challenge our 'will to truth' with a 'will to know'. The tension between these two terms is prominent in the work of French social theorist Michel Foucault (1926–1984) who, in turn, had taken them from the writings of the German philosopher Friedrich Nietzsche (1844–1900). Foucault was interested in how we come to think in a particular way at particular points and he believed that modern academic disciplines such as psychology and sociology have given us a 'will to truth', rather than a 'will to know'. Gore (1993: 10) explained how Foucault used these terms: '[Foucault saw] . . . the will to knowledge as the general desire to know, and the will to truth as the desire to know the difference between truth and falsity in particular disciplines or discourses.'

Foucault found the 'will to truth' highly problematic. Like other post-modern thinkers, he believed that there is no such thing as objective, neutral, simple 'truth'. Instead, he argued, what we regard as the truth is subjective, incomplete, multiple, contradictory and politically charged; and that these are characteristics of a local 'knowledge' (which may or may not be true else-where), not a universal 'truth' that is – by definition – true everywhere and always. From Foucault's perspective, we should seek *knowledge* about human-ity, rather than *the truth* about it. Why? When we seek truth, we seek certainty and one way forward for everyone; when we seek knowledge, we embrace uncertainty and the possibility that there are many ways forward and, there-fore, the chance to do things differently.

The 'will to knowledge' leads us to search for something beyond a uni-versal, neutral 'truth'; but this search shows that knowledge isn't objective, universal and neutral. Instead, knowledge is related intimately to power. Foucault believed that modern social institutions survive and thrive through creating and maintaining 'regimes of truth' about how we should think, act and feel towards ourselves and others; and that anyone who transgresses an institution's regime of truth faces institutional sanctions. Thus, for Foucault, 'Does truth exist?' is certainly a philosophical question, but it is also a practical and political one.

Alma and Amber were participants in a collaborative action research pro-ject about staff–parent relationships. Each of them addressed the power rela-tions between 'truth' and 'knowledge' in the form of communication between 'expert' staff and 'non-expert' parents. Alma realized that staff set themselves up as experts and draw a clear distinction between 'right' and 'wrong' know-ledge of children. In the following excerpt from her *Action Research Journal*, she expresses her belief that different 'perspectives' are neither true nor false; and she pits 'perspectives' against expertise:

Teachers' perspectives versus parents' perspectives – who is right?

Started thinking differently about parent knowledge. I was taught, teacher is 'expert' (and, therefore) 'right' – didn't challenge teachers when parenting – my child wrong / I'm wrong / teacher is right. Now I would challenge and question.

Amber believed that even though staff were experts, this didn't guarantee that they knew 'the truth' about children. Indeed, in her time in the early childhood field, Amber had seen the focus of staff's 'expert' knowledge of children shift from nurture and care to academic learning. How could both forms of expertise be 'true', especially if – as Amber believed – they contradicted each other? Amber's research confirmed what she believed already – that in shifting their focus from nurture and care to academic learning, staff's ambitions for children had diverged from those of parents. As part of her research, Amber asked parents at her centre how they would describe their child in a speech at the child's 21st birthday party. In this excerpt from her *Action Research Journal*, Amber reflected critically on parents' responses:

> It's really interesting – but not surprising – the focus on the social/ emotional outcomes, the value of being 'popular', 'respectful' and 'happy' (and) all have mentioned relationships and the value and importance of having good friends/family, 'to love and be loved', 'always an open door', have and maintain healthy relationships and diverse range of people, surrounded by supportive friends/family. . . . Reading responses has made me think about and value parents. . . . It seems to me that over the 11 years that I have been in the industry, the focus has shifted from being less nurturing/caring to more academic/learning based. . . . Teachers are far more stressed trying to impart knowledge rather than relaxing [and] enjoying being with the children and the children being with them. Thus, where is the nurture of the social/emotional child? Too busy!! Time!! Must meet tasks!! Need results!

Critical reflection in action research for *professional* change

In action research for *professional* change, critical reflection involves individuals interpreting and re-interpreting their practice so that they can act more 'wisely', i.e. more carefully, thoughtfully, considerately, intelligently and selflessly (e.g. Mezirow 1990; Brookfield 1995; Cranton 1996; Bleakley 1999). This means that they become curious about their daily practice; they think openly about their daily practice by using hermeneutic reasoning to identify and interpret 'wise' practice; and then they work to increase the 'wisdom' of their daily practice.

Becoming curious about daily practices and thinking openly about them

Action research for professional change starts when people become curious about their everyday practices and how they think about them. For example, while Mindy (whom we met earlier) reflected on her current practice, she started to think openly by including the ideas of equity and bias. Her reflections led her to consider whether she was involved in the presence/absence of equity in her programme, as she noted in her *Action Research Journal*:

> Collating a 1-page collage of photos of each child was a great way to highlight what children's interests are. Also confronting, as some children only had 1 or 2 photos. Are they invisible / quiet achievers / or not engaged?
>
> Am I biased? Am I interacting equally with all children? Are we catering for all children?

Increasing the 'wisdom' of daily practice through thinking openly

In action research for professional change, critical reflection aims to generate wisdom-in-action for an early childhood practitioner through hermeneutic reasoning. Drawing on Arlin (1999), we can say that a wise educator:

- understands the limits of what they know and what they can know;
- seeks and values the perspectives of others to deepen what they know;
- understands ambiguity;
- recognizes how contexts influence what happens and what is known;
- is cautious and thoughtful about what they do and the meanings they give to something.

Take a moment to revisit Mindy's reflections (above). Her efforts to open her thinking to ideas of equity required her to question the wisdom of her practice. She asked questions specific to her particular role in her specific circumstances and realized that as yet, she doesn't have the answers.

Critical reflection in action research for *social* change

In action research for *social* change, people reflect critically on their circumstances to change them by making them fairer and more equitable. This means that they become curious about the politics of difference in their daily practice; they think openly about their daily practice by analysing knowledge–power relations and by 'troubling truths'; and then they work to make their daily practice fairer and more equitable.

Becoming curious about daily practice

Action research for social change starts when people become curious about the equity and justice of their everyday practices. For example, Lydia became involved in a collaborative action research project (*RESPECT* project) because she was concerned about what she saw as inequalities between herself and parents at her centre:

> I have felt for a long time now that I have unequal relationships with the parents/families I work with. For example, some I tend to gravitate towards, others I often try and avoid. I also feel that while we say we incorporate children's and parents'/families' voices into the early childhood curriculum, often it's only the voices that we want to hear or that suit and fit with our images of how the classroom should look in practice.

Thinking openly by analysing knowledge–power relations and by 'troubling truths'

Action researchers for social change think openly by drawing from several traditions in critical theory. From its foundations in conflict models of society (including Marxism), critical theory has expanded and diversified to embrace feminist post-structuralism, critical 'race' theory, queer theory, postcolonial theory, critical whiteness theory and critical disability theory. Each of these more recent theories has its own ways to think openly for social change, but all draw on postmodern and post-structuralist theorists of knowledge, especially Michel Foucault. Foucault argued that in any society, the truths of that society make the existing power relations appear natural (rather than cultural). Consequently, if we wish to combat the existing power relations (and their oppressive and discriminatory effects), we must first understand how the truths of society make them appear natural. This entails analysing the relations between knowledge and power – the foundation of the existing power relations – and 'troubling our truths' about them.

Analysing knowledge–power relations

Knowledge–power analysis has two steps: (1) showing how the links between knowledge of a topic and the power it confers benefit some people at the expense of others; and (2) redressing that imbalance and promoting equity and justice by 'troubling' our truths about the topic. Links between knowledge and power are forged in the continuing competition between social groups. Foucault believed that there is never just one truth about us and our social/cultural world. Instead, multiple truths co-exist and compete for the status of the most valid. In any society, each 'truth' is associated with a particular social group; and each social group tries to persuade everyone else that what they know about a topic is the truth, because truth carries authority and if you have authority, you can get things done (Foucault 1977).

For example, developmental psychology explains and predicts normal child development, enabling developmental psychologists to identify developmental delay and abnormal development. Developmental psychologists try to persuade everyone else to accept what they know about children as the truth, because this gives them authority as 'experts' whom no-one (including parents and early childhood practitioners) would think to challenge. To analyse the knowledge–power relations associated with developmental psychology, we need to do two things: (1) show how the links between knowledge (developmental psychology) and power (authority as 'experts') benefit some people at the expense of others; then (2) seek to redress that imbalance and promote equity and justice by 'troubling' our truths about how young children grow and change.

Troubling our truths

The continuing competition between truths for the status of 'the truth' is rarely apparent for all to see and comment upon. The more embedded and secure a truth becomes, the harder it is for other truths to be seen, let alone considered as valid alternatives. 'Troubling our truths' brings this competition between truths into the open. 'Troubling our truths' involves:

- searching for different ways to understand what we know and do (i.e. searching for multiple truths);
- showing how truths that are associated with privileged groups benefit them at the expense of other groups;
- showing how our truths silence or marginalize other truths associated with other groups (especially oppressed or marginalized groups);
- deliberately choosing a truth that can guide our work to make our daily practice fairer and more equitable.

Glenda devised and uses an exercise to encourage people to 'trouble their truths'. She calls it 'The truth of the chair' that you can download from the CEIEC website: Dimensions for Action Research for Equity, available at: http://www.edfac.unimelb.edu.au/CEIEC/DARE/

Making daily practice fairer and more equitable

Just what 'fairer and more equitable' means will depend on your research topic and your research question. As an illustration, Lydia's concerns (above) about the 'unequal relationships with the parents/families I work with' led her to decide that, 'the main thing that I would like to change is how I create time and space for children, families, teachers and the wider community to have a real voice within the service.'

In action research for social change, critical reflection involves sharing your own perspectives and learning those of others, in order to assess whether what you know and do currently is equitable and just. Consequently, it requires time and space to converse with supportive colleagues.

Taking Step 6: a case from practice

As part of her work towards a doctorate in early childhood education, Karina Davis initiated an action research group to explore the inclusion of Indigenous cultures and people in curriculum. In the following excerpt from her thesis, Karina writes about the role that critical reflection (and its foundation in critical theory) played in her research. Her writing is, in itself, a powerful illustration of critical reflection:

> Critical theorists believe that if we follow the path to self-enlightenment, we can end domination and oppression and achieve freedom. . . . I understood critical theory and aimed to use it in action research to explore the inclusion of Indigenous cultures and people in curriculum. However, I did not engage with discourse analysis. [My action research group] discussed issues faced by Indigenous peoples, we problematised practice and discussed how to position Indigenous people in ways that disrupted othering and essentialism, but we did not explore how colonial and white discourses influenced our approaches to curriculum. Further, we resisted exploring the personal and attempted to engage only with our professional practice. The consequence was that we didn't challenge the discourses constructing our curriculum practice. . . . Understanding how discourses operate involves understanding that silences do not always reflect voiceless-ness. Instead of explaining silences solely in terms of powerlessness, we could explain silences as reflecting many possible factors, includ-ing resistance, lack of interest, and introversion. Each of these avoids positioning silent people as necessarily passive. . . . In this project, Indigenous peoples were certainly invited to speak . . . but only at specific places and times. While it is important that people and groups who are silenced have spaces and places to find and use their voices, it is also imperative that they choose where and when this happens.
>
> (Davis 2004: 7)

Taking (and retaking) your sixth step: your actions and reflections

Step 6 begins as you reflect on your research topic and your research question; and it continues, even as you formally end your project. We can see this in reflections by Ronnie Smith (2001) – a teacher in the USA – on an action research project for professional change:

> I believe the answer to my action research question is, in the end, a very simplistic one: 'Equality as a part of Algebra: How far can one kindergarten class go?' The answer is simply, 'As far as we'll let them'. What I need to reflect on now is, How far did I let them go? Were there ways I could have helped more? Were there stumbling blocks I didn't see? Was it a logical sequence? Was it enough of a foundation? Other questions have come up throughout the year also. These questions have been both specific and generalized. I'm wondering, for instance, about signs. Is it best to introduce them all at once or randomly or in a sequence? I'm also wondering about other algebraic concepts. What foundation could I be helping to build there?
>
> (Smith 2001: 10)

Reflection and critical reflection are the motor of action research cycle. They initiate it and they keep change happening throughout it, often spiralling unexpectedly towards another new way to think or act when you least expect it. Karina encountered deeper, more critically informed ways to think as she revisited the literature and began to re-theorize her research topic. Her experience reminds us that in real-life action research projects, each step is not separated from the others as clearly as in this book. In a specific action research project, the steps merge and reappear in different combinations throughout the life of the project.

Take a moment to reflect on what you have learnt through this chapter, especially on reflection 'in action' and 'on action'. How do you think that reflection and critical reflection might drive the coming steps in your action research project?

Further resources: going deeper

In print

The action research cycle in practice

O'Brien, N. and Moules, T. (2007) So round the spiral again: a reflective participatory research project with children and young people, *Educational Action Research*, 15(3): 385–402.

Some classic texts on reflection and action

Brookfield, S. (1995). *Becoming a Critically Reflective Teacher*. San Francisco: Jossey-Bass.

Carr, W. and Kemmis, S. (1983) *Becoming Critical: Knowing through Action Research*. Victoria: Deakin University Press.

Friere, P. (1972) *The Pedagogy of the Oppressed*. Harmondsworth: Penguin.

Parker, S. (1997) *Reflective Teaching in the Postmodern World: A Manifesto for Education in Postmodernity*. London: The Open University Press.

Schön, D. A. (1982) *The Reflective Practitioner: How Professionals Think in Action*. New York: Basic Books.

Online

Schön, D. (1987) Educating the reflective practitioner, presentation to the American Educational Research Association. Washington, DC. Available at: http://www-pcd.stanford.edu/other/schon87.htm

Links between Critical Thinking and Habermas's Critical Theory. Includes a brief but clear introduction to Habermas's work. Available at: http://www.phy.nau.edu/~danmac/habcritthy.html

Step 7 Map the practicalities of researching in your context

- Make *inquiries* to see if we can access the *school gymnasium* and equipment for *more physical games/activities*. Make greater use of the *oval/* school play ground. *Purchase some more balls* so that they can be used individually in a group activity on the oval/gym.
- Start the kindy routine with both outdoor and indoor activities so that boys can be active from the time they arrive. We could possibly have a longer indoor time after mat time, or include a fine motor activity in our small groups, to ensure children don't miss out on fine-motor activities. We could also *provide more fine-motor activities outside.*

_...... ...._... and drama to help children_

Figure 7.1   Excerpt from Lillith's *Action Research Journal*.

The initial focus of Lillith's action research project (*Student Engagement: Starting with the Child* project) was how to improve boys' engagement in preschool learning. In the excerpt (*Figure 7.1*) from her *Action Research Journal*, she began to map the practicalities of researching in her context. As part of planning for what was their first action research project, Lillith and her team brainstormed the practical resources they would need to change how they worked with the boys in their preschool programme.

Step 7 is the last of the six steps in 'Phase Two: Planning for change'. Creating change is always a *practical* process and good planning early in your project helps you to anticipate what you will need to complete it successfully. Imagine what would have happened if Lillith and her team had started their project on the assumption that they had access to the school gymnasium . . . and found that they hadn't! In this respect, action research is like much Chinese cooking – it's all in the preparation!

What you'll need to take Step 7:

Time
- to read this chapter, to reflect on its content and to complete its *Thinking Boxes*;
- to inform those who will be involved in your project;
- to plan your first steps.

Knowledge
- What are some basic planning questions I need to ask?
- Who can help me with planning the project?
- How can I overcome any hurdles that might face me in the first stages?

Other resources
- Access to materials and people you need to bring together to do your planning.

Find helpers and anticipate hindrances

In broad terms, one or more of these characters (each of which could be an individual or a group) might help you as you undertake your action research adventure:

1   THE BUDDY listens as you tell the story of your adventure. S/he reflects with you on what's happening and reminds you that your fellow participants in the adventure will be happy to help you.
2   THE INSPIRER cuts through the daily details of your project and reminds you of the 'big picture' within which you are acting and which you are trying to change. S/he reminds you why you decided to undertake your action research project and why and to whom it matters.
3   THE EQUITY PROMPTER helps you to examine your assumptions and taken-for-granted beliefs about social relationships and social practice. S/he helps you to reflect on whether and how your action research project will make relationships between children, between adults and between children and adults more or less equitable and respectful.
4   THE RESOURCER helps you to find the resources you need in your action research project. (For example, time to do your project, private space in which to think about it and reflect on it, information and advice about doing action research, examples of successful action research projects equivalent to yours.)

Try to anticipate the events, schedules or resources that hinder your work by causing the mess and muddle (for example, people who don't support your project or even work actively against it). The more you anticipate them, the better you can plan to avoid them. *Figure 7.2 Planning for problems* comes from an action research project in an early childhood setting aimed at involving parents in a literacy research partnership. It shows how a group of action researchers planned to avoid some of the initial problems they knew they might encounter.

What you can do now:

1   Use *Thinking Box 7.1 Planning for helpers and hinderers* to identify specific people you can enlist as helpers and specific hinderers you can anticipate.
2   Find one person whom you think can be a helper. Make contact, share your hopes, dreams and desires for your project with them and enlist their help.

Problem 1
Parents are often hesitant to make a commitment to being involved in a partnership with schools/centres.

Possible solution
Ask permission to visit them informally at home for a coffee and chat in order to explain the purpose of the group. Use this time to take photographs of the family which can be used at a later date.

Problem 2
Written invitations are not always read, read properly or responded to. Reasons include: some parents have limited literacy skill or confidence; the Kitchen Bench Syndrome; the Bottom of the Bag Syndrome; and the Paper Warfare Syndrome.

Possible solution
Approach each parent personally and individually, inform them that written information is on the way, and mail out the information.

Problem 3
Making written information easy to understand is an art.

Possible solution:

Keep it simple.	*Make it fun.*
Keep it bright.	*Use graphics.*
Keep it clear.	*Give a contact number.*
Post it!	

(Department of Education 2004: p. 34)

Figure 7.2   Planning for problems.

3   Think about your potential hinderers. Make a list of things you could do to overcome them or lessen their potential effects on your projects.

Thinking Box 7.1 Planning for helpers and hinderers	
THE HELPERS	WHO MIGHT THIS BE?
The Planner	
The Buddy	
The Inspirer	
The Equity Prompter	
The Resourcer	
WHO/WHAT MIGHT HINDER THE PROJECT?	WHAT CAN I DO TO PREVENT THEM OR LESSEN THEIR IMPACT?

Inform relevant others about your project

It is likely that there will be people whom you should inform before you start your action research project; indeed, in some circumstances you may need their permission to start it. These people include your supervisors (at work and/or at college), your colleagues at work and the potential participants in your project. Try to seek permission to proceed with your project as soon as you can, because this may involve formal meetings of committees or groups, such as human research ethics groups. These groups generally plan their meetings months ahead, so missing a meeting may delay your project considerably.

There are many means of informing these other people about your project, including telephone calls, mail, e-mail and personal visits. If your project involves substantial resources and/or numbers of participants, you may issue a media release or advertise your project in a local community or professional newsletter.

You should tell people the following:

* why you want to do the project and what it aims to achieve;

- the project's likely benefits for others (be specific);
- why you would like them to participate (if relevant);
- your contact details (for people who have queries or who would like further information).

(Averill 2006)

What you can do now:

- Identify the individuals or groups (and their contact details) you need to talk to in order to start your project and decide when and how you will contact them.
- Find out what ethics process applies to your project if you haven't done so already in Step 5. If you must inform a formal meeting of an ethics group, find out its schedule of meetings and deadlines for submitting applications and decide when you will submit your application.
- Produce an information sheet about your project to give or send to the relevant people.

Plan your first steps

Now it's time to consider just how you will start your action research project and how this fits into your overall project plan. As you do this, you should draw extensively on your review of the relevant literature (see Step 4) and ask yourself:

- When am I likely to receive (ethics) permission to start my project (Step 5)?
- How and when will I start my project?
- What resources will I need to start my project?
- Will anyone else be involved in starting my project?
- What data about starting my project should I collect?
- What will I do if my project doesn't start as I planned it?

It can be hard to spend time planning how to start your project when you're keen to actually start it! Try to use your 'waiting time' to get as much nuts and bolts planning done as possible. Waiting for permission to proceed can be frustrating, as Debbie Ryder, a New Zealand early childhood action researcher, found:

> We ploughed our way through the research proposal and ethical consent process. As teachers, we could not understand why we just could

not get on with it – why did we have to wait until the proposal was approved? It was an extremely busy time for all, and for many of the teachers it must have been hard for them to feel fully committed to something that, at that point, they did not have a full understanding of.

(Meade et al. 2004: online)

What you can do now:

1   Complete *Thinking Box 7.2 Planning your first steps.*
2   Read Step 10 on collecting data.

Thinking Box 7.2 Planning your first steps	
QUESTION	ANSWER
When am I likely to receive (ethics) permission to start my project?	
What will be my first steps and when will I take them?	
What resources will I need to take my first steps?	
Will anyone else be involved in my first steps? (If yes, list them.)	
What data about my first steps will I collect?	
What will I do if my first steps don't go according to my plan?	

Even when you've completed planning how to start your project, your plan may still feel messy and muddled . . . but it's time to act! Remember: in the early phases of an action research project, it's not unusual to feel unclear about where to go or what to do next. Starting your project is the best way to leave the mess and muddle behind . . . or, at least, to set it aside for a while!

If you are planning a large-scale, multi-site, long-term action research project, it's worth using some project planning and management software. During the project, it will prompt you with questions and help you to track your decision-making. There are many project planning software packages available and at the end of this chapter there is information about some free packages online that you can explore to decide whether such software would help you.

Taking Step 7: a case from practice

What follows are examples of 'mapping the practicalities' from the journals of two groups of early childhood practitioners who were participants in the *Student Engagement: Starting with the Child* project. Neither group's 'mapping' was especially extensive or time-consuming, because both undertook small-scale action research projects in their workplace and with their employer's knowledge and consent. Each group used very simple tools and questions to prompt their planning and to get their project started.

Group One (Byways OSH) undertook their action research project within an out-of-school hours (OSH) programme. Their research question was: *How can we, as OSH professionals, review how gender influences engagement in the OSH programme?* Their early planning involved answering a series of questions, recorded in this excerpt from their *Action Research Journal*:

> What steps/processes will you use to investigate this question?
>
> - observations
> - data collection
>   gather some qualitative data – staff thoughts, staff surveys
> - photographs
>   look closer at the types of engagement and gender
>   getting children to take photos of other children being engaged
> - question children – how does it feel when you become frustrated?

Group Two (Wise Bay) undertook their action research project within a preschool programme. Their research question was: *How can we include children's voices in the curriculum?*, which was directed more clearly at creating change than was Group One's question. Their early planning also involved answering a series of questions, but their questions were oriented more directly towards the practicalities of starting their project than Group One's.

> What is one change you will make tomorrow?
>
> 1   Child-initiated curriculum starting with one child per session.
> 2   Incorporate time, resources and experiences and curriculum in response to children's ideas.

> Who will I need to negotiate with or involve? Staff, parents and children at the site.

What resources will I need? Funding to purchase resources as children's interest/exploration/learning lead us.

How will I document my actions and their effects? In weekly journal, photographs, dialogue with staff, written learning journeys, children's work samples.

What steps/process will you use to investigate this question? Use focus children – what are they engaged in, why, how, when, etc. Who is disengaged? What can we do in the environment to facilitate this engagement? Brainstorm with children, interview parents. Changes they would like to see. Negotiate with children.

How will you document your investigation? Journal, photos, video, anecdotes, transcribe what children say.

Taking your seventh step: your actions and reflections

You should now be in a position to implement your plans and to start your project. You might find it useful to put this chapter's *Thinking Boxes* in your *Action Research Journal* to help your planning.

Further resources: going deeper

In print

Averill, J. (2006) Getting started: initiating critical ethnography and community-based action research in a programme of rural health studies, *International Journal of Qualitative Methods*, 5(2): 2–8. Especially helpful if you are planning a large action research project.

Bello, E. (2006) Initiating a collaborative action research project: from choosing a school to planning the work on an issue, *Educational Action Research*, 14(1): 3–21.

Hatch, A., Greer, T. and Bailey, C. (2005) Student-produced action research in early childhood teacher education, *Journal of Early Childhood Teacher Education*, 27(2): 205–12.

Online

Action Research at Queens's University. A very useful archive of students' action research projects to help you to plan and start your project, because they show action research unfolding in different ways. Available at: http://educ.queen-su.ca/~ar/oerc97/

Whitehead, J. (2007) *Action planning in creating your own living educational theory.* Available at: http://www.jackwhitehead.com/jack/arplanner.htm (Accessed 30 November 2007).

Free project planning software online

Mind Tools has details of a number of planning and management tools. Available at: http://www.mindtools.com/pages/main/newMN_PPM.htm

University of Technology Sydney (UTS) has an open access site with a number of project management planning tools to download. Available at: http://www.projects.uts.edu.au/stepbystep/planning9.html

Step 8 Plan to make your research rigorous and valid

By actively creating the space for open sharing (Scheurich 1997) about the data, and about my ongoing and emergent interpretations of this data, participants were able to critique my use of their storylines and have input into the analysis.

(Taylor 2007: 85)

In the excerpt (above) Louise Taylor has allowed co-participants in her action research project to examine and critique her data interpretation. Checking your data with others is a way to make your action research project rigorous and to ensure that your data is valid. In practical terms, checking with others means that any conclusions that you draw from your data and analysis (in Step 15) can withstand critical scrutiny.

The extent to which you need to consider rigour and validity will depend on the scale and scope of your action research. For example, a large-scale action research project involving large numbers of participants at several sites needs to be more rigorous than a small-scale project involving a few colleagues at one site; and an action research project that is submitted for a PhD needs to be open to greater critical scrutiny (especially concerning the validity of its data and analysis) than one that an individual undertakes to improve their professional practice.

What you'll need to take Step 8:

Time
- to read this step and to reflect on its content;
- to talk with those who will be involved in your project about the issues this step raises.

Knowledge
- How will you validate your results (i.e. which approach to validity will you adopt)?

- Who is likely to assess the validity of your research (this may depend on how/where you share the results) and what approach(es) are they likely to take?

Introducing rigour and validity

Rigour and validity are principles that are used to measure and judge the quality and truth of a specific piece of research and its findings.

Defining rigour

Put simply, rigour refers to the thoroughness and care with which you conduct your research project from your initial thought, through data collection and analysis, to the conclusions you draw from it. The rigour of a research project is a hallmark of its quality. The more thorough and careful you are in planning your project, collecting data, analysing it and drawing conclusions from it, the more rigorous your research project.

Different research traditions have different criteria for judging rigour. Scientific researchers have very specific standards of rigour. Social science researchers, including some action researchers, will use these standards to judge the quality of research. You will meet the key criteria for judging rigour in action research later in this step.

Defining validity

Validity refers to how you conduct your research project to ensure that its findings are sound and carry weight and authority. It is a measure of the truth of your research findings based on specific criteria for judging if a claim you make is true or not. As you will read shortly, there is considerable debate at present in social research about how you establish the truth of a research claim.

As with rigour, different forms of research have different criteria for judging validity. The debates about validity in action research are extensive. We will briefly explore these later in this step and introduce you to some current ways of judging validity in action research.

Planning for rigour and validity

Rigour and validity do not just happen. You need to plan for them at the outset of your action research project and use rigour and validity checks at key points in your project to ensure you are on track for quality research and sound research findings. For this reason, it's crucial that you learn about rigour and validity at the beginning of your action research project.

'Fit-for-purpose' rigour and validity: considering scope and scale

In deciding how you will plan for rigour and validity in your research project, you need to consider its purpose, scope and scale. The more that you intend to use your research to convince others about your findings, the more you need to consider how you plan for and argue their rigour and validity.

If you are a student researcher, you will need to convince your research supervisor and perhaps external examiners of the quality of your research and the soundness of its findings. Check with your supervisor for any specific criteria that may be applied. An individual early childhood researcher may need to convince colleagues, parents and/or children. If you are trying to convince policy-makers, trainers or a large professional group to make changes based on your research, then learning about the standards against which they judge quality research and sound findings will be important.

Scientific rigour

Action research is often seen as 'soft' research in contrast to the 'hard' research done by, for example, natural scientists and by social researchers who use scientific methods. Action researchers can find it hard to meet two defining characteristics of scientific research: identifying clear causal relationships (what influenced what?) and generalizing your findings to times and places other than your own. The absence of those two characteristics in most action research leads critics to say that its methods lack rigour and that its outcomes can't be validated.

The dominance of science

Scientific rigour isn't the only form of rigour that a researcher can demonstrate and in the next section of this step we examine some alternative forms of rigour. However, science is so influential that researchers who choose alternative ways to produce knowledge are often called upon to justify their choice, while scientists rarely face such scepticism. Further, such researchers generally have to justify their approach to knowledge not on its own grounds and in its own terms (as scientists do) but as a deviation ('unscientific') from the alleged norm – scientific research. Consequently, as an action researcher argues that they have conducted their research rigorously and that its results are valid, they must generally pre-empt criticism that their work is 'unscientific'. That is why we examine scientific rigour briefly in what follows.

How is science rigorous?

Scientists believe that their research is rigorous because their methods are described tightly and prescribed strictly. In scientific research, independent, objective observers collect measurable data and express the results numerically; then they share their results with their peers, who replicate the procedures. If the procedures produce the same results consistently, then the original research is described as rigorous. Scientific research often takes the form of testing something, then subjecting it to some process, then testing it again to see whether and how the process has changed it and, if it has, stating the nature and extent of that change.

For example, a scientific researcher who wishes to investigate the effectiveness of a particular literacy programme would measure the reading ability of a group of young children who are about to start the programme, then measure it again at the end of the programme and look for any differences between their two measurements, e.g. '20 per cent of the children in the programme improved their reading ability significantly; the ability of the remaining 80 per cent remained the same.' If this researcher's work was rigorous, any other researcher who replicates it should produce the same results.

Scientific rigour is appropriate in some contexts. Indeed, if you wish to measure the effectiveness of a programme, or the safety of a piece of equipment, then your methods need to be as rigorous as possible. However, just because scientific rigour is welcome in specific circumstances, that doesn't make it the only form of rigour that a researcher should demonstrate. Especially in social research, the lone, authoritative voice of the objective, detached scientific observer can fail to capture the complexity of a social event; whereas several observers' different perspectives on that event can produce the rich, detailed picture that is needed to capture complexity. For example, a teacher's account of an event in a classroom may be authoritative, objective and detached, but what do you think would be the effect of setting it alongside accounts from the children involved in the event?

Point for reflection

How relevant is scientific rigour for your action research project and the key stakeholders involved in it?

Alternative forms of rigour

An action researcher – like any other researcher – wants to perform their research rigorously (thoroughly and with care) because they want its results to be respected. However, scientific rigour is generally inappropriate in action research, because action researchers are generally anything but detached and objective observers of events. Instead, they are active participants in a process of change.

While action researchers regard scientific rigour as generally inappropriate in their work, they retain a basic principle of scientific rigour – methods of working that are described tightly and are prescribed strictly because they are reliable. Rigour then becomes a matter of choosing and applying the method/s most appropriate to the action researcher's aims and to their specific circumstances. This enables the researcher to affirm that their results, analyses and conclusions have solid foundations. As Swepson (2000: 8) put it: '[T]he methodology is fit for a given function [i.e.] it best allows the researcher to conduct systematic inquiry in order to present a warranted assertion.'

Rigour and reliability in quantitative and qualitative research

Quantitative research produces data in the form of numbers and relationships between numbers. Consequently, demonstrating that such methods are rigorous and reliable is a fairly simple matter of demonstrating that they produce consistent results. If two or more researchers using the same quantitative research methods achieve the same results and/or if a single researcher using the same quantitative research methods at different points in time achieves the same results, then those methods will be considered rigorous and reliable.

Demonstrating the rigour and reliability of qualitative data is not so simple, because qualitative data from two qualitative research projects is rarely consistent in the way that quantitative data can be – even if the two projects investigate the same topic in different circumstances. Qualitative researchers have responded by developing an array of procedures to establish the rigour and reliability of their data. One popular procedure is to 'triangulate' your approach to your research topic, i.e. examine it from diverse vantage points to ensure that you understand it comprehensively. There are four main types of triangulation:

- triangulation of data: use diverse sources of data about the topic;
- triangulation of methods: use multiple methods to study the topic;
- triangulation of investigators: use several researchers to study the topic;
- triangulation of theory: use multiple theories to interpret a single set of data about the topic.

Other procedures to establish the rigour and reliability of qualitative data include (but are not limited to):

- collecting data from multiple sources and multiple perspectives and then cross-checking the data from different sources to detect consistencies and inconsistencies;

- embracing (rather than suspecting) inconsistencies as an inevitable feature of the complexity of human behaviour and social circumstances;
- ensuring that participants agree that data associated with them is an accurate representation of their behaviour, attitudes, etc.;
- creating an 'audit trail' of data-collection procedures for others to assess;
- ensuring that influences on the final state of data are explicit by thinking and acting openly and reflexively.

In her research for her PhD, Louise Taylor (whom you met at the beginning of this step) cross-checked her data with her co-participants in her project and she gathered data from many sources:

- semi-structured interviews which she audio taped and transcribed;
- feedback forms that participants completed post-interview;
- group sessions which she audio-taped and transcribed;
- her action research journal that included her own reflections on group sessions;
- notes and memos from follow-up phone calls, e-mails, and face-to-face conversations.

Rigour in action research

In action research, rigour refers to the care and thoroughness with which you collect and analyse your data in each action research cycle. We have drawn on the work of several action researchers to identify four characteristics of rigorous action research. To ensure that your research is rigorous, you should be able to demonstrate (not just assert) that your project features each one of them.

1 Data was collected using several diverse methods

Using several diverse methods (e.g. observations, surveys, document analysis) to collect data builds rigour because it means you have a more comprehensive sense of what is happening in a situation (Branigan 2003). Each method of data collection will have its limits and its strengths. Using more than one method helps you to draw on the strengths of each method and reduce the limits overall in your data collection methods.

2 Data was analysed from several perspectives

Analysing your data from multiple perspectives gives you the most comprehensive understanding possible of events in your circumstances. They may be the perspectives of children, parents, colleagues or other researchers; and they may be various theoretical perspectives. Recording how you found different views of events and different interpretations allows you to show and see what has influenced your project over time.

Being open and transparent throughout the process of collecting data ensures that you seek and record disagreement as well as agreement (Crane 2004). In turn, this ensures that your analysis is sufficiently complex, rather than a simplistic overview that glosses over contrasting viewpoints.

Taking what Branigan called a 'participative' (2003: 38) approach to analysis requires researchers to seek diverse interpretations of events (Coghlan and Brannick 2004) through which to build a more comprehensive picture of what is (and isn't) happening and why. (We return to this in Step 12.) To analyse your data from several perspectives, look for the voices that are present in your data and those that are absent. In particular, consider the politics of difference and how gender, class, 'race', ethnicity and ability are (and aren't) influencing which voices are present in your data and which ones are absent.

By grounding your interpretations and diagnoses rigorously in scholarly theories and by showing how each theory supports, challenges or refutes your project outcomes, you can show that you have set your project in a broader professional conversation about your research topic. It also enables you to show that your project is generating new knowledge. Further, by reflecting on the content, process and premises of your data and analysis, you can test your assumptions about events and interpretations continuously and build new knowledge in all aspects of your project (Coghlan and Brannick 2004: 28).

3 Values were explicit

In your continuing reflection and self-examination, you need to be explicit about the values that are driving you to be systematic in collecting and analysing your data and to acknowledge the context of your research (Branigan 2003). Making these values explicit will lessen the chance that you will assume that others share your beliefs.

4 The action research cycle was enacted systematically

Enacting the action research cycle systematically builds rigour in your research as its cyclical nature means that data and interpretation from early cycles can be tested and evaluated in later ones (Dick 1999a; Branigan 2003; Crane 2004). Further, by showing how you diagnosed, planned, acted and evaluated at each stage of your project, you can demonstrate your thoroughness in acting for change (Coghlan and Brannick 2004).

Approaches to validity

In general usage, something is valid if it is based on truth; to validate something is to confirm or corroborate it; and to verify something means to prove or confirm that it is true. Researchers' use of validity is sometimes more specific. For them, a valid statement is an accurate or true representation of the thing to which it refers; and this is a reason to accept it. In Hammersley's (1992: 69) terms: 'An account is valid or true if it represents accurately those features of the phenomena that it is intended to describe, explain or theorise.'

Validity is linked closely with rigour. This is especially the case for scientists, who argue that their results are valid because they are the outcome of the rigorous scientific method of inquiry. More broadly, quantitative researchers argue that consistent (numerical) results reflect rigorous methods of inquiry. Like these other types of researcher, an action researcher must ensure that the results of their research are valid and can be verified, otherwise they have wasted their time (and the time of any other participants in their project) in producing them.

A common way to confirm the validity of research results is to call on other, independent researchers to corroborate them. Unfortunately, however, researchers differ on whether and how research results can be valid and verified – and some researchers are highly sceptical about the whole idea.

A 'procedural' approach to validity

Adherents to this approach believe that we *can* know whether research results are valid or true. They argue that if research is conducted rigorously (i.e. if the researcher followed the prescribed procedures correctly), then its outcomes are true. 'Proceduralists' often cite triangulation as a way to ensure validity; other instances of 'proceduralism' include scientific method (the consistent application of which is meant to produce consistent results) and the various prescriptions concerning qualitative research that we met in a previous section ('Alternative forms of rigour').

An 'agnostic' approach to validity

In contrast to the 'proceduralists', the 'agnostics' argue that we *can't* know whether research outcomes are valid or true, because we don't know what absolute truth is. The 'agnostics' believe that there is such a thing as truth, but they assert that we can't know if/when we've found it because we don't know where it is or what it looks like. A practical instance of this apparently arcane and abstract position is the idea that our understanding of something depends on the particular language in which we describe it. For example, a developmental psychologist and a children's rights activist use different 'languages' to talk about children.

A postmodern approach to validity

A postmodern perspective consists of four elements, each differentiating it from a traditional, scientific perspective. Postmodernists claim that they locate dynamic, multiple truths in specific local circumstances; and that each truth is inseparable from the circumstances of its production and of its consumption, especially the links between knowledge and power that characterize those circumstances. Consequently, postmodernists believe that validity is plural, 'local' and immanent in our practices of inquiry; and that knowledge is validated continuously in/through 'local' practices, rather than validated once and for all as 'universal'. In contrast, scientists claim that they offer an accurate account of real, objective objects, laws, rules and relationships that occur in the world of natural phenomena independently of any observer.

Scientific researchers virtually ignore participants' voices, often including them in summary and paraphrase, rather than as direct quotes. In contrast, postmodern researchers seek equitable relationships with their research 'subjects', in which researcher and researched are co-authors of continuing narratives of reality, rather than a knowing subject and an unknowing/known object respectively. Thus, postmodern research emphasizes participants' voices unmediated by researchers (while not claiming that these voices are necessarily 'authentic' accounts expressing 'the truth'); and a research report is just one stage of a continuing process of generating knowledge, not its end point.

Validity in action research

Action research seeks to improve social practices, so action researchers need means with which to verify statements about whether and to what extent the outcomes of their research projects are, indeed, improvements. In this section we examine alternative approaches to validity.

Validity through cycles of participation

One indicator of validity in your action research project is the extent to which your research goes through cycles of participation. If you go through cycles of data collection and reflection, then you are testing and retesting your data interpretation, ensuring its reliability and relevance to your specific context. If others participate in collecting and analysing your data, then this will enable you to use traditional approaches to data triangulation (Branigan 2003) to ensure the validity of your data and analysis. Diverse perspectives build validity by enabling analysis to move from individual viewpoints to common ideas that are the result of negotiation with others and thus closer to a modernist sense of the 'truth'.

Validity through using critical reflection and social critique to drive change and knowledge generation (action research for <u>social</u> change)

One indicator of validity in your action research project is the extent to which you use critical reflection and social critique to create change and understand the effects. You can use reflexive critique to question your judgements about your experiences, to show how your research is exploring questions of 'truth' and/or of 'truth games'. You can use dialectic critique to highlight any unities underlying apparently separate relations and also any internal contradictions underlying apparently stable relations and, again, to show how your research is exploring questions of 'truth' and/or of 'truth games'. You can show this happening in your research by recording how you interlink theory and practice as different yet interdependent and complementary phases of the change process. (Theory is based on practice, so when practice is transformed, so is theory [Winter 1989].)

Validity through 'moments of equity'

Berge and Ve (2000) were action researchers for social change who investigated gender equity in school classrooms. They linked the validity of their research to its social impact in the form of 'springboards to change' (2000: 34) that created 'moments of equity', when participants challenged traditional gender practices in their classrooms. You may need to reflect on what a moment of equity would and could look like in your project.

'Catalytic validity'

A catalyst is a substance that enhances the transformation of one thing into another and Lather (1991) coined the term 'catalytic validity' to describe 'reality-altering' research that creates the desire to create change. To establish the catalytic validity of your action research project, a key question is, 'To what extent did my research alter reality?' More specifically, 'To what extent did my research reorient, focus and energize (me) to know (my) reality in order to transform it?' (after Lather 1991: 61). Catalytic validity can be established in an action research project when someone says, 'Aha!', because they have just understood something differently, or when someone risks the uncertainty of creating change because they want to transform their practices and ideas.

'Provisional grounds' for validity

At times in your action research project you may find that you have 'provisional grounds' for planning your next action. Provisional grounds are

> claims, beliefs, theories we take to be useful and reliable, but whose obsolescence we can always imagine . . . (and we act on them because they are useful for) . . . opening up new paths of discourse, and revealing new ways to deal with situations, and new connections with the world.
>
> (Berge and Ve 2000: 34)

Recognizing that our claims, beliefs and theories are merely provisional keeps us open to the possibility that we need to learn something more – or different – about our research topic.

Validity through 'truth games'

Playing a game of truth entails following prescribed research procedures *in the belief* that the outcome will be the truth. It's a game because 'truth' can mean different things in different circumstances, so while we can pretend that we have grasped 'the real truth', we only ever grasp a 'local' truth. Adherents to this approach to validity reject the whole idea of truth. For example, Foucault (1984, in Rabinow 1997: xxvi) argued that claims to validity rest not on 'truth', but on 'games of truth': A game of truth is a 'set of procedures that lead to a certain result, which, on the basis of its principles and rules of procedure, may be considered valid or invalid'.

You can demonstrate this approach to validity in your action research project by acknowledging diverse accounts of events (and critiques of those accounts); and by posing questions and possibilities, rather than conclusions, at the end of your report.

Validity through 'an historical, reflexive, evocative narrative of the workable'

Heikkinen et al. (2006) argued that you can achieve validity in action research through building 'an historical, reflexive, evocative narrative of the workable'. Feldman (2007) criticized their argument and made some counter-proposals to ensure that research is valid and offered some alternatives. *Figure 8.1 Validity in*

Heikkinen et al. (2006) Proposals to ensure validity.	Feldman (2007) Critique and *counter-proposals.
Ensure that your account is part of a continuing historical narrative.	Chronology isn't the same as causality; and whether your account continues an existing narrative or challenges it, who assesses its quality and what criteria do they use? * Include clear and detailed accounts of *how* you constructed narratives from the data.
Ensure that your account is reflexive (i.e. self-questioning) and dialectic (i.e. includes multiple – possibly antagonistic – perspectives). This allows us to decide whether one perspective is better than another.	Authentic representation of people's words doesn't guarantee validity. It ignores ideology, delusion, the unconscious and the possible gap between perception and understanding. It can also lead to relativism because it implies that each person's view is as valid as anyone else's. * Explain *how* you used reflexivity and dialectics and *how* they led to your results. * Seek other ways to represent your data and use them to critique your own interpretations.
Ensure that your account is workable (i.e. if your outcomes are useful, then they're likely to be valid).	What's useful isn't always true! Once again, acknowledge the influences of ideology, etc. * It can be hard to specify cause and effect. Explain why you believe that your actions led to the results. * Ensure that your explanation can be applied elsewhere and is open to critique.
Ensure that your account is evocative (i.e. that it can evoke images, memories or emotions related to the topic).	However evocative your account, this doesn't guarantee that it is true. * Include clear and detailed accounts of how and why you collected your data.

Figure 8.1 Validity in action research: an exchange.

action research: an exchange summarizes their exchange. It reflects the vigorous debate between researchers as to the nature of validity, how to ensure it and how best to assess it.

You will need to decide how you will assess the validity of your research findings. If you are a student, this is best done in consultation with your supervisor who can tell you which measure of validity will be used to judge your project. If you are an early childhood practitioner, we suggest that you examine recent reports and policy documents relevant to your circumstances and determine what measure(s) of validity they have used.

Thinking Box 8.1 Checking rigour and validity in your action research project			
Criteria	**Initial plans**	**Reflections – end of cycle 1, 2, etc.**	**Final reflections**
Rigour – how am I . . .			
Selecting and using multiple methods of data collection?			
Seeking and using multiple perspectives on data?			
Making values explicit?			
Enacting the action research cycle?			
Validity – how am I . . .			
Driving change and knowledge generation using critical reflection and social critique?			
Enacting cycles of participation?			
Creating moments of equity?			
Altering reality (catalytic validity)?			
Demonstrating 'truth games'?			
Generating a historical, reflexive, evocative narrative of the workable?			

Taking Step 8: a case from practice

In her action research project with teachers, Louise Taylor took a postmodern stance on validity. In the following excerpt from her doctoral thesis, Louise describes how she used 'cycles of participation', 'critical reflection' and 'provisional grounds' to validate her research findings:

> In keeping with postmodern understandings, I have attempted to represent the multiple perspectives of participants and to offer them the opportunity for multiple readings of the data (Ryan & Campbell, 2001), right from the first interview through till the end of my writing. By actively creating the space for open sharing (Scheurich, 1997) about the data, and about my ongoing and emergent interpretations of this data, participants were able to critique my use of their storylines and have input into the analysis. I did however place boundaries around negotiations (Tripp 1983, cited in Lather 1991a), encouraging those who may have wanted to 'unsay their words' (p. 58) to consider their thoughts and comments as in progress, and I wrote the storylines accordingly. Additionally, I wrote around my own words in the same way I did theirs; experimentally and without locking any person or thought into a permanent position.
>
> (Taylor 2007: 85–6)

Taking the eighth step: your actions and reflections

How relevant are the alternative forms of rigour for your action research project and the key stakeholders involved in it? You can use *Thinking Box 8.1 Checking rigour and validity in your action research project* (p. 133) to help you to plan and reflect throughout your project.

Further resources: going deeper

In print

Avison, D. (1998) Rigour in action research: some observation and a plea, *Scandinavian Journal of Information Systems*, 10(1–2): 119–23.

Eikeland, O. (2006) The validity of action research – validity in action research, in K. Aagaard Nielsen and L. Svensson (eds) *Action and Interactive Research: Beyond Theory and Practice*. Maastricht: Shaker Publishing, pp. 193–240.

Hope, K. W. and Waterman, H. A. (2003) Praiseworthy pragmatism? Validity and action research, *Journal of Advanced Nursing*, 44(2): 120–7.

James, M. (2006) Balancing rigour and responsiveness in a shifting context: meeting the challenges of educational research, *Research Papers in Education*, 21(4): 365–80.

PHASE THREE
Creating Change

In Phase Three of your action research project, you collect data and analyse it as part of creating change. In your initial action research cycle, you should plan to collect and analyse data at least three times.

Lewin (1946) called the collection of data the 'first step' in the action research cycle. In our view, the first point of data collection is in Phase One of the action research cycle, because it is then that your early fact-finding occurs – you scan your local circumstances to see what's interesting, what's happening . . . and what isn't. At this point, your collection is brief and your data is broad.

The 'doing' in Phase Two of the cycle involves you discovering what you need to do and to know if your project is going to succeed. One way to do this is to read whether and how other researchers have explored your research topic and your research question. The 'thinking' involves drawing on your reading to plan how to create your first change using the action research cycle, then deciding how to collect data about the effects of that change. You can collect data in many different ways. Your choice will depend on:

- your particular preferences, skills and experience;
- the amount of time and other resources you have;
- the scale and scope of your project.

In Phase Three, the 'doing' is in three stages: gathering baseline data (i.e. data about the status quo); creating your first change; then collecting data about the effects of that change. The 'thinking' involves reflecting critically on your data. This will require you to organize your data somehow, looking for patterns, themes or issues in your data and asking 'What do I still need to know about my research topic and research question?'

As part of your critical reflections, re-visit the material that you read in Phase Two (i.e. what others have written and done about your research topic and research question) and then ask yourself:

- Has creating my first change altered my understanding of that written material? If so, how?
- Have my 'baseline' and my subsequent data altered my understanding of that written material? If so, how?

You will return to reflection and critical reflection in each cycle of your research.

Step 9 Form an action research group

> I have found that not only the group collaboratively has been powerful but that the opportunity to engage in some shared professional and social experiences provided the opportunity for greater insights and discussions which led to more support being given.
>
> (Sharon, *Action Research Journal*)

As Sharon researched how to improve her support to literacy learning in schools, she found that collaboration in an action research group was a great support. Step 9 explains how to form an action research group in which to collaborate with others; and how to ensure that each member can participate actively.

What you'll need to take Step 9:

Time
- to read this step and to reflect on its content;
- to talk with those who will be involved in your project – who may or may not be in an action research group with you – about the issues this step raises.

Knowledge
- What is an action research group?
- How can it be formed and maintained?
- What role do you want to play in an action research group?
- What are the challenges and possibilities in forming an action research group?

Other resources
- A place where your action research group can meet regularly and that is accessible to each member.

Why research collaboratively?

It can be hard for an individual to create change. It can be hard to convince others to join you, it can be hard to remember what you have learnt, and it can be hard to avoid repeating tried and trusted ways to do things. An individual has little hope of rejecting or reassembling what s/he already knows or of convincing other people to change the way they see the world and act in it.

In contrast, collaboration can offer you support, encouragement and inspiration as you plunge into new ways of thinking and acting. More specifically, collaborative research can offer action researchers support as they build:

- the *skills* to investigate and understand social issues in ways derived from 'leading edge' contemporary thinking, such as the work of feminists, postmodernists, postcolonialists, critical theorists and cultural theorists;
- the *passion* to advocate policies based on social justice that aim to create respectful, equitable and joyful societies;
- the *desire* to act together to create progressive social change and to extend democracy;
- the *commitment* to embed human rights in their work.

(After Mac Naughton 2005)

Forming a collaborative action research group

Collaborative research can be supportive but it can also have its challenges. It involves attempting to build an equitable relationship with your co-researchers and trying to ensure that the research questions being explored are of mutual interest and benefit. There is no formula or template to follow when you form a collaborative research group because, almost by definition, such groups reflect their members' particular circumstances and interests. However, some broad themes – culture, participation and diversity – run through the formation and operation of such groups, which this step examines in turn.

How a group develops a culture

The participants in a particular meeting may well have been meeting as a group for some time and may well continue to do so. They share a 'group history' or a 'group culture' that is more than the sum of its members' histories or identities. Therefore, to understand what happens when that group meets, you must understand its history.

Group cultures generally develop in four very broad stages:

Stage One: 'Forming'. A collection of individuals has identified a common purpose and meets to form itself into a group. Members try to get to know each other and each individual tries to establish an identity in the group. This can be a delicate, awkward process that results in a false consensus on the group's leadership, purpose and procedures.

Stage Two: 'Storming'. The group tests its preliminary (false?) consensus in practice and, if it proves inappropriate, the group seeks to modify it. As the issues become clearly defined, individuals may reveal their personal motives and goals, sometimes creating conflict.

Stage Three: 'Norming'. As a workable consensus emerges in the group, so do certain expectations and standards of behaviour. Individuals test the boundaries of these expectations and standards, seek approval for their ideas and decide on their (and others') levels of commitment to the group's existence.

Stage Four: 'Performing'. The group agrees a few ideas and members feel that they share goals. The group will have 'performed' at each of the three preceding stages – it is working as it develops – but only at this last stage is it fully productive.

(Hughes and Mac Naughton 1999, after Handy 1986)

Each stage is not clearly separated from the one/s before and after it and every group does not move through the four stages at the same rate. For instance, a group which has to focus urgently on a matter of great importance often appears to spend little or no time 'Storming' but goes straight from 'Forming' into 'Norming' or even 'Performing'. Such a 'leapfrog' can make 'Storming' unacceptable to a group which sees itself as 'beyond' that stage. If one participant – or even several – raises doubts about why the group exists or how it should conduct its business, the rest of the group may dismiss those doubts on the grounds that 'We all know why we're here and what we have to do!' Nonetheless, if genuine differences on goals, procedures, etc. are dismissed, they will reappear in destructive challenges to the consensus in the form of covert plotting and manoeuvring and overtly disruptive behaviours.

Maintaining participation in a group

There are many ways to take part in a group, so there are many views about what 'group participation' means. Simply attending a meeting is a low level of participation; actively shaping the group's policy direction is a high level. Someone's levels of participation generally reflect her/his levels of influence over the group: the higher their participation, the greater their influence.

Participation is most likely when everyone knows the following: the meeting's purpose, who will be present and how it will take decisions. A good leader can give a group this sense of structure, combined with a group culture that supports fair play, participative decision-making and an openness to change.

These considerations underpin six general strategies to increase participation – 'the six Ps'. Group leaders should ensure that each meeting has:

- *purpose* – why are we meeting?
- *procedures* – how will the meeting work?
- *pertinence* – does my participation matter?
- *participative decision-making* – does everyone have a say?
- *protocols for fair play* – how do we ensure that everyone is treated equally?
- *preparedness to change* – are we really willing to act on group decisions?

Each of these is examined below, followed by some 'quick fixes' to encourage participation.

Purpose

People attending a meeting need to know its goals. Where possible, they should be told this before the meeting (for example, by receiving an agenda) and be reminded as it begins. The group's leader should ensure that people know why they are meeting and what s/he hopes the group will achieve overall – and especially at this meeting.

Procedures

A group leader should ensure that people know in advance how the meeting will be run. For example, will discussion be restricted to formal papers with recommendations or can anything be discussed? What if someone cannot attend? An agenda plus attachments can help with this.

Pertinence

People should only be asked to attend a meeting that involves things that matter to them. Group leaders can increase participation in a meeting by ensuring that people invited to it have a clear interest in the matter/s to be discussed and a clear role in that discussion.

Participative decision-making

People are unlikely to participate in a discussion about an issue if they feel unable to affect the outcome. A group leader should actively seek people's involvement in group decisions and should allow and encourage the group to reach consensus over issues. S/he should ensure that each person has at least one opportunity to express her/his point of view. This can work well, but in the longer term, a group leader should ensure that people treat each other with respect and should enforce consistently any protocols (see below) established to ensure fair play.

Protocols

To maximize participation by everyone, a group may wish to establish and maintain protocols (rules and procedures) that ensure that everyone gets a fair hearing. These protocols should state what should happen when someone is speaking, how to deal with interruptions, how to prevent someone from dominating a discussion, etc.

Preparedness to change

Group members who will be responsible for implementing a decision taken by the group should listen and be flexible and open to new ideas. In particular, they must be prepared to innovate when the traditional solutions to a problem are clearly inadequate or inappropriate.

Some 'quick fixes' for non-participation

There will be times in most groups when efforts to increase participation fail. If this happens you could try one or more of the following:

- Ask for a show of hands on an issue. Once people show their hands, you can ask them to share the reasons for their decision. You can target (gently!) those people who have been quiet to date.
- Ask some open-ended questions to encourage responses which are 'off the wall' or 'at a tangent' to the subject being discussed.
- Ask some open-ended questions and ask each person to respond.
- Present the issue or question in written form and ask everyone to jot down their responses quickly. Collect the responses, read them to the group and ask the group for their reactions/comments. To start people talking with each other, ask them to do this in pairs.
- Invite non-participants by name to voice their views – 'Sally, we haven't heard your thoughts yet. What do you think?'
- Assign two or three people the role of devil's advocate and ask them to come up with any objections they can think of.
- Conduct an 'Affinity Process' exercise – see *Figure 9.1 The 'Affinity Process' exercise*.

This exercise gathers information quickly or gets to the heart of a problem in a way that ensures that everyone's voice is heard and counted.

Phase One
Divide the whole group into sub-groups of 4–8 people. Give each sub-group a large piece of paper on which is written the question or issue you want them to consider; and give them a pad of 'Post-its' and a pen. Give each sub-group these directions:

- You have three minutes to complete Phase One of this exercise.
- 'Brainstorm', i.e. give as many responses as possible to the question or issue written on the piece of paper, using just a few words in each response.
- Write each response on a 'Post-it' and place them randomly on the paper.
- Please do not talk during this process.

Phase Two
At the end of Phase One, give each sub-group these directions:

- You have 15 minutes to complete Phase Two of this exercise.
- Group together all your responses that seem alike. (If necessary, ask each one's author to explain or clarify their idea.)
- Discuss what makes each collection of ideas similar and devise a collective title for each collection.

Phase Three
Ask each sub-group to report their results, then invite the whole group to discuss the results, then ask them what they learnt from the exercise.

There are several software packages available to help you in this process if you want to record the results as part of your data collection (see, for example, http://www.skymark.com/resources/tools/affinity_diagram.asp).

(Based on Gaffney 1999)

Figure 9.1 The 'Affinity Process' exercise.

Planning for diversity

The membership of collaborative action research groups can be very diverse, reflecting members' different experiences and histories, and their particular circumstances and interests. Added to that diversity is members' different experiences of action research and the extent to which each one feels that they 'own' the project of which they are a part.

In a conference paper called 'Bungee jumping in the classroom: action research in early childhood', Sheralyn Campbell, Sharon Saitta and Kylie

Smith described how such diversity influenced the action research group that they formed in an early childhood centre. In the following excerpt from their paper, Kylie emphasizes the importance of planning for the likely diversity and describes how they did this:

> When the project began, there were different levels of involvement, commitment and understanding. Everyone was extremely interested in knowing about the project – particularly in terms of how it would impact on the room and children, and how they could be involved.
>
> However, there were also elements of doubt. These doubts were evident in some of the questions and statements staff raised. For example:
>
> - What do I know about action research?
> - How do I know what I'm doing and thinking is 'right'?
> - I don't have any qualifications – I won't be able to help.
> - I'd like to be involved, but I need to watch and see what happens.
>
> We found that it was important to recognize and validate each concern. Some of the ways we approached this were:
>
> - listening to each other;
> - encouraging each other;
> - reassuring each other that we could do anything we wanted with hard work;
> - unquestioningly accepting people who chose not to participate or to withdraw from the project;
> - asking questions;
> - sharing our laughter, tears and anger over inequities in our past and present lived experiences.
>
> Building supportive relationships and networks is probably one of the most important steps in beginning and continuing action research. What cemented the cohesion of our group and encouraged our ongoing participation in the project was an explicit understanding that we would not judge each other's knowledge, understandings of the world or involvement in the project. Our team of eleven people from diverse backgrounds of culture, age, class, race, education and history became a group of people who were able to unquestioningly trust each other with our professional and (in many ways) personal lives. Each person took on diverse and at times interchangeable roles and levels of involvement in the project, but everyone was essential to its life. For example, some people like Sharon and Meg were in the

middle – being recorded each week and revisiting their practices in the classroom; others like Tina made it possible for Sharon and Meg to be involved by relieving them in the Spider Room so they could meet with Sheralyn.

(Campbell et al. 1999: 11)

Maintaining critical reflection, maintaining relationships

Action researchers aim to create change by questioning taken-for-granted ways of doing things and of thinking about them. In an action research group, critical reflection must be collaborative. Here are some ways to facilitate such collaborative critical reflection:

- Meet regularly as a group to share individual members' research findings, understandings and practices.
- Structure group meetings to allow time for each member to share the data that they have gathered and for the group to talk (retrospectively and prospectively) about that data.
- Establish times for critical questioning, when group members ask each other questions about how and why things happened.
- Bring new ideas to the group to provoke members to think beyond the status quo and their taken-for-granted understandings. (For example, sharing literature about the group's Focus, inviting a critical friend to the group.)
- Summarize the group's progress (including any issues or dilemmas) regularly.

However reflective and well-meaning the (nominal) leader of an action research group may be and however closely they follow the advice in this step (!), problems can still arise. In these excerpts from her doctoral thesis, Karina Davis reflects on the effects of her particular approach to her role in 'her' action research group:

> In that I would bring theory to the research, I saw myself as one of those objective authority-figures, removed from the emotionality and subjectivity of discourse. The result was to silence those who reacted emotionally and subjectively (Luke 1992; Gore 1993). Specifically, as I had not explored how colonial and white discourses shaped my views of Indigenous peoples, I couldn't allow, encourage, enhance or guide such explorations within an action research group. . . . Through deconstructing the notion of the objective authority-figure and recognising that identities are constructed within and through discourses

in multiple and sometimes contradictory ways, action research could engage with discourse analysis to ensure all participants' real engagement as co-learners and co-constructors of knowledge.

(Davis 2004: 241)

Taking Step 9: a case from practice

Sia initiated an action research group in her local child care network because she was struggling with developing anti-racist policies and practices in her centre and wanted to create a collaborative action research group with colleagues who experienced the same struggles. Sia formed her group in three stages: (1) find people who share your interest; (2) call those people to a meeting; and (3) decide how to collaborate.

Stage 1: Find people who share your interest

Sia used two strategies to find her group. Each strategy sought to ensure that prospective participants understood that they were being invited to join a collaborative effort to create social change by challenging racism and working in anti-racist ways. Her first strategy was to recruit by word of mouth. She asked colleagues in her centre and throughout her local child care network if they knew of any early childhood practitioners who might want to join the project. She also took every opportunity to announce her project at formal and informal meetings of early childhood practitioners in her local child care network. Her second strategy was to advertise the project in early childhood newsletters in her state. Neither strategy brought her sufficient people to form a group, but after using both for two months, Sia had found ten early childhood practitioners who agreed to attend a meeting about her proposed research project.

Stage 2: Call people to a meeting

Sia used the initial meeting of the group to explain in detail how an action research project operates and what it would mean to be a participant in her proposed action research project. She encouraged people to discuss their own interests and the ensuing discussion covered four areas:

- Common 'niggles' and research interests.
- How the group might work together (e.g. taking notes and distributing them, doing readings, attending group meetings, bringing observations and journal notes to the group for reflection).
- How to ensure that each member has an equal say and that no one voice dominates group discussions.

- What next? The group agreed that each member would come to the next meeting with a practice or policy on which s/he wished to reflect critically – they called it their *Focus for Critical Reflection* (abbreviated quickly to their *Focus*).

Stage 3: Decide how to collaborate

In the group's second meeting, each member presented their particular *Focus* on issues of racism in their setting. (The group took care to ensure that each person had equal time to share their ideas.) Then the group identified ideas that were common to more than one specific aspect of anti-racist education and found that they could group all those common ideas fairly easily under the broad topic of respect for diversity.

The group agreed to find some reading about this common *Focus* that would challenge how they thought about it at present. Specifically, each member agreed to read a journal article about anti-racist education and to discuss it at the next meeting; and to include in their discussion some observations and/or reflections about the relevance of their reading to their current practice.

In the group's third meeting, each member in turn discussed the item that they had read about the common *Focus* and whether/how it related to their current practice. The whole group discussed the insights and challenges that had emerged from each member's readings, observations and reflections, then paused to ask 'What have we learned so far?' and to document their responses. Finally, the group reflected on what it could do next to challenge further members' practices and thinking around anti-racist education in early childhood settings, to make them more equitable and agreed its next steps.

The group's fourth meeting followed a similar format to its third, with members sharing knowledge and reflecting on it. One member – Brian – was concerned that perhaps the group might just fall into traditional ways to think about research and to do it because they are comfortable – 'like an old pair of slippers', as he put it. So he proposed that the group should try to inject at least one really challenging idea into each meeting – perhaps by inviting an 'outsider' to act as a critical friend to the group at key points. The critical friend would be a support to their thinking but would also challenge it. The group documented what it had learned so far and the meeting ended with a short discussion about how the group might present what it was learning to colleagues at, for example, local professional development sessions or conferences. The aim would be to help colleagues to become 'critically knowing' and to contribute to creating change in and through their own research.

Taking your ninth step: your actions and reflections

If you don't already belong to an action research group, it can take time to form one, as each of the two case studies showed. This step has offered you some strategies, but remember: Step 9 doesn't end once you have *formed* your group, because you need to *maintain* the group throughout the project. (This is another illustration that the steps in this book aren't always differentiated so clearly in real-life action research projects.)

Forming and maintaining a group can be a very real challenge for a first-time action researcher. When Louise Taylor initiated her first action research project, she certainly found this aspect a challenge. This excerpt from her action research journal demonstrates this very powerfully. It also illustrates the general point that the practicalities of action research can very often be much less clear-cut than the 'theory' leads us to expect:

> I was determined right from the beginning that I would work collaboratively with the teachers in this project; after all that is the goal of action research isn't it – or at least it is supposed to be. Putting this goal into practice is not as easy as it sounds, especially when the participants are telling me that they just want to talk – with no particular end in mind! How on earth am I going to track action research cycles when everyone is just talking? I thought that this project would have nice neat cycles that I could describe and report on but this isn't happening as I had hoped it would. This has become a real problem . . . I thought we would be inquirers together, and that I could write up about the progress each one of us was making on a kind of a project by just talking! Oh boy, how can I make this work? I need to be able to meet the demands of this project but I am committed to collaboration, this is confusing and stressful and it all feels so loose and uncertain. (JE/27/04/04)
>
> (Taylor 2007: 88)

As you form your collaborative action research group, be prepared for some bumps and humps along the way. Further, once the group starts to meet, you will probably encounter different ways to think about and act in the world that make your project more complex and contradictory. However, uncertainty and complexity are a necessary part of learning and we should embrace them, not resent them.

Forming and maintaining your group is part of your action research project (remember: Step 9 never ends!) and, as such, generates its own data. Note the events around your group, as this will help you to understand what and who is changing and what and who is not.

Further resources: going deeper

In print

Bray, J., Lee, J., Smith, L. and Yorks, L. (eds) (2000) *Collaborative Inquiry in Practice: Action, Reflection, and Making Meaning*. Thousand Oaks, CA: Sage.

Coyer, F. M., Courtney, M. D. and O'Sullivan, J. (2007) Establishing an action research group to explore family-focused nursing in the intensive care unit, *International Journal of Nursing Practice* 13(1): 14–23.

Jacobs, G. (2006) Imagining the flowers, but working the rich and heavy clay: participation and empowerment in action research for health, *Educational Action Research*, 14(4): 569–81.

Online

Fisher, K., Bennett-Levy, J. and Irwin, R. (2003) What a GAS! Action research as peer support for postgraduate students. Available at: http://ultibase.rmit.edu.au/Articles/nov03/fisher1.htm

Step 10 Gather 'baseline' data

> Discussed, discussed, discussed – decided to go back to basics first. Observed children to see if they did continue on from week to week.
>
> (Field notes, Loosley Early Learning Centre, *Student Engagement: Starting with the Child*)

Staff from the Loosley Early Learning Centre were researching the question, 'How can we reinvent our practices to ensure sustained engagement occurs when children only attend sessions once or twice a week?' First, they gathered baseline data on the pattern of children's engagement in specific learning experiences between kindergarten sessions. Rather than assume they knew what was happening, they decided to collect observational data on children's patterns of engagement, then analyse it to see how they might enhance learner engagement for those children who attended kindergarten on a part-time basis.

Step 10 in your action research project is to collect baseline data about the circumstances of your research before your initiate your project and create the first change in your first action research cycle. Your baseline data collection will be more or less extensive, depending on your resources, the time you have to complete your project and its scope and scale.

What you'll need to take Step 10:

Time
- to read this chapter and to reflect on its content;
- to collect your baseline data.

Knowledge
- What is likely to be the most appropriate strategy through which to collect my baseline data (both 'Observations' and 'Interactions')?
- How can I best document my baseline data?
- Has any form of action research been conducted already in my circumstances?

Defining our terms

Data and documentation

Data is information that researchers gather deliberately and systematically to answer their research question. It can take a variety of forms, including numbers, words, images and/or sounds; and it can be collected in a variety of media, including handwritten field notes, questionnaires, checklists, photographs, video- or audio-recordings. *Documentation* is the process by which researchers record and organize their data for interpretation. Researchers interpret their data, then draw conclusions from it. Data is the evidence that supports and substantiates a researcher's conclusions. An action researcher generally collects two forms of data: 'raw data' about events in their research project ('what happened') PLUS critical reflections by individuals or groups in the research project on (a) that raw data and (b) the learning and changes that they are experiencing in the project.

A hypothesis

A *hypothesis* is a statement that is meant to be tested by research. Typically, a hypothesis states a testable relationship between two variables (although it can refer to more than two). For example, 'People's attitudes become less flexible as they grow older'. A 'null hypothesis' states that there is no (statistically significant) relationship between the two variables, so any relationship that a researcher can demonstrate disproves the null hypothesis. For example, 'There is no relationship between children's attitudes and their age' is a null hypothesis; and if a researcher can demonstrate that, say, children's attitudes become less flexible as they grow older, then they have disproved that null hypothesis. The Loosley Early Learning Centre staff had hypothesized that part-time attendance had a negative effect on children's engagement as learners in their kindergarten programme. They gathered their baseline data as the first stage of testing their hypothesis.

Quantitative and qualitative data

There are two very broad approaches to research – 'quantitative' and 'qualitative'. Each approach produces a specific type of data: quantitative research produces quantitative data, i.e. primarily numbers; and qualitative research produces qualitative data, i.e. primarily non-numerical data. A research project may feature both approaches, depending on what the researcher wishes to discover about the research topic at particular stages of the project.

Quantitative research

In general terms, quantitative research aims to produce facts and figures – some form of numerical, possibly statistical data – about something. As its name implies, quantitative research is concerned with quantities – how to measure phenomena and how to express those measurements. A researcher who takes a quantitative approach to investigating a topic (e.g. the occupancy rate in long day care centres in rural areas) aims to learn more about it. Their research is guided by the belief that our knowledge of some-thing increases over time, step by step, piece by piece. For these researchers, knowledge is like gold dust – as you collect more and more, you get richer and richer.

Taking a quantitative approach to research implies asking questions about phenomena that have numerical answers. For example: How frequently does a specific child behave in a particular way? How many children in this centre prefer outdoor to indoor play? How much does the accreditation process influ-ence staff attitudes to curriculum? Consequently, researchers who take a quantitative approach often work within a paradigm called positivism, which 'frames' the world as a collection of apparently independent, unconnected phenomena to be counted, measured and otherwise catalogued as the prelude to deducing the hidden rules or laws that underlie these phenomena and connect them.

A very simple example of a quantitative approach to research would be a project that counts how many people behave in certain ways. A researcher could ask a group of early childhood practitioners if they approve of subsidized long day care and then count how many say 'yes', how many say 'no' and how many give another response. The resulting knowledge would be quantitative – the numbers (the quantity) of practitioners who responded in each way to the question. This very simple exercise is the basis of all quantitative surveys, each of which counts how many people respond in particular ways to particu-lar questions. *Figure 10.1 Baseline data record* (overleaf) shows how the Byways group collected quantitative data about children's engagement in pro-grammed and non-programmed activities in the OSH programme.

If you plan to collect your baseline data through a survey, you might like to use a free online survey tool such as *Survey Monkey* (http://www.surveymonkey.com) to design the survey. If respondents complete your survey online, *Survey Monkey* will generate simple reports on the data with minimum effort, saving you considerable time when you come to analyse your data (in Step 12).

Qualitative research

A researcher who uses qualitative research to investigate a topic aims to under-stand it in a new or different way. Qualitative researchers generally aim to

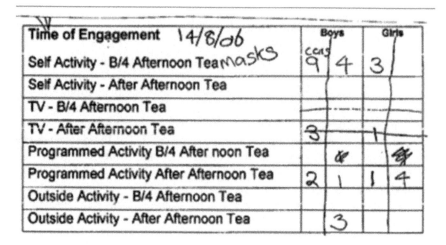

Figure 10.1 Basline data record.

show something's meaning or significance to particular people or groups of people. A researcher who takes a qualitative approach to investigating a topic (e.g. children's relationships with the media) doesn't seek to learn more about the topic itself, but rather how people understand and make sense of that topic. They do this by describing in detail how contexts affect what happens (Silverman 1993). Consequently, researchers who take a qualitative approach often work within the paradigms of interpretivism or post-structuralism, as each paradigm – in its own way – 'frames' the world as the outcome of people's continuing 'negotiations' with it.

A very simple example of a qualitative approach to research would be a project that asks people to explain their attitude to a particular issue. A researcher could ask a group of early childhood practitioners to state individually what they think about subsidized long day care. (Note the different wording – 'what do you think about it?' as opposed to 'do you approve [yes or no]?') The resulting knowledge would be qualitative – detailed descriptions of how and why individual early childhood practitioners felt about subsidized long day care. This very simple exercise is the basis of much qualitative research, which seeks to explain events and actions through the eyes and in the words of the people involved. For example, Eleanor was involved in the *Diversity and Children's Voices in the Early Childhood Curricula* project and she wanted to include children's ideas in her programme, so she established what she called 'planning committees', where she asked two children at a time what they would like in the room, offered them a choice of materials and gave them a space in which to develop their ideas. Eleanor photographed her 'learning committees' in operation, recorded what was said and then transcribed it. The resulting qualitative data was her baseline data and she used it as a guide as she planned the rest of her research project. What follows is the transcript of her recorded conversation with Jay and Trent. Eleanor had asked them, 'What would you like in the programme?'

Jay: I want a jungle.

Trent: Yeah! That would be good. We could have elephants, hippos and gorillas.

Jay: I want lions and tigers.

Eleanor: Where would you like to set up this area? How many children do you want to play in the jungle?

Jay: (Points to where he wants the area) I want it here. I think six children.

Trent: I want three children.

Eleanor: This area is very small. (It was usually only for two children.) Do you think six children will fit?

Jay: No.

Trent: No.

Eleanor: Maybe we could choose another area?

Trent: (Points to a larger area) We could have it there.

Jay: Yeah, more children will fit there.

Eleanor: If Trent wants three and Jay wants six, then you need to compromise.

Jay: OK. Is five children OK with you, Trent?

Trent: Yes, five is OK.

Eleanor: What sort of animals do you want? Small (plastic) jungle animals? Puppets?

Jay: We want to be the animals.

Trent: Yeah! We want to be the animals.

Eleanor: Do you think we could make costumes?

Jay: Yeah! And we can have some other toy animals, too.

Subsequently, Eleanor gathered more qualitative data to track what happened. This subsequent data included photographs and observations of life in the jungle area, which Eleanor turned into field note entries in her *Action Research Journal*. Here's one such entry:

Today is Friday and the jungle area has been extremely popular for the entire week. The children have been both using the animals in the area and pretending to be animals. Trent and Jay have done a good job developing negotiation skills and leadership roles. The children displayed ownership and a sense of pride in being heard; the involvement of other members of the group eager to assist their peers to achieve their goal (creating the jungle). I realised I need to let go of my expectations, really look at how the children respond and <u>then</u> judge whether an experience is working. Balance the power! (11/06/04.)

Deductive and inductive research

Whether a researcher takes a quantitative approach to research or a qualitative one, they will also have to make another choice: whether to answer their research question through deduction or through induction.

A researcher engaged in deductive research works from the 'top down'. They start with a possible answer to their research question (a hypothesis), then collect data to prove or disprove that possible answer: 'What can I deduce about my hypothesis from my data?'

A very simple example of deductive research would be a project that asked whether teachers in rural areas had different attitudes to after-hours care than teachers in urban areas. The researcher would start with a hypothesis – 'Teachers' attitudes to after-hours care depend on whether they work in a rural or an urban area' – and then try to prove or disprove their hypothesis by interviewing a group of teachers in a rural area and another group of teachers in an urban area and comparing their responses.

A researcher engaged in inductive research works from the 'bottom up'. They collect data about their research topic with no clear, preconceived view about whether or in what way that data will answer their research question. Then they examine their data to see whether and how it enables them to form a hypothesis about their research topic: 'Does my data enable me to say anything new about my research topic?' Inductive researchers seek understanding rather than explanation and they seek diversity and complexity in their data, rather than trying to impose controls on it, as in a scientific experiment (Mac Naughton et al. 2001: Glossary).

A very simple example of inductive research would be a project that asked what teachers think about after-hours care. The researcher would ask teachers from a variety of early childhood settings to state individually what they think about after-hours care; then they would examine their data to see if there were any links between particular responses and particular locations (e.g. rural, urban, suburban, in-school settings, free-standing settings).

Figure 10.2 Intersecting approaches to research shows how these choices intersect.

Quantitative research asks questions about events, issues, etc. that will produce numerical answers. E.g. how often does something happen, how many people act in a particular way, how widespread is a belief? A quantitative researcher is interested primarily in finding laws that govern social phenomena.	*Deductive research* is a 'top down' approach: you start with an idea (a hypothesis) and try to prove or disprove it. Thus, deductive research will prove or disprove a hypothesis.
Qualitative research produces 'meanings and understandings' and so its questions are likely to produce non-numerical answers. E.g. how do people achieve their goals, how do friendships form? A qualitative researcher is primarily interested in how people make sense or meaning of social phenomena.	*Inductive research* is a 'bottom up' approach: you collect data about an issue or idea with no clear, preconceived view about the significance of that data. Thus, inductive research may suggest a hypothesis.

Figure 10.2   Intersecting approaches to research.

An appropriate data collection strategy

To start collecting your baseline data, spend some time in the circumstances in which you will initiate your action research project (unless you're familiar with them already) to learn more about them by observing in detail who is there, what happens when, etc. This is your baseline data. Then make an inventory of the resources and people there relevant to your project. Set aside a section of your *Action Research Journal* to record details of where you'll initiate your action research project. For example, locations, key people and their contact details, key dates.

Just how you collect data depends on the sort of knowledge about your research topic that you want to produce. Thus, the choices between quantitative and qualitative research and between deductive and inductive research aren't just matters of personal preference (for example, 'I'll take a quantitative approach because it's simple and clear-cut' or 'I'll take an inductive approach because I don't trust big theories'). Nor are they arbitrary choices, to be made by tossing a coin; nor a matter of fate, indicated by throwing the I Ching. Instead, you need to choose a research approach that is appropriate to your research topic and to its context; and you need to choose a data collection strategy that will ensure that your data is timely, relevant and reliable.

Action researchers generally collect qualitative *and* quantitative data in the form of descriptive field notes. Generally, their data consists of people's own words (rather than a summary or précis by the researcher);

professional, official and policy documents and artefacts; together with critical reflections on that data by themselves and others in the research project. Their data also include evidence of the action researcher's influence on the research. Action researchers document their data using various media, including handwritten research journals, audio recordings and video recordings, transcripts of those recordings, and e-mail correspondence. They believe that this diversity of data and documentation captures the complexities and richness of people's lived experiences in ways that numbers and patterns alone cannot.

Critically reflective researchers use both observations and interactions to immerse themselves in the circumstances they are researching. Like any good researcher, critically reflective researchers investigate their research questions systematically, but what marks them out is that their investigations are also critical. They integrate their descriptions of events with theoretically-grounded explanations of those events. For example, they ask not only, 'How do people understand their circumstances?', but also 'How do people's circumstances (including their gender, 'race', class, ability, and power) influence their understandings?' Similarly, they focus as much on *how* people learn as on *what* they learn; and on how what they learn relates to their teacher's intentions.

For example, Marnie was investigating gender issues in children 0–12 years old as part of her work in the *Student Engagement: Starting with the Child* project. In this excerpt from her journal, she describes how the group collected its baseline data:

> As a team we have chosen to collect some baseline data before any intervention. Lisa will be formulating and distributing a proforma for easy data collection and then for later collation and review. We have decided to collect data for one month. We have also decided to collate as much past research as possible on the topic to present to our research team at our next meeting. Thought: do a journal search on the HOST search engine. See what I can dig up.

Figure 10.3 The data collection matrix shows the major decisions required to plan your data collection.

Sources of data

Sources of data fall into one of two very broad types: 'observations' and 'interactions'. Particular data collection techniques are associated with each type of data source and these are summarized in *Figure 10.4 The observation library* and *Figure 10.5 The interaction library*.

What you collect	*How* you collect	*Who* collects	*How much* do you collect?
Do you need to know? • if it happens • how it happens • why it happens • when it happens • where it happens • who it happens to or with • how often it happens • how many times it has happened • what it looks like when it happens • the relationships between two or more of the above. The 'it' is a key term associated with your research question.	*Observations* • direct or participative • structured or unstructured *Interviews* • direct or indirect • structured or unstructured *Documents* • Interviews • Transcripts • Work samples • Portfolios • Analyses of such documents *Mixed methods* • Some or all of the above	• Children • Teachers • Parents • Peers • Others	• How many children? • How many rooms? • How many centres? • An hour? • A day? • A week?
When you collect • Time intervals (how often?) • Timing (at what specific times or events?) • Duration (for how long?)	*Where* you collect • Naturalistic – in the classroom, the home, the wider community? • Experimental – in the classroom, the home, the wider community?	*How* you make make your analysis rigorous Triangulation of: • data sources • data methods • data collectors	*How* you organize data Organized for analysis by: • coding • annotating • labelling • selecting • summarizing

Figure 10.3   The data collection matrix.

Observations

Observing a particular event or circumstance is a way to see and hear directly what is happening, rather than having to rely on someone else's account of it. You may observe by yourself, i.e. as an 'outsider' (direct observation), or with others who are involved in an event, i.e. as an 'insider' (participant observation); and you may choose between a variety of tools of observation, summarized in *Figure 10.4 The observation library.*

TOOL	DESCRIPTION	PURPOSE	OUTPUT	ADVANTAGES	DISADVANTAGES
Anecdotal records	A short, informal note about a significant event and its context.	To examine a significant event and its context.	Qualitative data, i.e. descriptions of events and people's responses. Use this data as the start of systematic data collection.	Records events, rather than relying on memory.	They are unsystematic, so they may be inconsistent in form and content with other records.
Time and event sampling	*Time sampling* charts specific behaviours at specific intervals over a specific period. *Event sampling* charts a specific behaviour and its causes.	To examine a specific behaviour or event. E.g. how often, how long, how many, who, where and when?	Quantitative data, i.e. numbers, frequencies and duration of behaviours or events. Use this data to show patterns in behaviours.	Easily adapted to your own needs. Show patterns that anecdotal records may miss.	They can take time to do and to analyse. They can't explain what the behaviours mean to the people involved.
Socio-metric measures	A combination of time sampling and interviews.	To plot relationships and dynamics within a group.	Quantitative data, i.e. 'maps' of relationships and dynamics. Use this data to show a group's culture.	Objective measure of subjective things (i.e. emotions).	They need repeating regularly, as relationships change continually.

Activity logs	A comprehensive chart of an individual's or a group's activities – may include time and event sampling or checklists.	To plot patterns or consistencies in an individual's or a group's behaviour.	Quantitative data, i.e. a record of who did what, when and with whom. Use this data to show the effects of interventions.	A comprehensive picture of the circumstances that you want to change.	They can take time to do and to analyse. They can't explain what the behaviours mean to the people involved.
Checklists and rating scales	A *checklist* is a list of behaviours or events. A checklist often includes a rating scale. A *rating scale* shows how well/often a person does each item on a checklist.	A *checklist*: to discover if someone can or cannot do a specific thing. A *rating scale*: to discover the quality of the observed behaviour.	Quantitative data, i.e. numbers, frequencies and duration of behaviours or events. Use this data to show patterns in behaviours or events.	Pre-existing checklists and rating scales may save time, but may be inappropriate to a particular culture and/or context.	They rely on personal judgements. They tell you what a person can or cannot do, but can't explain it.

Figure 10.4 The observation library.

TOOL	DESCRIPTION	PURPOSE	OUTPUT	ADVANTAGES	DISADVANTAGES
Sociogram *	A 'map' showing group members' preferred companions.	To discover sub-group organization and relationships.	Qualitative data, i.e. people's expressed preferences.	Explains group functioning and may suggest how to improve it.	Doesn't normally address power relations and/or hidden prejudices.
Document review	Review of written documents such as performance ratings, programme logs, tally sheets and other existing indicators.	To discover how an organization monitors and evaluates its activities.	Quantitative data, i.e. a summary of evaluations and scores.	Answers 'What?', 'When', 'Where' and 'How many?'	Can't – by itself – explain why an organization achieves particular scores in its evaluations.
Interview	A recorded conversation with an individual, based on questions that are more or less 'open' to interpretation.	To discover an individual's views on specific issues or topics.	Qualitative data, i.e. a recording of people's views.	Answers 'What?' and 'Why?' Richer data than questionnaires.	Needs transcribing for easy access and analysis. Can't – by itself – situate responses in any social context.
Questionnaire	An individual's written responses to written questions that are more or less 'open' to interpretation.	To discover an individual's views on specific issues or topics.	Qualitative and, if required, quantitative data concerning an individual's views.	Answers 'What?' and 'How many?' Data is accessible easily for analysis.	Can miss nuances in responses that a conversation (especially face-to-face) can capture.
Focus group	A recorded, moderated discussion between several people on a particular topic or issue.	To discover the views of a type of person on specific issues or topics.	Qualitative data, i.e. a recording of people's views.	Answers 'What?', 'How?' and 'Why?'	Needs transcribing for easy access and analysis. Can be mistaken for a 'randomized sample' of quantitative research.

* Walsh's Classroom Sociometrics programme can simplify the whole process (not for Macs).

Figure 10.5 The interaction library.

Melanie (see above) used observations to gather baseline data on gender issues. She detailed these observations in her journal. *Figure 10.6 Notes on observations* summarizes her notes:

FOCUS OF OBSERVATION	RESULTS
Number of children engaged (at 4.30 time slot) in staff-programmed activities, rather than their own	Average 23.32% (Monday 15%, Tuesday 30%, Wednesday 48%, Thursday 14%, Friday 9.6%)
Total number of children in various areas according to gender	More girls used the indoor (craft) area on average Many more boys than girls used the outdoor area
Staff in the areas versus staff engaged with children	Staff engagement at the end of the day (5.30 approximately) was minimal, as staff performed routine tasks, e.g. cleaning
Total number of children engaged in staff-programmed activities	Children chose to complete more imaginary-based activities rather than our programmed activities

Figure 10.6   Notes on observations.

Lillith collected similar data but in a different way (see *Figure 10.7 Data collection using visuals*).

Name: How does staff engagement in activities impact on children's engagement

Anecdote:
I collected data on the number of children at an activity without teacher present, then approximately 5 minutes after a teacher joins the activity and later again approximately 5 minutes after the teacher left the activity.

Activity	No of children before teacher joins in	No of children with teacher at activity	No of children after teacher leaves
Sorting	♟ ♟	♟ ♟ ♟ ♟ ♟	♟ ♟ ♟
Tessellation (shapes)	♟	♟ ♟ ♟	
Sand	♟	♟ ♟ ♟ ♟ ♟ ♟	♟ ♟
Drawing (outside)		♟ ♟	
Puzzles (outside)	♟	♟ ♟ ♟	
Construction	♟ ♟ ♟	♟ ♟ ♟ ♟ ♟ ♟	♟ ♟ ♟ ♟ ♟ ♟
Collage	♟ ♟ ♟ ♟ ♟ ♟ ♟ ♟ ♟	♟ ♟ ♟ ♟ ♟ ♟ ♟	♟ ♟ ♟ ♟

Figure 10.7   Data collection using visuals.

Interactions

While observing an event or circumstance enables you to watch and/or listen to it directly, the event itself may be only half the story. The other half consists of people's understandings of that event and their reactions to it. Observation, by itself, may give you a clue (sometimes a very strong clue) as to how someone understands something, but if clues are all you have, you can never be sure that you're right. The only way to ensure that you understand correctly how someone makes sense of something is to ask them (and hope that they reply truthfully!). These interactions can take a variety of forms, summarized in *Figure 10.5 The interaction library*.

Here are some examples of action researchers in early childhood settings using interactions as a way to gather their baseline data:

- Melanie used interactions and observations to gather her baseline data on gender issues (a common practice). For example, having noticed that boys used the outdoor area more than girls, she asked a selection of boys why they used the area more; and she asked a selection of girls why they used the area less.
- Alma wanted to improve communication with parents at her centre and she designed a written questionnaire to discover parents' views about communication between staff and parents at present. Among the six questions were: 'What do you expect from staff in the way of communication?' and 'Which type of communication do you find most effective? (A list followed) Why?'
- Nina was concerned that her centre was offering food that wasn't necessarily appropriate to all of the cultures represented by the children and families that used it. She wrote a short list of questions about this issue and used the list as a basis for conversations with parents and with staff. (Nina chose conversations over a written questionnaire partly because several parents had English as their second language.)

Documenting your data

Whatever your source(s) of data, you will need to document the data you collect. The simplest way is to use pen and paper, but there are various more sophisticated options, as summarized in *Figure 10.8 The documentation library*.

MEDIUM	ADVANTAGES	DISADVANTAGES
Handwritten notes	Capture events, actions, contexts and reflections as they happen. Access requires no specific playback technology!	Can distract you from what's happening, because you're concentrating on capturing as much as your writing speed allows. Allied with this: handwritten notes may require transcribing for others to read! Things can happen faster than we can write about them! Captures only your perspective unless you specifically seek others' perspectives and make notes about them at the time.
Still camera (includes phone cameras)	Captures events, actions and contexts as they happen. Access requires no playback technology. Digital photographs can be included quite easily in written/printed documents, e.g. reports.	Captures only your perspective. (Give each participant a camera?) Photographs give the illusion of impartial accuracy, but are always the result of the photographer's choice of what and how to photograph.
Audio recorder	Captures events, actions, contexts and reflections as they happen and more comprehensively than handwritten notes or a still camera.	Access requires specific playback technology. Audio recordings can't be included in written/printed documents, e.g. reports. Only transcriptions can be included. Audio recordings give an illusion of impartial accuracy (the lack of visuals reduces this), but are always the result of the operator's choice of what and how to record.
Video recorder	Captures events, actions, contexts and reflections as they happen and more comprehensively than any other medium. Can capture others' perspectives (unlike still photographs), but the perspective of the camera operator (e.g. you) can still dominate.	Access requires specific playback technology. Video recordings can't be included in written/printed documents, e.g. reports. Only transcriptions can be included. Video recordings give a greater illusion of impartial accuracy than a photograph, but are always the result of the operator's choice of what and how to record.

Figure 10.8 The documentation library.

(Continued overleaf)

Figure 10.8 continued

MEDIUM	ADVANTAGES	DISADVANTAGES
Transcriptions	Makes recorded speech more easily accessible to analysis. Access requires no specific playback technology. Transcripts can be included quite easily (in whole or in part) in written/printed documents, e.g. reports.	Can miss non-verbal cues in an audio recording (and visual cues in a video recording) unless these are described in the transcript. Very time-consuming to create (e.g. a one-hour conversation between two people can take three hours to transcribe; and if it's between five or six people, it can take up to six hours to transcribe).
Participants' presentations	No intermediation by the researcher. Presentations can help participants to regard the project as their own, as well as the researcher's.	There's a risk that they'll be seen as 'authentic' or 'the truth' because they are participants' own words, images, reflections, etc. May require specific playback technologies (e.g. video, computer projector), but this can be avoided by 'keeping it simple'. If anyone is featured, they will need to consent to being featured or referred to in public presentations.
Work samples	No intermediation by the researcher. Immediate demonstrations of what the project is achieving (or not!).	If anyone is featured, they will need to consent to being featured or referred to in public presentations.
Participants' journals	No intermediation by the researcher. Capture participants' perspectives on events, actions, contexts and reflections close to when they happen. Access requires no specific playback technology!	There's a risk that they'll be seen as 'authentic' or 'the truth' because they are participants' own words, reflections, etc. Captures only one person's perspective at a time, so each one needs to be read alongside others.

Taking Step 10: a case from practice

Kara from the *Student Engagement: Starting with the Child* project (whom you met in Step 1) had a comprehensive list of the different types of data that her action research group could collect, as she recorded in her journal:

> MEETING . . . We had a meeting . . . [at which] . . . we have decided to focus our research on gender. L. will do some observation proformas for everyone to use. We will be doing observations on 'Play choices in their play environment'. About twenty observations before we meet again.
>
> Ideas.
>
> - Survey about roles in family. 'Washing dishes', etc.
> - Make a photo of a child and get that child to put petals around it to form a flower. Choice of petals – pink and blue.
> - 'Get to know your friends' booklets. 'Out of your friends, who do you see as a secretary, a child care worker, a painter, a cook, a police officer and why?' See what gender of friend they use.
> - Make two colours of playdough – pink and blue – and see who will play with what colour.
> - Check *Playstation* list to see if boys use it more than girls.
> - Watch ads to see differences between 'girl' and 'boy' ads.
> - Bring gender issues articles/books.
>
> . . . LET'S EXPLORE GENDER.

Subsequently, Kara collected data using each of those techniques and presented the results in her journal in various ways, including:

- interviews to discover children's opinions about their favourite pet, toy, colour and activity; and charts to document differences and similarities between girls' and boys' responses;
- interviews to discover children's opinions about what job they would like to do when they grow up; and charts to document differences and similarities between girls' and boys' responses;
- photographs – accompanied by handwritten notes – to document children's preferences for pink and blue playdough;
- time and event sampling to show who uses the computer and *Playstation*;
- a document review to contrast adverts aimed at girls and at boys.

Taking your tenth step: your actions and reflections

Use the data collection matrix and the three data collection libraries in this step to decide what baseline data you will collect and how you will collect it. Note these decisions in your *Action Research Journal*. Then, collect your data as you planned and note any difficulties, obstacles or issues that are associated with this – especially those for which you hadn't planned! Note these, too, in your *Action Research Journal*.

Further resources: going deeper

Online

Data Use: School Improvement Through Data-Driven Decision Making. Available at: http://www.ncrel.org/toolbelt/index.html

North Central Regional Educational Laboratory. Access to web-based tools for collecting information in educational settings, including checklists and surveys.

Teachers and Students as Action Researchers: Using Data Daily. Available at: http://www.ncrel.org/info/nlp/lpsu00/resrch.htm

Tools for data gathering on gender in schools. A list of useful tools for observation and data gathering in schools, that are downloadable. Available at: http://www.education.qld.gov.au/students/advocacy/equity/gender-sch/action/action-data.html

Survey tools on values in schools. Available at: http://www.valueseducation.edu.au/values/val_survey_tools,10794.html

Data collection tools. Available at: http://www.broward.k12.fl.us/hrd/action researchstudies/datacollection/index.htm

Step 11 Create a change and collect data about its effects

Alice (Child Care professional) was a participant in the *Diversity and Children's Voice in the Curricula* project. Her research question was, 'How can I positively include quieter children's voices in the programme?' Four children from her room agreed to participate in her project. Rather than trying to determine why they were quieter than others by 'assessing' them, Alice asked them directly why they were quiet. She spent time with each child individually, asking each child the same nine questions then asking them to draw a picture.

(CEIEC 2006: 22)

Step 11 in your action research project is to create a change in your circumstances and collect data about what happens. Alice (see above) decided to interview the quiet children in her room, so her action was linked closely with her data collection. In this step, we share examples from practice of the many different ways that early childhood action researchers take action. It can be hard to decide just how to act to create change and you might worry about whether or not you're creating the 'right' or 'best' change. However, now it's time to brush aside such caution (while remembering all your planning, of course!) and just . . . act! Once you create your first change, your action research project will build its own momentum and direction.

What you'll need to take Step 11:

Time
- to read this chapter and to reflect on its content;
- to do what you have planned.

Knowledge
- What is my first action?
- How will I record it and its effects?
- How will I keep the momentum going?

Other resources
- These will vary, but you should have assembled them as part of your planning.

Taking Step 11: cases from practice

The learning to learn (learner engagement) project

Researchers in this project started their work in various ways, including reading, brainstorming, reflecting, observing, meeting, talking with colleagues, collecting data and attending training sessions. *Figure 11.1 Starting to improve student engagement* shows how researchers at two different sites started their projects and their simple memo notes on what they did.

Question	Steps to date
How do I re-examine my practices in relation to encouraging positive engagement in middle primary aged children within FDC?	• Sid – Met with children and got their ideas about what they need, would like to do, etc. Own sons, aged 8 and 9, helped others write theirs down. Has spoken with Annie ???, coordinator, re use of learning stories • Kate – researched info on middle primary aged children and their learning. Posted out some material with possible activities for kids. Meeting attended with other FDC providers and coordinators to expand own ideas on that age group
How do I rethink the use of visual cues and prompts to increase children's engagement?	• Spoken with families through HACC programme that access me for care • Accessed resources with the families through websites – found pyramid Aust. Catalogues with symbols they use. • Looked through children's comics folders • Looking to discuss with children on how to use comics – size, colouring, sharing and how and where to put them • Meeting to discuss progress with JP • Engage children to produce own compics

Figure 11.1   Starting to improve student engagement.

Louise Taylor started her research on rethinking professional learning with teachers by interviewing the teachers in her project, as she explains in this excerpt from her doctoral thesis:

The first cycle was one of reconnaissance and involved semi-structured interviews designed to ascertain the experiences and desires of teachers in relation to their professional learning; each interview lasted between 1½ to 2 hours. First and foremost these interviews were about hearing what teachers had to say about their teaching and learning experiences, in an open-ended and uncensored context. This information was then used in an emergent way to inform the next cycle.

(Taylor 2007: 96)

Cassie was involved in a project on increasing children's voices in the early childhood curriculum (CEIEC 2006; Olcay 2007). Her research question was, 'How can I involve children in the routines I participate in?' Cassie started by inviting children individually to help her to make up the beds at sleep time, as she believed that this would give them a say in what happened at sleep time. In this excerpt from her *Action Research Journal*, Cassie described the initial events:

> I thought: it won't matter if I run behind schedule a bit. I put out the beds with the bed bags nearby. I thought I would ask one child at a time if they would like to make their bed. I went outside and saw Child A1 busily washing a doll. I thought he is having such an enjoyable time he won't want to stop. However, when I asked him whether he wanted to continue washing the doll or help make his bed, he nodded his head and turned and headed indoors straight away. . . . As he was making the bed, two more children came in – Child A2 and Child Y. Child A2 wanted to make his bed, too, and began to do so. Child Y went to bend down and then straightened and shook his head. Child A1 and A2 made their beds and chose to move to another bed and make that one, too. . . . When I checked the time, I discovered that I had not lost any time at all. (08.04.05)

That excerpt shows Cassie creating change, collecting data about that change *and* reflecting on it – another illustration that the clear-cut distinctions in action research 'theory' don't always apply so neatly in practice.

Rebecca was in the same project as Cassie. To find a focus for her action research, she reviewed routines in her child care centre to see, 'who has the majority of power to make decisions?', as she wrote in her journal. Rebecca's review led her to ask, 'How do we change the balance of power and make it more fair and equitable for all?' In the next excerpt from her journal, Rebecca lists her first actions:

- To talk with children about their ideas about how meal times should look. At the moment children seem to enjoy and eat better when the lunch routine is not hurried and when we give children a choice in what they eat. For example, L will often have two to three servings of rice but if we add the casserole to his plate his refuses to eat at all;

- To talk with parents about their ideas about how to run this routine. For example many of the parents have said that allowing children to serve themselves and select their own food is a good idea as like with adults children also have certain food preferences;
- To work with N. (her co-worker) in establishing a routine that is consistent and then follow through with other teachers and kitchen staff in how routine should run even if N. and I are not in the room; and
- To organise a table where we can serve lunch from and get the children to scrape their plates into a scrape bowl.

Taking your eleventh step: your actions and reflections

Your eleventh step will be based on the data you collected in Step 9; and data collection will be central to Step 11. As you take your eleventh step, remember to keep comprehensive records in your *Action Research Journal* about what you do and what happened in consequence. In the heat of the moment when you create your change, you may feel confident that you'll have total recall of events but, precisely because you'll be so involved, total recall is even less likely than usual.

Further resources: going deeper

In print

Averill, J. (2006) Getting started: initiating critical ethnography and community-based action research in a programme of rural health studies, *International Journal of Qualitative Methods*, 5(2): 1–8.

Online

Classroom Action Research. Visit this site to see how other action researchers took their first steps. Available at: http://www.madison.k12.wi.us/sod/car/search.cgi

Department of Education (2004) *Research into Action*, Department of Education, Hobart, Tasmania. (Can also be downloaded from the website – http://www.ltag.education.tas.gov.au/references.htm)

Step 12 Analyse your data

> We have more than one week of data collected over ½ hour intervals. Very frequently, under 20% of children were involved in our offered activities.
> (Marnie and Cindy Biway OSH, June memo, *Student Engagement: Starting with the Child* project)

Collecting data does not – in and of itself – tell you why it is significant. For example, Marnie and Cindy had more than a week's worth of data on children's patterns of involvement in their programme, collected at half-hourly intervals, but to see its significance, needed to organize it. To summarize the patterns that they had seen in their primary data, they converted them into percentages and then presented them as charts with baseline data, graphs to show results, photo snapshots and staff 'thought pages' so that they could reflect on the implications for their practice.

In Step 12 in your action research project, you begin to analyse the data you have collected about the change that you created in Step 11.

What you'll need to take Step 12:

Time
- to read this chapter and to reflect on its content;
- to talk with those involved in your project about the issues this chapter raises.

Knowledge
- How do I best analyse my data?
- Do I need to do a quick overview at this point or a deeper analysis of data?
- What software packages might help me with a deeper analysis?
- What literature might help me go deeper with my analysis?

Other resources
- A data archive, a coding book (or similar) and a set of coding instructions for others to use and/or for you to use to validate your coding should there be a challenge to your research results.

What is 'data analysis'?

Researchers use the term 'analysis' in one of three ways:

- analysis as obtaining data (e.g. analysing a book or a person's behaviour);
- analysis as interpreting data (e.g. analysing a recording or a transcript);
- analysis as the result of an analytical process (e.g. an analysis of a programme).

(After Charles 1998: 154)

Here, we use analysis in that second way, i.e. interpreting data. Data analysis is a process of organizing and sifting your data, then looking for and mapping any patterns or regularities in your data as a way to interpret it. Blaxter et al. (2001: 206) put this very well: 'Analysis is about the search for explanation and understanding, in the course of which concepts and theories will probably be advanced, considered and developed.'

As you look for patterns and as you interpret any that you find, you should ask yourself whether and how this helps you: (1) to answer your research question; and (2) to plan your next action in the action research cycle.

In action research, data analysis involves four tasks, each of which we examine below:

1 Organizing the data for analysis.
2 Coding the data.
3 Sifting the data for patterns.
4 Analysing the data and displaying the results.

Organizing the data for analysis

Good data analysis starts with good organization. Before you start to analyse your data, spend time organizing it in ways that enable you to review and retrieve it easily. Different researchers do this in different ways but most do it in four broad stages: label the data, transform it, check with participants and then skim the data.

Label the primary data

1 Label each item of data with relevant background information (e.g. date and time it was gathered; its source).
2 Anonymize data (if your ethics organization has required this) by substituting pseudonyms and/or a code for each participant, centre or context.
3 Create a *Data Archive* – a book or file in which you list the following details about each item of data:
   - Item code
   - Type of data (e.g. audio-recording, painting, questionnaire)
   - Date collected and phase of the action research cycle
   - Means of collection
   - Participants involved
   - Participants consulted (Yes or No)
   - Anonymized (Yes or No)
   - Primary or transformed data
   - Comments.

Transform the primary data

You may need to transform your data into a form that can be organized, reorganized and reduced. For example, questionnaires may need to be photocopied, recorded interviews transcribed, images scanned and printed and analogue photos digitized. As you transform each item of data, remember to code it accordingly ('Primary or transformed data?') and note the additional coding in your *Data Archive*.

Check with participants

Before you start analysing your data, ensure that the participants associated with it approve it and do not want it changed in any way. For example, once participants read a transcript of their interview with you, they may feel that they did not say just what they intended to, or they may wish to tell you that their circumstances have changed, casting a different light on their original comments.

Skim the primary data

Your penultimate step in organizing your primary data is to familiarize yourself with your data as a whole by skimming it, i.e. reading it swiftly for structure, more than for content. Skimming your data enables you to complete three tasks:

1   Build a 'big picture' of your data overall.
2   Add small notes, questions and thoughts about your data that you can explore in detail once you start your analysis. Try some different methods (e.g. written notes in the margins, 'Post-its' on the data, notes in a computer) to find one that suits you.
3   Choose how to analyse your primary data – to categorize and/or to connect.

- *Categorize your data.* As you sift your data, you may find significant similarities and/or differences between different elements. You can arrange these into categories that address specific questions, e.g., 'What is changing [or not] and why?'; 'What needs to change and why?'. Thus, as part of preparing to organize your data, you should code it so that you can then sort, arrange and rearrange it into various categories.

and/or

- *Connect your data.* As you sift your data, you may build stories that show relationships between changes and events in a specific context. Ways to connect data include creating case studies, profiles, vignettes, or narratives; 'reading for voice', critical discourse analysis and ethnographic microanalysis.

(After Maxwell 2005)

Coding the data

Having organized your data, you are now ready to code it. A data code is simply a label that you apply to your data. There are various forms of data code, including letters, numbers, colours and symbols, but whatever form of coding you use, it should be comprehensive and consistent (i.e. it should include all your data and it should code the same type of data the same way throughout); and the codes should be mutually exclusive (i.e. each label should apply to one type of data only and exclude all other types).

Codes can simplify and standardize data ready for analysis – for example, assigning a label to a characteristic such as gender, location or age. Codes can also reduce the quantity of data by assigning a label to a group of data – for example, grouping participants according to age range and/or qualifications. If your data is in physical form (e.g. drawings, field notes, transcriptions of interviews), then you can apply your labels physically (e.g. using a highlighting pen, making a handwritten note); if your data is in electronic form (e.g. in a word-processing or spreadsheet programme), then you apply your labels electronically (e.g. using the program's colour highlighter function).

Once you have decided how you will code your data, you will need to create a code book (where you list the codes that you are using) and to write some coding instructions, so that other researchers can code your data in the same way as you to ensure that the data is coded consistently and is valid. Ensuring the validity of your coding is a four-stage process:

1   List your coding categories.
2   Define each category so that you are clear what it includes and excludes.
3   Identify the rules by which you assign content to a category.
4   Provide an example of each category, so that others can check how you have categorized your data.

(After Mayring 2000)

Start with 'economical' coding strategies

In action research, the distinction between collecting data and analysing it isn't always clear-cut, because the action research cycle consists of both action and analysis (reflection). You often code your data 'on the run', because you need to interpret what has happened so far in order to decide what to do next. Consequently, you need 'economical' strategies (Dick 1999b) that enable you to code your data as quickly and efficiently as possible.

Mark the data in colour
A simple way to code data (especially data in the form of text) is to use colour to identify a specific component or pattern in your data. For example, you can colour-code your data (with a highlighter pen or using the colour highlighter function on your computer) to highlight a particular phrase, or idea, or action; and then look for recurrences, sequences or associations.

Assign a number or letter to each component
This strategy identifies a specific component or pattern in your data. It uses letters or numbers as labels and uses a word-processing or spreadsheet pro-gramme to attach a label to each component or pattern and then to track the distribution of each label (i.e. each letter or number) throughout the data.

Coding by colour, letter or number allows you to identify and track recurrent events, behaviours, etc. For example, if you want to identify effective ways to encourage children to pose questions as part of their learning, you could apply a particular colour, letter or number to each type of question that children raise at a particular time (e.g. around science experiences) and then look for (1) recurrent questions, and (2) associations between a recurrent question and a particular prompt by the teacher. Alternatively, you could apply a particular colour, letter or number to each question that a particular child poses; then look for variations in the frequency with which she poses them, or in their magnitude (i.e. their significance for the child's learning); then look for associations between those variations in frequency and/or magnitude and a particular prompt by the teacher.

Identify key terms

You can use the 'find' function in a word-processing program to locate key terms in any text data and to mark them (e.g. using different font styles or colours). This is an 'economical' way to code individual items of data, but 'find' won't find chunks of data. Further, this strategy requires you to decide your key terms and then apply them *to* your data, rather than allowing key terms to emerge *from* your data. To that extent, this strategy presupposes its outcomes (Winter and Munn-Giddings 2001).

Attach analytic memos

This involves making notes about your data and then using them to track any recurrences of similar ideas, issues, etc. Your notes about a piece of data are your coding label and you can attach them to the data in many ways, e.g. writing on the data itself (e.g. on a transcription of an interview, on your field notes), sticking a separate written note onto the data, or making a note at the appropriate section of your electronic data.

This strategy is a little more sophisticated than the previous three, in that it does more than just identify items of data – it begins to show their significance to your research question. For instance, you can use analytic memos to identify outposts or absences (the latter can be hard to colour-code!) and then track them over your data as a whole. Similarly, you can use this strategy to identify power effects as you find them, making initial connections with particular people, events, institutions, etc.

Figure 12.1 'Economical' coding strategies summarizes these four coding strategies and their major advantages and disadvantages.

Mindy and Martha were curious about whether their relationships with parents affected children's engagement with their programme (*Student Engagement: Starting with the Child* project). They distributed pro-formas for staff at their centres to complete over a term, then collected and collated the results. *Figure 12.2 A pre-coded data collection pro-forma* reproduces their pro-forma. It shows how each pro-forma incorporated colour coding and coding by letters.

Once they had collected their data, Mindy and Martha skimmed it and then Martha noted the results in her journal as follows:

What's it telling us (first glance)?

- we don't know many parents' / caregivers' name;
- some parents aren't getting any contact;
- the wet area is the most frequent meeting place;
- talks are more socially oriented and only some shared information;
- talks were more informal.

Coding strategy	Foci	Advantages	Disadvantages
Colour, letter or number	Settings, actions, speech, text, structures, processes, formal relationships.	Quick and easy way to 'set the scene' for subsequent analysis.	Descriptions involve no analysis.
Key terms	Presence/absence of key terms in descriptions and accounts.	Confirms or refutes your first interpretation of events, etc. as they happened.	Imposes pre-existing categories on your data.
Analytic memos	Outposts, absences and power effects.	A first step beyond simple description.	Requires you to return to develop the analysis later.

Figure 12.1 'Economical' coding strategies

Legend for data collection

(Please circle)   A.M.   P.M.   ALL-DAYERS

(Please circle)   Monday   Tuesday   Wednesday   Thursday

Name of the child:

Do you know the name of the child's carer/s?

Have you met or talked to the carer/s?

Where?   O – Office   FD – Front Desk   RR – Reading Room
         W – Wet Area   PH – Over the phone

What was the type of conversation?

         I – Information   SC – Social
         M – Meeting   Q – Quick   D – Detailed

Who are you?

         Maria – Blue   Maureen – Green
         Joanne – Red   Lisa – Yellow

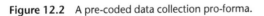

Figure 12.2 A pre-coded data collection pro-forma.

Move on to 'sophisticated' coding strategies

The detail and sophistication of your coding data analysis should reflect the scope and context of your action research project. 'Economical' data coding strategies may well be sufficient for your action research project. There is no value in pursuing sophisticated strategies if your data or research questions don't warrant it. However, some action research projects may require sophisticated data coding strategies. For example, projects receiving funding from an external source, or that are part of studies for a doctorate, are often expected to be broader in scope and more sophisticated in their analysis. If this is the case for your action research project, ensure that there is someone associated with the project who is familiar with sophisticated data coding strategies.

Several computer-based programs – both qualitative and quantitative – can assist you to code your data. (Refer to the *Going deeper* section at the end of this step). They are especially useful if you have large amounts of data, but if your project is relatively small, then it is probably not worth spending the time required to learn how to use one. However, if you are familiar with such a programme already, you will know whether it can assist you to code even a relatively small amount of data.

If you need to develop sophisticated data coding strategies (because you need to undertake sophisticated data analysis), please consult the list of further resources at the end of this chapter.

Sifting the data for patterns

> I went out with some ideas of what I would find with my baseline data and every day with another level of data collection I became more surprised and intrigued.
>
> (Marnie, Byway OSH)

Your next task is to choose between the coded components of your data for the ones most likely to help you to answer your research question; this enables you to identify any patterns in the arrangement and occurrence of those components. Its important at this point to be open to all possibilities. It's important to look for what surprises and intrigues you.

Choosing between the components of your data

Your data will have different components, including:

- Ideas – the opinions, beliefs, impressions, plans and suggestions of people associated with your project.

- Issues – the concerns or debates that people raise in the course of your project.
- Questions – people's doubts and uncertainties that either form part of your project's beginning or emerge as the project progresses.
- Dilemmas – the especially difficult choices, quandaries or predicaments that may face people associated with your project.
- Principles – people's rules or standards for acting.
- Events – things that happen that are significant for your project.
- Topics – the subjects that people in your project talk or write about.
- Emotions – feelings that people in your project have as the project progresses.
- Relationships – links between people, between events, between institutions and practices.
- Decisions – people's choices as they face changes in their circumstances.
- Values – the ideals, morals and ethics that guide the people associated with your project.
- Discourses – how people 'frame' events to understand them.

To start your search for patterns in your primary data, identify components of your data that you think might help you to answer your research question and group them with any others with which you think they might be related. Just how you approach this will depend on the stage of your project. For example:

- *The start of your action research project.* Here, you need to understand what is happening or what needs to change, so you should examine components of your primary data that are likely to give you this sort of information. Ideas, issues, questions, dilemmas, principles and values are likely to feature in the circumstances in which your project starts and to be major drivers of events in it.
- *Later in your project.* Here, you also need to understand whether and how change has happened, so you should look to components of your primary data that are associated with change. For example, emotions, relationships, decisions are likely to be associated with changes and discourses will influence how people understand changes and their effects.

In reality, your circumstances are likely to be more complex than in those two examples. The data from the start of your project will not necessarily feature the particular collection of components in the first example and data you collect as your project progresses and change starts to occur will not necessarily feature the components in our second example. For instance, if you were to ask children about a specific piece of equipment, your resulting data may include the children's:

- opinions about the equipment ('ideas');
- reasons for using it or not ('decisions');
- feelings about the equipment ('emotions');
- experiences of the equipment ('events').

Further, you are unlikely to be able to give all the components of your data equal attention, especially if there is a lot of data and/or if it concerns a complex issue. Consequently, as you start to sift your data, choose which components of your data are related most directly to your research question, because they will be most likely to help you to answer it. For example, in your research about a specific piece of equipment (see above), start by analysing time and event sampling of children's activities on that piece of equipment and leave any other equipment until later. Start with one or two components, to keep your analysis manageable and economical. If you feel that you need to examine more components, then at least you will have some idea of the time and other resources you will require to do so.

Identifying patterns in your primary data

Remember: you can look for categories or connections in your primary data. Thus, as you analyse your data, you can look for patterns around a specific component or for patterns in relationships between two or more components. For example, you could look for patterns of play around the piece of equipment in which you're interested, or you could look for patterns in relationships between children's play on that piece of equipment compared with another.

The four 'economical' coding strategies (coding by colour, by letter or number, by key term and by analytical note) can begin to show simple patterns in your data. You can rarely foresee the sorts of patterns that emerge from your primary data, but here, at least, is a beginning list of some of the more common patterns to emerge from an action research project's primary data:

- *Recurrences* (often called 'themes'). These show you an event, behaviour or way of seeing that keeps happening. It may be your target for change ('I want to stop this recurring') or it may be a part of your process of change ('People respond this way consistently').
- *Associations*. These show you two or more components of your data co-existing. They may do so for many reasons, including: one is caused by another, one depends on another, or both have the same origins.
- *Sequences*. These show you things that happen in a particular order.

For example, 'B' always follows 'A'. Sequences may suggest causes; but a sequence may just be an association between events, behaviours or ideas: just because 'B' always *follows* 'A', that doesn't always mean that 'B' is *caused by* 'A'.

- *Frequencies*. These are the rates at which things happen in a given period of time, so they can tell you whether things are changing (e.g. increasing in frequency, decreasing in frequency) or staying the same (i.e. happening at the same frequency). Frequency patterns can also tell you how often components are associated with each other, how often a sequence of events occurs and how often events recur.
- *Magnitudes*. These are the quantities or 'sizes' of events, behaviours and ideas, so they can tell you the significance of a particular component (e.g. the emotions associated with a particular event) or of the relationships between two or more components (e.g. how strongly is this action associated with that emotion?).
- *Outposts*. These are events, behaviours, ways of seeing, etc. that are consistently on the outskirts of the norm or the group or separate from it. They raise the question, 'What is it about the norm or the group that excludes or marginalizes these outposts?'
- *Absences*. These are gaps or holes in your primary data. They identify a certain type or component of data that you need to answer your research question but that you haven't collected so far or that has been excluded or silenced by your methods of data collection . . . or even by your research question.
- *Contradictions*. A pattern of contradictions can underlie what people say or do and may, indeed, drive their behaviour ('I'm doing this, even though . . .'). They may show that what people consider right or normal behaviour is, nonetheless, not free of controversy.
- *Power effects*. These show you distribution of influence and control. For example, patterns of power effects can illustrate how the politics of difference works in your project.

Lena was concerned that her centre's 'Background Information' sheets effectively told parents what the staff wanted to know, rather than inviting parents to say what they thought staff needed to know:

> What I thought I was doing was telling parents that I value their knowledge and insight, but actually what I was doing was telling them what I think is important for me to know and in so doing benefiting myself, because it makes my job easier.

This would mean that when she came to analyse the data that she collected using these sheets, she may have found absences (information that parents didn't feel they could provide), contradictions (information that parents provided may well not have been what they thought) and power effects (the data reflected her centre's agenda, not that of the parents). Consequently, to prevent these problems emerging in her analysis, she collected her data using more open-ended questions that allowed parents to respond as they wished.

Figure 12.3 A data pattern matrix will help you to decide where to begin your search for patterns in your data. It lists the possible components of your data, together with the common patterns in data. The matrix will also help you to track which data components you have analysed and what (if any) patterns you found as you did so.

Analysing the data and displaying the results

Having found some patterns in your primary coded data, you now have to explain what those patterns mean, why and to whom they matter and whether/how they help you to answer your research question. You are likely to accumulate both quantitative and qualitative data throughout your action research project and below we examine how to analyse each type.

Quantitative data and descriptive statistics

Using statistical analysis of quantified data, you can demonstrate particular issues and events simply yet powerfully in graphic forms such as diagrams, tables and graphs. The simplest form of statistical analysis – descriptive statistics – enables you to summarize and analyse your data in the form of fairly simple numerical relationships. For example: 'How many times did children do activities in the written programme?'; 'How many children played at the new tables?'; 'How often was bullying associated with the absence of a staff member?'; etc.

Some basic terms/ideas

You will probably be familiar with at least some of this list of the basic elements of descriptive statistics:

- *A number.* A quantity of units. For example, the number of children in a classroom.
- *A fraction.* A ratio between two numbers. For example, 'Ten of the twenty children were boys.' or 'Half the children were boys.'
- *A percentage.* The proportion or rate per hundred parts. For example, 'Fifty per cent of the children were boys.' (If there were one hundred children, fifty would be boys; if there were twenty children, ten would be boys, etc.)

Types of pattern

Data components	Recurrences	Associations	Sequences	Frequencies	Magnitudes	Outposts	Absences	Contradictions	Power effects
Ideas									
Issues									
Questions									
Dilemmas									
Principles									
Events									
Topics									
Emotions									
Relationships									
Decisions									
Values									
Discourses									

Figure 12.3   A data pattern matrix.

- *Percentile.* A measure of your standing or status compared with others. For example, a centre that was told that it had scored 70 per cent in an accreditation exercise wouldn't know whether that was a good or bad result; but if it was told that its result put it in the 80th percentile, it would know that it had done as well as or better than 80 per cent of all centres that had been accredited.
- *The range.* The 'distance' between the highest score and the lowest. For example, 'The children ranged from one to five years old.'
- *The median.* The mid-point between the two ends of a range. For example, 'The median age of children under five years old is 2.5 years.' Note its difference from 'the mean'.
- *The mean.* (Also known as the average.) The result of dividing the number of units in a category by the number of sub-categories of that category. For example, add up the number of young children in a particular centre who are aged five and under; then divide that number ('the number of units in the category') by five ('the number of sub-categories of the category') and you will find the average age of a child under five in that centre. If there are few children under one, this will tend to make the average age higher than if there are few children between four and five.
- *The mode.* The most frequent score. For example, 'Asked to reply "Yes", "No" or "Don't know", most people replied "No", i.e. "No" was the mode.'

Quantitative data and more sophisticated statistical analysis

There are three levels of quantitative analysis beyond descriptive statistics, but in most cases, descriptive statistics will meet your needs adequately. Much of your data will be qualitative, not quantitative and so much of your data analysis will be non-numerical. We will just summarize the other three levels here; if you wish to learn more, please see the resources at the end of this chapter.

- Inferential statistics enable you to assess the statistical significance of your data and results, e.g. chi-square, Kalmogorov-Smirnov and student's t-test.
- Simple inter-relationships enable you to measure relationships between two components of your data ('variables' as the statisticians call them).
- Multivariate analysis enables you to measure relationships between three or more components of your data, e.g. multiple regression, cluster analysis and factor analysis.

(After Blaxter et al. 2001: 216)

Analysing qualitative data

The analysis of qualitative data requires a researcher to interpret their data actively, in order to elicit the various meanings that they represent. The analysis of qualitative data requires you to describe and theorize social relationships and to explain how the people involved in those relationships make sense of them, because social relationships exist only as meanings made by their members. (For social scientists, a 'meaningless relationship' is an oxymoron!) In contrast, descriptive statistics require a researcher merely to 'read off' the simple numerical [quantitative] relationships that they represent, because statistical relationships require no-one to 'make sense' of them for them to exist.

There is a multitude of forms of qualitative analysis, but we are presenting just five forms with which you can analyse the sorts of qualitative data that you are likely to generate in your action research project. *Figure 12.4 Analysis of qualitative data* summarizes these five approaches to analysing qualitative data and their advantages and disadvantages. If you wish to learn about other forms of qualitative analysis, please see 'Further resources: going deeper' at the end of this chapter.

Form of analysis	Foci	Advantages	Disadvantages
Thematic analysis	Major themes and categories	Generates a 'big picture' of your data	Can blinker you to later, alternative, interpretations
Exemplars	Case studies, profiles or vignettes of major themes	A first step beyond simple descriptions of events	Can reinforce a theme, rather than pose alternatives
Narrative	Events, actions, etc. that, taken together, form a coherent story	Can show multiple viewpoints, each telling its particular story	Assumes a linear coherence of events that isn't always the case
Reading for 'voice'	Presence/absence of the 'voices' of specific groups in what is said and done	Goes beyond appearances to power effects; highlights multiple viewpoints	Requires the researcher to know that 'voices' exist that are inaudible
Critical discourse analysis	Presence/absence of particular 'frames' (i.e. ways to explain speech and action)	Goes beyond appearances to the power effects of dominant discourses	Needs integrating with 'voice' to show practical implications

Figure 12.2   Analysis of qualitative data

Thematic analysis

As its name implies, this form of analysis looks for major themes and categories in your coded data. Indeed, since the point of coding your data is to highlight similarities between components of your data, coding may well be a precursor to this form of analysis. Thematic analysis gives you an overview or a 'big picture' of your data. It won't necessarily give you a detailed picture, but it will highlight any issues or questions that need further analysis. A note of caution: your first, thematic analysis of your data can be fairly straightforward and can produce clear results, so it can blinker you to other – possibly competing – interpretations of your data.

Exemplars

Again, as the name implies, this form of analysing qualitative data looks beyond first appearances for indicators of major themes and big ideas. Such indicators include case studies, together with less substantial exemplars such as vignettes and profiles (short stories) that illuminate broader trends and issues. Exemplars can work in two ways: they can illustrate themes that have emerged already; or they can come together to demonstrate that a theme exists. Either way, exemplars can reinforce the problem associated with thematic analysis, i.e. they can blinker you to other – possibly competing – interpretations of your data by providing 'evidence' of particular themes.

Narrative

Through narrative analysis, you can make sense of patterns in your data by linking them in a story (a narrative). Further, narrative analysis need not stop at one story: it can show two or more stories co-existing or competing in your data. As such, it is especially useful for demonstrating different perspectives on events, which is a feature of action research data. The disadvantage of narrative analysis is that it explains events, etc. in the linear terms ('beginning, middle, end') of the classic story, which don't lend themselves easily to representing co-existing perspectives, especially when those perspectives conflict with each other.

Reading for 'voice'

In this form of analysis, you examine your coded data for the 'voices' that are present – and for those that you might expect to be present but that are absent. We are putting 'voices' in single inverted commas to indicate that it refers not just to speech data but to the whole range of discourses and theoretical 'frames' that shape events and actions (including speech) in your specific circumstances. Reading for 'voice' takes you beyond mere appearances to the power relations represented by the presence and absence of specific voices in your coded data. It can also highlight multiple perspectives, enabling you to move beyond the linear logic of narrative analysis. The strength of reading for 'voice' lies in its ability to show not just whose interests were served in particular circumstances but also whose weren't and to explain that in terms of context-specific power relations. Its weakness is that it relies on the researcher being familiar not just with the 'voices' that are present but also with those that are absent . . . and yet it's hard to recognize voices that are inaudible!

Critical discourse analysis

Critical discourse analysis takes a step beyond reading for 'voice', in that it identifies the discourses and other theoretical 'frames' at work in your coded data. It can be an abstract exercise, but when you integrate critical discourse analysis with reading for 'voice', you can see the power effects of specific discourses and 'frames' in the circumstances of your action research project.

Displaying the results of your analysis

If you have found patterns in your primary data that may help you to answer your research question, you need to display them – both for your benefit and for the benefit of the other participants in your project – and to show their significance to your research project. You can do this graphically or textually.

Graphic presentations

Descriptive statistics lend themselves to graphic presentation and this can lead you to see patterns in your data easily and quickly. You have seen examples of summary tables and matrix displays already in this chapter. There are various forms of graph, including the classic 'line' graph, the bar chart, the pie chart and the scatter graph. Each one is a graphic representation of numerical information and you may use one or more types of graph to summarize numerical information associated with your action research project. (Data analysis software can help you to generate simple graphs, decision trees, etc.) Concept maps and/or decision trees are further graphic ways to present your data.

As an illustration: Staff in the Biway Out of School Hours programme were interested in whether and how gender affected children's participation in the activities provided (*Student Engagement: Starting with the Child* project). They measured how long girls and boys spent in a particular area over a week and what they did there; and they summarized and presented their observations as a series of bar charts, one for each day of the week. *Figure 12.5 Wet area summary chart* is one of their summary charts for the wet area on a Monday.

Reviewing and summarizing these graphs they found that, over time, on average 67 per cent of boys used the outdoor area and only 37 per cent of girls used this area. They also found that on average only 15 per cent of children participated in the service's written programme during the data collection period. They also found that children (in general) choose to participate in

Wet area

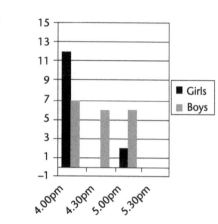

Monday 14th November

Activities

- Drawing
- Dancing
- Reading
- Tamigotchi's
- Guinness book of records
- Mobile phones (toys)
- Wrestling

Figure 12.5 Wet area summary chart.

more imaginary play-based activities than the formal activities that were pre-pared for them. This analysis led them to ask:

- Why do the differences exist?
- Can we make a difference?
- Can we increase both the boys' and girls' participation in the outdoor area?
- How can we improve staff engagement?
- Are we really hearing children's voices around programming?

Textual presentations

You can display patterns in your qualitative data such as themes, exemplars, narratives, reading for 'voice' and critical discourse analysis through textual devices such metaphors, stories, vignettes and case studies. In the next section, we present an excerpt from an analysis of some action research data that shows many of these textual devices at work.

Taking Step 12: a case from practice

The authors ran a collaborative action research project in Melbourne, in which eleven early childhood practitioners in long day care services explored how their understandings of parents' role affect their current relationships with parents (the RESPECT project). The following is an excerpt from their analysis of the data from the project. It includes references (in italics) to several of the ways to analyse and present data that you have met in this chapter.

Two *themes* ran through participants' data consistently. The first theme was the 'expert' teacher. All participants raised concerns that parents and colleagues regarded them as 'experts' and that this created an inaccurate dichotomy between staff (professional, expert) and parent (carer, nurturer). The emergence of this dichotomy is a long *story*, which is reflected in the data. It starts with Plato's distinction between family and state; it develops through the emergence of the teacher-as-professional (detached and rational) in the USA in the late nineteenth and early twentieth centuries; and it continues as the dominance of the contemporary early childhood field by developmental 'expertise'. The staff–parent dichotomy rests on the assumption that some forms of knowledge – especially developmental psychology – are more important than others, such as parents' skills and lived experiences; but that parents can become apprentices to practitioners by learning their expertise. The popular television programme, 'The Supernanny' is an *exemplar* of this approach; and Jennifer's project was a *case study* of this approach in action. Jennifer believed that parents could be involved in programme planning if they learnt what knowledge was valid and useful in supporting their child's development.

In contrast, this little *vignette* from Lydia's journal shows that it is possible for staff to recognize that while parents' knowledge is different from theirs, it should still be respected:

> *In reflecting on conversations with parents since being part of this project, I feel that I have a better understanding of some of their struggles each day. As a result, I have tried to be less flippant in reassuring them that their child will be OK when they have to leave them in a screaming heap at the beginning of the day and I will now often e-mail or call them to let them know that their child has settled in.*

The second theme was time and space. All the participants mentioned this as a factor in their struggles not only to engage with parents but also to reflect on their relationships with parents and the effects for parents, for themselves and for the children. They showed how their use of time and space is governed by a particular *discourse* of professionalism that *prescribes* two hours a week for qualified staff to leave the classroom and work elsewhere on programme planning and evaluation; *proscribes* using those two hours to, for example, read the latest research and reflect on its implications; and excludes the possibility that unqualified staff can plan and evaluate their work, let alone read and reflect on research. That discourse of professionalism was reasserted and reinforced by the constant *'voices'* of the national Accreditation Council and the local regulatory bodies; but the discourse excluded children's voices, despite the fact that they are allegedly meant to be its beneficiaries.

Taking your twelfth step: your actions and reflections

It's now time for you to analyse your data, using one or more of the techniques for data analysis that we have provided, in the form of lists, charts, tables and boxes. You might compare and contrast the understandings that you gain from each technique and then decide which one is the most useful to you as you analyse your particular collection of data. As you apply each of your chosen techniques, note the results in your *Action Research Journal*, as this will give you stronger foundations for: (1) comparing and contrasting the techniques; and (2) drawing conclusions from your data.

Further resources: going deeper

In print

Maxwell, J. A. (2005) *Qualitative Research Design: An Interactive Approach*, 2nd edn. London: Sage.
Harvey, G. (2007) *Excel for Dummies*. Chichester: John Wiley & Sons, Ltd.
Schmuller, J. (2005) *Statistical Analysis with Excel for Dummies*. Chichester: John Wiley & Sons, Ltd.

Online

Ereska, T. M. (2003) How will I know a code when I see it? *Qualitative Research Journal*, 3(2): 60–74. Available at: http://www.latrobe.edu.au/aqr/journal/ 2AQR2003.pdf (accessed: 20 July 2007).
de Wet, J. & Erasmus, Z. (2005) Towards rigour in qualitative analysis. *Qualitative Research Journal*, 5(1). Available at: http://www.latrobe.edu.au/aqr/journal/ 1AQR2005.pdf (accessed 10 October 2006).
Marshall, H. (2002) What do we do when we code data? *Qualitative Research Journal*. 2(1). Available at: http://www.latrobe.edu.au/aqr/journal/1AQR2002.pdf (accessed 10 October 2006).

McKee, A. (2001) A beginner's guide to textual analysis. Metro, 20 May. Available at: http://0-elibrary.bigchalk.com.library.ecu.edu.au:80/Australia (accessed 20 July 2007).

Exploring Data. Available at: http://exploringdata.cqu.edu.au/

Software for 'sophisticated' data analysis

The most widespread quantitative data analysis software in social science and education departments is *SPSS* (Statistical Package for Social Sciences) and *MINITAB*. These allow users to conduct a range of simple statistical analyses.

Many spreadsheet programmes and databases also allow users to undertake simple quantitative analysis.

The UK Economic and Social Research Council (ESRC) has established a website offering online training in statistical analysis. 'Teaching Resources and Materials for Social Scientists' is at http://tramss.data-archive.ac.uk

The most common software packages for qualitative analysis are probably *Ethnograph*, *QSR NUD*IST* and *ATLAS.ti*.

SCOLARI (a division of the publishers Sage) produces many qualitative software packages and offers free demonstrations on its website: http://www.scolari.com

Other sites to visit for information on qualitative analysis software:

- American Evaluation Association. http://www.eval.org/Resources/QDA.htm
- Economic and Social research Council (ESRC) has established a website offering information about qualitative analysis software: http://caqdas.soc.surrey.ac.uk

Step 13 Deepen and broaden your data and understandings

> How does this data differ between teachers / what characteristics are children
>   drawn to?
> What would this data look like with a male teacher?
> What about children's independence versus teacher–child engagement?
>   (Sandy, *Action Research Journal* and presentation to colleagues,
>   *Student Engagement: Starting with the Child* project)

Sandy collected data on student engagement and in the above excerpt from her journal she asks questions about how her context influenced her data. Such questions could lead her to gather more data that is deeper and broader, which, in turn, could deepen and broaden the meanings of the patterns that she saw in her data when she began to analyse it. Step 13 eases you towards creating new knowledge and new strategies for change in your project.

What you'll need to take Step 13:

Time
- to read this step and to reflect on its content;
- to talk with those involved in your project about the issues this step raises;
- to review your data and plan your next action.

Knowledge
- What does 'deeper and broader' data look like?
- Are there implications of deepening and broadening my data?

Where next?

So you have collected, coded and analysed your data. Now is the time to deepen and broaden your understanding of it. Before you do, pause for a moment to assess how far you've come by looking at your data and your analysis from the perspective of an outsider:

> At the same time as recognizing and asserting your own perspective on your data and analysis, it is important not to get too embedded and bound up in this view. . . . It is healthy, therefore, to stand back for a time and attempt to view your research from the more dispassionate perspective of an outsider.
>
> (Blaxter et al. 2001: 219–20)

As you collected and analysed your data, you tried to remain alert to conflicting and contradictory viewpoints of events. Now is the time to be alert to interpretations of your data that may conflict with or contradict yours. This may not be easy, but it is a way to re-charge your batteries, as Foucault (1985: 8) reminded us: 'There are times in life when the question of knowing if one can think differently than one thinks, and perceive differently than one sees, is absolutely necessary if one is to go on looking and reflecting at all.'

Figure 13.1 A complexity/understanding matrix shows you broad strategies through which to broaden and deepen your data. In this matrix, we use 'narrow' and 'shallow' purely to describe the nature of your first batch of data, rather than to judge its quality. However, the point about action research is to increase our understanding of change – how to create it successfully, the factors that support or hinder it, etc. As you move through the action research spiral, you should find that your data about your circumstances – and, therefore, your understandings – become broader and deeper. There are various ways to broaden and deepen your data and your understandings, as summarized

NARROW AND SHALLOW DATA	NARROW AND DEEP DATA
• Snapshots/anecdotes of one or two factors • A quick overview, often in numbers	• Detailed, in-depth data about one or two events or factors • Complex analysis of one or two events or factors
BROAD AND SHALLOW DATA	BROAD AND DEEP DATA
• Snapshots/anecdotes of several factors • An overview of several factors, often in numbers • Brings complexity, but not understanding in depth	• Combines snapshots with detailed, in-depth data about several factors • Brings complexity and understanding in depth

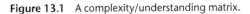

Figure 13.1   A complexity/understanding matrix.

in *Figure 13.2 Broadening and deepening your data* and *Figure 13.3 Broadening and deepening your understandings*. You can choose which techniques to use, depending on which aspect/s of your data you think might be broadened and deepened most profitably. However, we suggest that you combine at least two techniques.

BROADENING AND DEEPENING YOUR DATA			
Five Ws and an H	*Any other types of data?*	*Any others' views?*	*How is it significant?*
• Who? • What? • When? • Where? • Why? • How?	• Numbers • Words • Images • Stories • Anecdotes • Observations	• Parents • Colleagues • Children • Supervisors • Others	• Is it unusual? • Is it part of a pattern? • Does it link with other data? • Why (and to whom) does it matter?

Figure 13.2   Broadening and deepening your data.

BROADENING AND DEEPENING YOUR UNDERSTANDINGS			
Reflecting	*Reflecting critically*	*Returning to the literature*	*Taking 'lines of flight'*
What are your: • questions? • issues? • dilemmas? • lessons?	Whom does your data: • include? • exclude? • silence? Who benefits from those inclusions, etc.? Did gender, 'race', class affect events? How?	How have theorists from different areas addressed your topic? Will their views affect your next step? How?	What texts link to this one? What does each text 'say' about your topic and what light does it throw on your present analysis?

Figure 13.3   Broadening and deepening your understandings.

Broadening and deepening your data

This section introduces four techniques to broaden and deepen your data, each of which is based on the ideas in Step 10 'Gather "baseline" data'. In that step, *Figure 10.3 The data collection matrix* summarized your major types of data; and Figures 10.4, 10.5 and 10.8 were detailed libraries of techniques to *collect* your data. So before you read this section and decide how best to broaden and deepen your data, you might like to revisit Step 10.

Five Ws and an H

In this technique, you ask: does my data enable me to explain events or are some things still unclear? Thus:

- Who? Have you included all the relevant actors?
- What? Have you included all the relevant perspectives on events?
- When? Do events follow a clear (logical and chronological) sequence?
- Where? Have you located all the sites where relevant events occurred?
- Why? Whose explanations of events are present and absent?
- How? Whose descriptions of events are present and absent?

Any other types of data?

In this technique, you ask: are my current types of data sufficient to enable me to explain events, or do I need any of the following?

- numbers
- words
- images

. . . in the form of . . .

- observations
- interviews (from anecdotes to narratives)
- documents.

Any others' views?

This technique links with 'Five Ws and an H' – it asks whether your data includes all relevant perspectives and explanations of events. Here's a short checklist:

- parents
- colleagues
- children
- supervisors
- others.

How is it significant?

When you ask yourself, 'What does this aspect of the data *mean*?' you are starting to judge its significance. Here are some other questions to help you to do this:

- Is it unusual?
- Is it part of a pattern?
- (How) Does it link with other data?
- Why (and to whom) does it matter?

Sandra and Elizabeth (*Diversity and Children's Voices in the Curricula* project) wanted to improve their approach to consulting children about daily routines and events. They collected and analysed data about their current approach and noted (in their *Action Research Journal*) how reflecting critically on their data had prompted them to deepen their data (by speaking to children individually rather than in groups) and to seek parents' perspectives on what children were saying. The result was a deeper understanding of how introducing what they called a 'rest bag' at sleep time was affecting children:

> We felt that we were consulting with the children. We were confident that this new routine would work as it was based on the children's desires and voices. . . . However, after session 2 of the project, we thought about some of the discussions we had had. We began to suspect that we had only really listened to a certain group; the predominant group.
>
> On reflection, we realised that an open forum where a question was asked of the whole group and each child was expected to respond was not likely to be the optimal method to use if we wanted the voices of each child to be expressed. We began to ask ourselves whose were being heard loud and clear and whose voices were being marginalised.
>
> So then we had more individual chats with children. We were also interested in what their parents had to say on the subject since we assumed that the children were likely to talk about their concerns with them. As a result of these more meaningful conversations, we

discovered that this rest bag routine was not what all the children wanted.

A particular parent came to us, and spoke of his child's dislike of rest time. This child disliked the rest bag so much that he did not want to come to kinder. The child had not spoken about these feelings to us. This was quite a disturbing and shocking insight and brought home to us how easily we can unwittingly cause distress when we fail to seek out a child's real voice.

(CEIEC 2006: 38)

Broadening and deepening your understandings

As you broaden and deepen your data, you will probably also broaden and deepen your understandings – of your circumstances, of the change/s you have brought to them through your action research project and of processes of change. This section introduces you to four techniques to broaden and deepen your understandings that will focus any broadening and deepening that is occurring already.

Reflecting

In the heat of the (research) moment, it can be hard to find time to reflect on your data – to 'mull it over' – but it can both broaden and deepen your understandings of it. Ask yourself these fairly simple questions about your involvement so far with your action research project:

- What questions do I have about (1) changes in my circumstances and (2) the meaning/s of those changes?
- What issues have emerged for me so far?
- What dilemmas am I facing?
- What lessons have I learnt so far?

Reflecting critically

You can broaden your understandings still further by reflecting critically on your data. (You might like to return to Step 6 to remind yourself of the significance of the 'critical' in critical reflection.) To revive or reinforce your critical perspective on your data, ask yourself questions such as these:

- Who is present in my data? Who is absent from my data?
- Who benefited (and how) from the events in my data? Does my data show this clearly?

• How (if at all) did gender, 'race', class (singly or together) affect the events in my data? Does my data show this clearly?

Mindy and Martha (whom you met earlier) made the time to reflect on the data they collected about their relationships with parents. In their journal, they raised issues, dilemmas and lessons very clearly:

> When we ask parents 'What is a welcoming centre?', whose voices do we privilege through having the questionnaire in English? Whose voices do we hear? Is it the same ones all the time (people who are confident communicators)? If you look at who is responding to the questionnaire, it would have been the English-speaking parents. We need to re-examine the questionnaire for non-English-speaking parents and parents who are not confident communicators.

Returning to the literature

This can be a time not just to reflect but also to return to the literature to help you to broaden your understanding of your topic. As you return to the literature, see whether there are ways to see, think and talk about your topic other than the one/s you have used so far. In other words, ask whether and how theorists from different areas or fields (e.g. psychologists, feminists, constructivists, 'brain theorists') have addressed your topic.

As part of her doctoral action research project on observation, Kylie Smith interviewed early childhood staff. Having collected and analysed this data, Kylie deepened her analysis by 'returning to the literature' – specifically, an article by Davies (1994), where she analysed gender inequalities in the classroom, using the post-structuralist concept of binary oppositions. After re-reading this article, Kylie wrote a short paper (to share with her fellow postgraduate students) that deepened her understanding of her data by generating new questions about it. The following is an excerpt from that short paper.

> Deconstruction
> The identification of these binary opposites within the text will assist me to identify categories that support people in positions of privilege within lived experiences and disrupt and deconstruct the binaries to create multiple discourses that provide more socially just categories. For example, within the male/female dichotomy, male is the dominant position as male is the invisible, unmarked category, while the female is the visible, marked category (Davies, 1994). Hence, in the early childhood classroom, all children can have access to the block corner, but the boys will have an unconscious and often

invisible privilege to access to the play in this area as a 'masculine' activity. Within early childhood, the anti-bias curriculum (based on critical theory) guides early childhood professionals to challenge inequity where boys have dominance over girls and to create space for 'everyone' to play, whether you are a boy or a girl. This holds intact the ideas of maleness and femaleness as binary opposites and the disruption to binary thought as transgressive, not a move towards multiplicity, as critical theory positions gender (being male or female) as universal (Davies, 1994). Davies (1994) argues that while patterns of desire are constructed in relation to a binary gender order, males will find ways to maintain their ascendancy (p.16). Post-structuralism – in the form of deconstruction – provides strategies for disrupting and undermining the hierarchical dualism that creates those patterns of desire.

Beginning to deconstruct early childhood professionals' interviews on their understandings of early childhood observation.
Early childhood professionals were asked the following questions in regard to observation within the service:

- How would you define observation within an early childhood setting?
- How do you use observation in this service?
- What do you observe?
- Who has access to these observations?
- Who performs the task of observation in this service?

One of the binary dualisms to emerge from this data is the early childhood professional/parent or expert/apprentice. For example:

- How do you use observation in this service?

Kylie included several examples of binary dualisms in reponse to her question. Here are just a couple:

AT1 25.9.98
36. Onya: So they're used ... obviously, between each other, they're used for programming purposes but, of course, I also can use them as a backup when I speak with families. Um ... I haven't ever shown any of my families my written observations because I can talk about them off the cuff and when I've met with families the folder's been there, but I haven't had to use them – I can just talk straight out with the family. I don't like to compare and show them

checklists and stuff like that because, you know, it could lead to mis-understandings and things like that. Yeah. So observations are used, yeah, with families, with each other and with other staff at the centre as well.

AT2 25.9.98

35. Lucinda: Well, they are used within ... um ... the pro-gramme, so we set up the programme for the children and also, I think the observations are used, too, if we have problems with the children and we want to discuss with the parents or if the parents are worried about the child's development or behaviour problems, we can use these observations as a guide. And perhaps to help them solve the problem that they're having.

(Smith, K. Unpublished data analysis presented to the CEIEC postgraduate group, 28 May 2002)

Taking 'lines of flight'

Another way to broaden and deepen your understanding is to take a 'line of flight' (Mansfield 2002: 146) from your data to texts that you might not, at first sight, regard as relevant to it. The aim of taking 'lines of flight' is to resist or silence aspects of your data that are normally dominant and privileged, which is why Fleming (2002: 202) described lines of flight as 'tangential cata-pults that fling us out of the spiral of domination'. To 'fling' ourselves away from the viewpoints of dominant or privileged groups requires us to 'fly' to texts about our topic created by people who have experienced injustice or oppression. For example, if you are trying to deepen your understandings of gender's influences in early childhood settings, you could take a 'line of flight' to texts written by women who have experienced sexual discrimination, rather than read more texts by men who have perpetrated it. Similarly, if you are trying to deepen your understandings of racial injustice in early childhood settings, you could 'fly' to texts by those who have faced racial discrimination, rather than those who benefit from it.

We use 'texts' to mean not just books and papers, but anything that we can 'read' for meaning in the way that we read a text. In this usage, 'a text' can refer to books and papers, but it can also refer to paintings and drawings, an interview, a set of observations, a video recording, etc. Consequently, you can take 'lines of flight' to texts in very diverse places, including biographical texts, newspaper stories, historical texts, research texts or texts from popular culture.

A 'line of flight' generally takes us to texts that are outside of our discipline or area of work. Thus, broadening and deepening your understandings of your data by taking a 'line of flight' will probably lead you out of the early child-hood field to radical political texts that examine justice and competing discourses through the eyes of the oppressed, the silenced and the marginalized. Against that background, Mac Naughton (2005) suggests four ways to take 'lines of flight':

1 Ask questions of your data that focus explicitly on equity issues. For example:
   • What is happening in this observation?
   • Which texts would I normally refer (defer) to for an answer?
   • Which children's voices are present in (or absent from) my observations?
   • What are the consequences for a child who is present in (or absent from) my observations?
   • Do my observations privilege one child's voice and silence another's?
   • How can I use my observations to enable a silenced child to speak?
   • How can I use my observations to honour children whose voices are heard only rarely?

2 Be 'nomadic' and follow your lines of flight to texts you think might be relevant but which would not normally be included in a research project about your topic. To assess the relevance of a text you find on a line of flight, ask of it questions such as these:
   • Who created this text and whom does it benefit?
   • Whose voice dominates this text and whose is marginalized?
   • Where else can I find the ideas in this text? Whom do those texts benefit?
   • When was this text created and has anything changed since then?
   • How does this text encourage us to 'read' it one way and not others?
   • Why is this text (or texts of this type) not generally regarded as relevant to a research project such as mine? What happens when I refer (defer) to this text for an answer to my questions?

3 Read what each text you find on a line of flight has to say about the issues you are exploring in your data, then ask of it questions such as these:
   • Does it reinforce your present analysis? Does it change it?
   • Does it challenge, conflict with or contradict your present analysis?
   • Does it broaden or deepen your present analysis . . . or point it in a different direction?

4 Once you have read the texts you found on a line of flight, ask yourself whether they prompt you to think differently about your data and to draw different conclusions from it.

In a project on children and 'race', Karina Davis, Kylie Smith and Glenda Mac Naughton tried to think differently about their data on young children's racial understandings by moving beyond traditional early childhood research on children and 'race'. They wanted to see how texts that told stories about the experiences of racism in Australia from an Indigenous perspective might take them to new insights into the processes of 'racing' young children. Consequently, they took 'lines of flight' to texts that included voices that are absent consistently from Australian early childhood texts and that speak to specific political struggles over 'race' in Australia. One such text was Aunty Iris's biography, which described her experiences as an Indigenous Australian woman growing up in 1920s and 1930s Australia. In another such text, Judy Atkinson (an Indigenous Australian academic) used stories of Indigenous women's and men's lives to begin 'healing' the generational trauma produced by the violent, racist treatment of Indigenous communities in Australia. From this text, the three researchers chose Lorna's story, in which she described her childhood as a political struggle against a masculine white hegemony that positioned her as inferior and undesirable because of her 'black' identity (Davis et al. 2005).

Taking Step 13: a case from practice

Sandy (whom you met at the start of this step) was part of a collaborative action research project on student engagement in early childhood settings. At the start of the project, the participants wanted to know which children engaged with their programme, so they gathered, coded and analysed data about students' engagement with a programme. To broaden their understanding of their data and of the issue of student engagement, they returned to the literature, where they found different ways to think and talk about student engagement, each of which is more or less influential than the others. For instance, some theorists focus on *levels* of engagement, while others focus on *forms* of engagement. Further, they found that there are several different forms of engagement, including:

- frustrated engagement
- unsystematic engagement
- disengaged engagement
- critical engagement
- structure-dependent engagement
- self-regulated engagement.
              (http://cela.albany.edu/newslet/winter99/bbdtable.html)

Their return to the literature led the group to ask different questions about student engagement, such as: 'Do children engage with our programme in different ways?' In this new question, engagement isn't simply something that does or doesn't happen. Instead, it is a more complex form of behaviour that can vary between individuals and groups of children in particular circumstances.

The group then broadened its understanding of student engagement still further by trying to reinterpret their data in the light of their new questions. They looked again at their analysis of their data and asked questions such as:

- As well as my first analysis, can I now find in my data other ways to think and talk about student engagement, such as different forms of student engagement?
- How can I code and categorize (types, forms, etc.) these different forms of student engagement?
- How can I rate these different forms of student engagement? (Indeed, is it possible or realistic to rate them?)
- How can I best explain and represent these different forms of student engagement (e.g. graphs, charts, metaphors, analogies)?

Sandy's questions – with which we opened this step – were as follows:

- How does this data differ between teachers/what characteristics are children drawn to?
- What would this data look like with a male teacher?
- What about children's independence versus teacher–child engagement?

As she reviewed her data with her new questions in mind, this is what she found:

- In 16 out of 17 observations, teacher's participation in an activity resulted in an increase in the number of children who participated. Further observations also indicated longer participation, enhanced communication with teacher and other children and increased creativity.
- On average, the number of children almost doubled (48 per cent increase) when a teacher joined the activity and then decreased by 56 per cent after the teacher left.
- In one instance, a group of boys left the room as soon as a teacher joined the activities inside. They were observed to continue moving about the preschool with little time spent at any activity. They also appeared to prefer secluded areas away from teachers.
- In 15 out of 17 instances, children's numbers decreased within

five minutes of the teacher leaving the activity. Some children 'went looking for teacher company', others moved to another activity.

Taking your thirteenth step: your actions and reflections

It's now time for you to deepen and broaden your understandings by using one or more of the techniques that you have just met.

Further resources: going deeper

In print

Ragland, B. (2006) Positioning the practitioner-researchers. Five ways of looking at practice, *Action Research*, 4(2): 165–82.

Step 14 Choose a further social practice to change or improve, perhaps guided by a new research question

Tip of the ICEBERG . . .

The journey so far has led the team to some amazing discoveries (some obvious, some not). However, it seems that the journey has just begun and that the more we look for the answer, the more we find <u>some</u> answers but many more questions.

(The Biways Out of School Hours team. PowerPoint slide presentation to colleagues at the final meeting of the *Student Engagement: Starting with the Child* project, November 2006)

Like the Biways team, most action researchers enter the final phase of their first action research cycle with new questions. Step 14 in your action research project is both an end and a beginning. It is the final step of your first action research cycle and the first step in your second cycle. The transition from the first cycle to the second isn't automatic – you *can* get off the bus! You may decide that now is not the right time to start your second cycle because, for example, you no longer have access to the sorts of resources that sustained your first cycle and/or because your action research group is dispersing; or perhaps because you just need time to reflect on what you learnt from your first cycle.

What you'll need to take Step 14:

Time
- to read this chapter and to reflect on its content;
- to talk with those involved in your project – who may or may not be in an action research group with you – about the issues this chapter raises;
- to plan what action you will take to initiate your second cycle.

Knowledge
- What have I learnt to date from my action research?
- What is my next step? Why?

Other resources

- You may wish to start a second *Action Research Journal*, reflecting the fact that you are exploring a new social practice through a new research question.
- You may need to create another literature search diary (print or a computer file), together with another indexable means (paper or computer folder) of organizing and storing the results of your literature search.

Choose another social practice to change or improve

The second action research cycle is likely to take less time than the first, because it consists of just 11 steps, not 14. You will have done most of the preparation in Steps 3–6 and, if you are researching as part of a group, then you will have taken Step 7 already. *Figure 14.1 The second action research cycle* summarizes this shorter action research cycle.

Another social practice

Your aim in your second cycle is the same as in your first – to improve your practice both by changing it *and* by finding new ways to think about it. Thus, your second cycle should allow you to improve another social practice by changing it and by creating new knowledge about it. In Step 1, we defined a social practice as one whose meaning depends not just on our intentions in performing it but also on other people's interpretations of it. You may have seen this dialogue at work as you analysed the data in your first cycle, especially in your reading for 'voice' and your use of critical discourse analysis, each of which examines whose interpretation or understanding of a situation is accepted as the 'right' one.

A new 'niggle'

It is quite likely that you will initiate your second cycle with a good idea of the social practice on which to focus, because unless something was 'niggling' you, why would you initiate a second cycle?! Even if you have a new 'niggle', it's worth reflecting on whether and how it corresponds to one of the three very broad strands of thinking about social and educational change – technical, ethical and activist – that underlie the action research family and that you met in Step 3. That is likely to influence how you approach your new niggle and it may be a different approach to the one you used in your first cycle. Further, you should reflect on the differences between the action research family's two branches (action research for *professional* change and

---

Phase One. Choosing to change
Thinking

| STEP 1 | Choose a social practice to change or improve |
| STEP 2 | Ask a question about your chosen social practice |

Phase Two: Planning for a change
Thinking

| STEP 3 | Map the practicalities of researching in your context |

Phase Three: Creating change
Doing

| STEP 5 | Create a change and collect data about the result |

Thinking

STEP 6	Analyse your data
	Do you have new questions about your chosen social practice?
STEP 7	Deepen and broaden your data and understandings

Phase Four: Sharing the lessons
Doing

| STEP 8 | Check that your results are rigorous and valid |
| STEP 9 | Draw conclusions from your analysis |

Thinking

| STEP 11 | Start the action research cycle again |

Figure 14.1   The second action research cycle.

action research for *social* change) and then decide which is appropriate to your new niggle. Finally, you should decide whether you can explore your new niggle best through an individual or a collaborative approach.

Return to the literature

Since you are now focusing on a different social practice, you may wish to undertake another, different search of the literature to discover whether and how other researchers have thought about it and investigated it.

New ethics permission

You may have to seek fresh approval from the ethics organization to which you submitted an application concerning your first cycle. This will depend on whether you received permission to undertake a continuing spiral of action research or just a specific, clearly limited first cycle.

Taking Step 14: some cases from practice

Case 1 Lydia

In her first action research cycle, Lydia had investigated how to include diverse stakeholders' voices respectfully and meaningfully in the early childhood curriculum (*Diversity and Children's Voices in Early Childhood Curricula* project). As she prepared to initiate a second cycle, Lydia outlined her short-term and long-term actions in her *Action Research Journal*:

> I have started to think about ways to weave children, parents/families, teachers and the wider community into the curriculum next year. I would like to start to explore ways of opening up and creating more meaningful documentation that meets the diverse needs and desires of each person in the room. . . . To do this, I will need to talk about the various ways I can go about this process so that it is not seen as tokenistic or making children and families 'apprentices' to the teachers. . . . Time and space will once again play a vital role in how this goes and also parents'/families' and children's reactions to these ideas.
>
> Now:
>
> • Ensure that all families know where children's journals are and that they are updated throughout the year.
> • Provide a brief summary of the questionnaires for families in the room and for staff at the centre.
>
> Next year:
>
> • Look at diverse and (hopefully) innovative ways of including families more into the curriculum in the babies room that are meaningful and respectful of each person's values, needs and desires.
> • Some ways may be to look at providing e-mails of programmes. 'Thinking out aloud' books, snapshots of the day, photos, documentation in a variety of ways, asking parents to think about – and maybe design – the type of information they would like.

- Look at genuine ways to include children's voices into the curriculum.

Case 2 Mindy and Martha

Mindy's and Martha's initial curiosity about their relationships with parents (*Student Engagement: Starting with the Child* project) had led them to distribute a questionnaire about what parents thought was a welcoming centre; and their analysis of the resulting data had led them to question whose voices they were hearing. They implemented a range of measures, observed their effects and decided that these measures had, indeed, made parents feel more welcome. They used PowerPoint slides to share their experiences of doing action research with colleagues in neighbouring centres; and the text of their final two slides showed them preparing for another action research cycle:

> Penultimate slide
>
> 'Now that we have improved relationships with parents, does it follow that student engagement has also improved?'
>
> Final slide
>
> 'Questions!' (accompanied by images of question marks and compasses)

Case 3 Biways Out of School Hours programme

In their second action research cycle, the Biways OSH team explored boys' and girls' engagement in the outside play area, focused on the question, 'How does gender influence children's engagement in the outdoor environment?' The team began their second cycle by mapping what they called 'side tracks and future directions' for their future work and in the slide from their PowerPoint presentation about their first cycle, they presented what they called the 'spiralling questions (their new question) brought them' (*Figure 14.2 Spiralling questions*, overleaf).

Taking your fourteenth step: your actions and reflections

So, where to next for your project? As you choose your new focus, the action research cycle of think–do–think begins again. Like the Biways OSH team, you may face many possibilities. Like Lillith, you may initiate a second action research cycle simply and informally. In the following excerpt from Lillith's *Action Research Journal*, she reviewed her data, found a new niggle and planned new changes in her practice with the simple, 'Hmm! What to do?' (*Figure 14.3 Excerpt from Lillith's Action Research Journal*, on page 211).

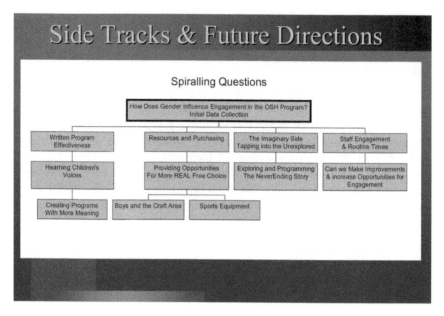

Figure 14.2 Spiralling questions.

In contrast, a project's cycles are differentiated more formally. An example is the 'RESPECT' project. There, participants identified and reflected critically on their dilemmas, niggles and uncertainties about their relationships with parents, implemented strategies to change them and evaluated the results. Participants proceeded through three cycles of action and reflection:

> *First cycle.* Participants reflect critically on how they understand and practise parent involvement at present and on what they think that good parent involvement means; develop 'critical questions' about their present relationships with parents; and formulate strategies through which to answer their questions.
>
> *Second cycle.* Participants reflect critically on their progress on enacting the strategies identified in the first cycle; and use project support materials to plan their next actions, based on what they learnt so far.
>
> *Third cycle.* Participants reflect critically on the overall lessons of the project and decide how to evaluate it formally.

The level of formality associated with moving to the next phase of your action research project will in part depend on the nature of your project. In many action research for professional change projects undertaken by individual

④ Mat Time Engagement

Staff took data on boys and their engagement
at mat time – 15 mins.

Lucas   f f f T🙁

Haydn   an T T

Philip   f T T

Arron   f an T f T f T ff T T f (This one was interesting)

Ryan   f (talking)

Vienna   f T f T f̶o̶r̶ ̶2̶n̶d̶ T

Harrison

f – fidgeting with things around them

T – Teacher called child back h attend

an – annoying another child nearby.

Hmm! What to do.

IDEAS
     – Visuals
     – Shorter mat time
     – Strategically placing children at front/
        away from friend
     – Things to feel / hold
     – Spots to sit on.

Figure 14.3 Excerpt from Lillith's *Action Research Journal*.

students, there is time to engage with one action research cycle only. In longer-term projects, more cycles are possible and generally planned. The more formal your project, the more likely it is that you will plan formally to move from one cycle to the next.

A fitting way to end this step on beginning again is to returning to the beginning of this step-by-step guide – 'bungee-jumping' with early childhood action researchers Sheralyn Campbell, Kylie Smith and Sharon Saitta:

> [T]here was not a single 'bungee jump', but many, each time:
>
> - coming back to the ladder and having to climb it again (when we gathered information and recognized a problem);
> - standing at the top and look in/down (when we critically reflected and planned to address the problem); and
> - leaping again (when we acted to create changes that would make things better).
>
> . . . In these cycles of action/reflection we came to see that there are no final words, answers or understandings – but that questioning, uncertainty, and personal confrontation, are a liberating and inspiring part of how we understand ourselves as good critical early childhood professionals involved in the pleasures and dangers of making a better world.
>
> (Campbell et al. 1999: 30)

Further resources: going deeper

Ferrance, E. (2000) *Action Research*, Brown University, Providence, USA. This publication includes several case studies in which teachers reframe their questions for the second cycle of action research. Available online: http://www.alliance.brown.edu/pubs/themes_ed/act_research.pdf

PHASE FOUR
Sharing the Lessons of your Change

Phase Four of your action research consists of Steps 15 and 16, in which you draw conclusions from your analysis of your data and then share what you've learnt from the project overall. The fact that these are the last two chapters in this book doesn't necessarily mean that they are the last two steps in the action research cycle. Some action researchers have the resources to undertake more than one cycle in their project; others have to restrict themselves to just one cycle. For the former, it may be some time before they reach Phase Four; the latter, in contrast, skip Step 14 and go straight from deepening and broadening their understandings to drawing conclusions from them.

As we've said, everyone has to 'get off the bus' at some time. Whether you have undertaken one action research cycle or more than one, you will decide that it is time to reflect one last time on your work to date, draw conclusions from it and then share them with the rest of the world! Welcome to Phase Four, in which you do just that.

Step 15 Draw conclusions from your analysis

> I'll never go back to what I was at the beginning of this project. I have changed my way of thinking.
>
> (Tania, Early Childhood Worker, presentation to colleagues *Student Engagement: Starting with the Child* project)

In the final cycle of your action research project you reach Step 15, in which you draw conclusions from your data and analysis. Drawing a conclusion about your action research project requires you to decide what has (and hasn't) changed since you began your project, explain why and then decide what you have learnt as a consequence. The changes may be material and/or they may concern how you think and act, so that – like Tania – you can never revert to how you thought and acted at the start of your project. Alternatively, it's possible that while your project didn't change your circumstances, it generated new questions about them.

What you'll need to take Step 15:

Time
- to read this step and to reflect on its content;
- to talk with those involved in your project – who may or may not be in an action research group with you – about the issues this step raises
- to revisit your data and analysis and draw conclusions from them.

Knowledge
- In what format should you present your conclusions?
- To whom will your conclusions be directed (for whom will you write them)?
- What do you intend to happen as a result of delivering your conclusions?

The limits of general advice

As you may appreciate by now, action researchers seek to increase understandings at the local level, rather than create new knowledge that can be generalized beyond its local origins. That is a general statement about action research, but it is becoming less and less appropriate to refer to your project in such generalized terms. As a result of collecting and analysing your 'baseline' data and your data about the change you initiated, you will now have a very specific perspective on your topic and question that other people may not share; and your analysis of your data will reflect your specific experiences to date in your project. Consequently, our advice in Step 15 is in very broad, general terms, leaving you to interpret it in the light of your specific circumstances.

To conclude or not to conclude?

'To conclude' can mean 'to terminate' or 'to end'. This usage can be a little tricky in action research: how do you (the action researcher) decide that your project is complete? Ideally, action research never concludes – each cycle generates new questions, initiating a further cycle. In reality, any action researcher has to stop researching at some point – especially if they have reached the end of their resources (e.g. a student has reached the end of the semester allowed for their research project). But when?

'To conclude' can also mean to reach a final, reasoned decision or judgement and it is this second usage that we will discuss. As you conclude your project, you should summarize your data and your analysis of it; then explain why and to whom your data and analysis are significant. For example: What were the lessons of your action research project? Does it imply or require any changes in policy? Your conclusion is your final, considered and reasoned decision or judgement about your project and, as such, it should include no new data or analysis.

How to conclude

Any conclusion is generally an outcome of reflection. The more careful and critical the reflection, the more considered the conclusion; and 'jumping to conclusions' can lead to trouble because it allows little or no time to reflect. A considered conclusion will have substantial foundations in your data and in your analysis, so to start drawing your conclusions, reflect once more on your data and analysis. You might find it helpful to assess whether the techniques (Figures 12.1, 12.3, 12.4, 13.2 & 13.3) in Steps 12 and 13 will help you to draw conclusions. Below, we examine three areas about which you might want to draw conclusions: your research topic, your research question and your learning.

Your research topic

1 What can you state with certainty about your research topic?
2 What continues to puzzle you about it?
3 What do you still want to know about it?
4 What questions about it do you have now?

If you are unable to state anything about your research topic with certainty, this doesn't mean that your project has failed. A 'negative' outcome from a research project can be just as significant as a 'positive' one; and an inability to make statements about a topic with certainty may well be as significant as an ability to make many statements about it. It may reflect continuing uncertainty or instability – or a major change – in the circumstances of your project; it may point to the need to collect more (or different) data; it may indicate that you need to make your analysis of your data deeper and/or broader; and so on.

If you are unable to work any longer on your project, this doesn't preclude drawing conclusions from it. Use your data and analysis to explain why further work is required – this is a substantive conclusion of your project, in that it tells us something about your project's context. Questions 2–4 in this section imply that your project is incomplete, but in a positive way – an action research project is never really complete.

In what follows, action researchers draw conclusions from their data and analysis about their research topics:

> Sharon (Early Childhood Literacy Advisor, the *Trembarth* project).
>
> *Research topic*
> How best to support teachers to reflect critically on their literacy practices.
>
> *Conclusions*
> Barriers to my process: I have not been able to focus on a group of teachers that I see often enough to build a climate of collaborative supportive discussion time around a focus. I believe that this is vital in order to be able to support a deeper reflection process on practices.
>
> The other factor that is important is also supporting teachers by *giving them time* to engage in a reflection process rather than expecting them

to engage in reflection on top of all the other expectations we have of them.

(Excerpt from Sharon's *Action Research Journal*)

Jane (Family Day Carer, *Student Engagement: Starting with the Child* project)

Research topic
How best to engage the children in her care in meaningful learning, using visual prompts.

Conclusions
From my research with the children and our journey together with our visuals I have concluded that they become engaged in something when there is an interest, it involves them on a personal level, when they have a say, when I as the adult am involved and allow open-ended curiosity and respond to them in a positive manner and allow their engagement and involvement in an activity even if it does not necessarily lead where I thought it may go.

Age makes a difference to the level and depth of engagement. Time of involvement varies greatly from child to child but can be expanded if I the adult become involved and make a comment that is open-ended and challenging. I have learnt that engagement can be a voluntary and an involuntary involvement and that may lead to the children having to stay 'on-task' and not 'in-task'.* The level of engagement may be more deep when something is fun. I have learnt to recognize the different signs physically and how to respond to them.

I have learned that engagement is ever changing and evolving and tomorrow may bring a whole new level as the children and I learn together. My poster is very visual and textured and shows our journey together from start to now. Look at them very carefully and see if you can pick up the significance of the colours, textures and pictures of our story – if so, hopefully, I as an educator of children have learned the art of meaningful engagement and allowed the children here to have a voice.

(Excerpt from the transcription of Jane's presentation to colleagues,
November 2006)

* One of the readings associated with the project had differentiated between 'in-task' and 'on-task' engagement.

Your research question

1 Have your answered your research question?
2 Do you still regard it as you did at the start of your project?
3 Would you ask it again if you could start your project again?
4 Do you have new questions and issues as a result of your project?

If you haven't answered your research question, this doesn't mean that your project has failed. Even if you followed the advice in Step 2 assiduously, this is no guarantee that you will have asked the 'right' research question. As your project has progressed, you have learnt more about your research topic and/or you have changed your perspective on it and, therefore, it is quite possible that you now want to ask a different question about it. Again, use your data and analysis to explain why – with hindsight – you now regard your original question as inappropriate. This is a methodological conclusion of your project – it tells us about the sort of question that needs to be asked about the context of your project. Questions 2–4 imply that you view your original question differently as a result of your involvement in your action research project, but in a positive way because an action research project should generate answers *and* more questions.

Kara, Kindergarten Teacher

Research topic
How can we further develop learner engagement through children's voice?

Conclusions
We have learnt that defining and measuring engagement is very challenging. Engagement is very complex. The first day we wrote down easily what we thought engagement was . . . There are different types and levels of student engagement and its different for everyone and different for different situations and its ever changing. Over the past 18 months looking at student engagement has just posed more and more questions . . . The more we look deeper, the more questions that arise. We didn't have the answers, just more questions . . . Our aim now is to really listen to children and move deeper.
(Excerpt from the transcription of Kara's presentation to colleagues, *Student Engagement: Starting with the Child* project, November 2006)

Your learning

1 What is the most significant thing you have learned about your circumstances from/through your action research project?

2   What is the most significant thing you have learned about action research (as a way to create change) from/through your action research project?

3   Was any theory (or theories) especially helpful in explaining the events in your project?

4   What was the most significant aspect of your action research cycle/s? Do you have an example or (preferably) a case study of this aspect?

The questions in this section don't have 'yes/no' answers, because they are intended to prompt you to make some judgements about your project overall. Questions 1–3 ask you to make judgements about the substantive, methodological and theoretical knowledge that you have gained from the project. However, the backdrop for each question is the change that you created in your circumstances through your project and so your answer to each one should address this.

You will probably find it hard to answer Question 4, but it could encourage you to 'stand back' from the project that you have been involved in so closely. If you had to say just one thing about the project to an outsider, what would it be? Your answer might refer to a substantive aspect, a methodological one or a theoretical one; and if you can illustrate it with an example or a case study, so much the better.

Sharon (Early Childhood Literacy Advisor, the *Trembarth* project).

Research topic
How best to support teachers to reflect critically on their literacy practices.

Conclusion
The other factor I have found when trying to reflect on my own has been how difficult it is when the train of thought or feeling about my focus is interrupted with phone calls, people needing you and then you can't get that thought or feeling back in the same way.

Being part of a collaborative group enables you to be in a 'reflection mode' and time for being in that group helps you maintain that reflections on your focus. . . . The collaborative discussions, even though about different topics or focus, still enabled us to connect with each other's focus and draw parallels to our own.

Critical reflection is bound up in relationships because critical reflection is a social process – interaction of our thoughts and observations with others – linked to your own learning style.

In this excerpt from her Masters thesis, Millie does a good job of integrating theory with her conclusions:

> A distinction can be made between the contribution of the partici-pants in their attempts to include children's voices at an individual level, and the challenges and possibilities that emerged at a systemic level [social, structural and institutional]. Specifically, the conditions reported by the participants for optimising children's participation in curriculum decision-making related to the importance of a shared philosophy around listening to children; the acknowledgement and negotiation of power relations; supportive and trusting relationships between staff, children and their families; skills [intrapersonal and interpersonal], time and funding.
>
> Despite these challenges, the experiences of the participants as action learners involved in this study enabled the pedagogical possibilities to emerge for honouring children's voices in curricula. Access to current research and literature and resources such as support, skills, time and funding were reported to enable and sustain children's participation in decision-making processes. In particular, access to discourses of participation provided participants with an alternative framework to conceptualise children's voices in early childhood. A poststructural approach to analysis of the empirical data was identified as useful to the participants in their attempts to re-think practice in the light of contrasting images of the child.
>
> (Olcay 2007: 103)

Taking Step 15: a case from practice

The authors were involved in an action learning project concerning 'children who challenge', i.e. children who are, e.g., physically violent, verbally abusive and discriminatory in their relationships with other children. The project enabled and encouraged teachers to reflect critically on their approaches to 'children who challenge' and then to use their critical reflections to strengthen their capacity to work with these children. In our subsequent journal article, we drew several conclusions about:

- our research topic (children with challenging behaviours);
- our research question (can teachers use critical reflection to improve their relationships with such children?);
- our learning from the project.

We didn't identify our conclusions in that way in the article, but we'll do so here.

> *Conclusions about our research topic*
> [The *Children Who Challenge* project] rejects the mainstream's focus on individual children defined in biological terms as exhibiting a pathology or deficit; and it rejects the mainstream's reliance on intervention by an outside 'expert', such as a pharmacist or behaviourist. The focus of *Children Who Challenge* was children-in-contexts, defined socially through one or more competing models (children as possessions, as subjects, as participants and as social actors).

> *Conclusions about our research question*
> Early childhood staff and centres are significant elements of a child's contexts, so the founding methodological and strategic assumption of *Children Who Challenge* was that when staff reflect critically on their current practices around children who challenge, this is a prelude to changing those practices. . . . [E]ach of the thirteen participants reported that they had increased their confidence and ability to respond to children who challenge and that they had initiated strategies in their classroom that had reduced disruptive behaviour, increased children's participation and reduced adults' and children's stress.

> *Our learning from the project*
> [The *Children Who Challenge* approach] counters not just the 'medicalisation' of behaviour defined as problematic or challenging, but also the drift to a technocratic, top-down micro-management of education and, by implication, of children. *Children Who Challenge* poses an alternative – an autonomous, reflexive practitioner-researcher who is a member of a reflexive community that is committed to improving young children's lives by emancipating them.
>
> (Mac Naughton et al. 2007: 54–5)

Further resources: going deeper

In print

Lather, P. (2003) Issues of validity in openly ideological research: between a rock and a soft place, in Y. Lincoln and N. Denzin (eds) *Turning Points in Qualitative Research*, Blue Ridge Summit, PA: Rowan Altamira Press, pp. 185–216.

Reason, P. and Bradbury, H. (eds) (2001) *Handbook of Action Research: Participative Inquiry and Practice*. London: Sage.

Online

ALAR. Action Learning and Action Research Journal. Available at: http://www.alara.net.au/publications

Local stuff. A site on local government in South Australia and inquiry learning with students. Available at: http://www.lga.sa.gov.au/site/page.cfm?u=639

Step 16 Share the lessons of your project

Jane's poster presentation of her action research journey elicited these comments:
> 'I think you told an amazing story of a professional learning journey.'
> 'You may not have PowerPoint, but you have passion and emotion.'

When action researchers (indeed, any researchers) disseminate the lessons of their project, they bring together theory, practice, data, analysis and conclusions. You can share the lessons of your project formally and/or informally. Jane (see above) made a colourful collage to share her journey. Her presentation, while informal, was powerful because she spoke passionately about what she had changed and learnt through her action research project.

If you work in an organization, then how you share the lessons of your action research project will depend on its scope or significance and on your status in the organization. At one end of the scale, you may be required to produce a simple report to your immediate superior, or have a brief meeting with her/him; at the other end, you may be required to produce a substantial report for internal circulation and/or to make a presentation to a small group of colleagues (as Jane did), to a department or to the whole organization.

What you'll need to take Step 16:

Time
- to read this chapter and to reflect on its content;
- to talk with those involved in your project – who may or may not be in an action research group with you – about the issues this chapter raises.

Knowledge
- What have you learnt through your project?
- Who do you want to share your learning with and why?
- What options do you have for sharing your work?

Other resources
- funds to produce reports and/or to attend conferences;
- access to the Internet to upload your stories to an action research site and/or to learn about conferences, journals and other ways in which you can share your work.

A formal, written project report

A formal, written project report organizes your information, ideas and arguments in a clear and coherent way that comes to a conclusion about your research question. It is a highly structured essay, which documents the facts it presents and the sources on which it draws. It describes how and why your project was started; how it was conducted; its results; and the conclusions you drew from its results. As the author of a formal report, you shouldn't assume that your intended readers will have any technical, specialist knowledge (for example, about the action research cycle or the theories underlying it), but you can assume that they have broad general knowledge and are used to analysing written documents such as your report.

A formal project report aims to communicate particular ideas and information to its intended readership to prompt them to act on them. Generally, it is written in the formal, impersonal language of a bureaucrat, because its intended readers are likely to be managers and policy-makers in various bureaucratic organizations in the early childhood field, who read such documents daily as part of their jobs.

Why would I write a formal project report?

Generally, you will write a formal report about your project if you undertook it as part of your job or as a consultancy; or if you received funding (other than from your employer or client) from an external source that was conditional on you writing a formal report.

What is a <u>good</u> formal project report?

In a way, you start to write your formal project report as soon as you start your research project. A good formal report has these characteristics:

- *Clarity*. Write for your intended readership, who may lack your familiarity with the content.
- *Conciseness*. The report should be only as long as it needs to be to achieve its aims. Length is no measure of quality and effectiveness!
- *Comprehensiveness*. The report should contain all the information

necessary to achieve its aims, but include background information (e.g. statistics to justify your claim about the prevalence of a problem) as an appendix to your report, to avoid disrupting the flow of your argument.

- *Accuracy.* Provide accurate information on which readers can base sound decisions to act.

How do I write a good formal report?

There is no comprehensive formula or template for producing a good formal report, as each report has a specific purpose, a specific intended readership and specific criteria of excellence. However, there are some very general steps that the writer/s of any formal report would take:

1 *Plan.* Create a basic structure and then adapt it to acknowledge any specific characteristics of your planned report. For example, a report to an Education Department probably wouldn't include a description of the education sector and a review of the research literature on current curriculum practices, but a report to a government Education Minister may well include such material.

2 *Research.* Define your report's purpose, scope and intended readership. Map the possible sources of information about the report's topic or issue. Find the relevant information, keeping careful track of each source for inclusion in the References/Bibliography.

3 *Organize.* Decide on your chapter headings and on each chapter's sub-headings. Ensure that each piece of information that you have collected relates clearly to your purpose in writing the report – and reject any information that doesn't. Arrange your information into areas or groups with common characteristics, list these areas or groups and then decide the order in which to include them. Arrange your material logically – lead the reader from what they know to the new information and ideas that you are presenting. See *Figure 16.1 The structure of a standard formal report*.

4 *Write.* Keep your formal report simple, concise and to the point. Use short, clear sentences. Each paragraph should present one idea or piece of information; and each paragraph – even each sentence – should relate to the report's topic. Keep your hierarchy of headings as simple as possible; ideally, use just three levels – heading, sub-heading, sub-sub-heading. *Figure 16.2 A model table of contents of a formal research report* uses a three-level hierarchy of headings: '2.1' is a heading, '2.1.2' is a sub-heading, '2.1.2a' is a sub-sub heading.

COVER	Report title; your organization's logo
TITLE PAGE	Title of the report Addressee (for whom it was written) Author/s (name and organization) Date of completion Copyright and ISBN (if appropriate)
TABLE OF CONTENTS	Shows how the report is organized. Lists the chapters and each chapter's major headings, the references and the appendices (if any).
EXECUTIVE SUMMARY	A short, succinct summary of the report and a list of recommendations (if any).
INTRODUCTION TO THE REPORT	
Ch. 1 *Introduction*	States who commissioned the report and why; states the project's terms of reference. Describes the problem at hand, states the research question that drove the project and outlines the significance of the problem and of the research question ('Why and to whom does this matter?'). Summarizes the main points of the report and its major recommendations (if any).
BODY OF THE REPORT Presents current thinking (e.g. research findings) on the report's topic; describes how you collected and analysed your data; and presents the data and your analysis of it.	
Ch. 2 *Literature review*	Presents other researchers' and commentators' results and conclusions about the research topic; highlights their significance (if any) for this project.
Ch. 3 *Methodology*	Presents the project's theoretical foundation and its associated methodology and methods.
Ch. 4 *Results*	Presents the results of collecting information about the topic, oriented to answering the project's research question.
Ch. 5 *Analysis*	Describes how the results link with the project's theoretical foundation and with its methodology. Explains the results from the project's perspective.

Figure 16.1   The structure of a standard formal report.   *(Continued overleaf)*

Figure 16.1 continued

CONCLUSIONS AND RECOMMENDATIONS	
Ch. 6 *Conclusions*	Summarizes the results and analysis and explains why and to whom they are significant. Presents no new material.
Ch. 7 *Recommendations*	Presents options for action, based on the report's conclusions. May recommend a best option.
REFERENCES/ BIBLIOGRAPHY	Lists (using a standard referencing system) the print and online resources the report refers to.
APPENDICES	Supporting data, e.g. tables, charts.

5 *Substantiate*. Substantiate each claim as you make it. Ensure that your conclusions and recommendations draw visibly on your substantiated claims.

6 *Recommend*. Make definite recommendations. If something must be done, say so; if the issue needs more investigation or examination, say so. If you think that a recommendation will not be accepted, offer alternatives. Provide specific information about each recommendation (e.g. its likely costs, benefits and disadvantages).

7 *Read and revise*. Read your report slowly and carefully to detect typographical errors. If possible, ask someone unfamiliar with the report to read it for you – fresh eyes often see mistakes that authors miss as they read their words yet again. (A spell-check programme spots only mis-spelt words; it won't spot inappropriate words or words remaining from a cut-and-paste.) Then read your report again through the eyes and experience of its intended readership, to see whether they will find it easy to read.

8 *Prepare your report for submission*. See *Figure 16.3 A checklist for writers*.

9 *Prepare your report for printing* (if appropriate). See *Figure 16.4 A pre-print checklist*.

Winter (1989) suggested that, unlike a standard formal project report, in an action research report, 'situations cannot be reduced to a consensus, but must be presented in terms of the multiplicity of viewpoints which make up a situation' and that an action research report should have a, 'plural structure . . . [of] . . . various accounts and various critiques of these accounts, and ending not with conclusions (intended to be convincing) but with questions and possibilities (intended to be "relevant" in various ways for different reasons).'

(i) Executive summary

1. Introduction to the report
   1.1 The project's topic and terms of reference
   1.2 The project's research question

2. Review of the research literature concerning the topic
   2.1 The substantive literature
       2.1.1 The history of the topic
       2.1.2 Current approaches to the topic
             a) 'Top down' approaches
             b) 'Bottom up' approaches
   2.2 The methodological literature
   2.3 Relevance of the literature to this project's approach to the topic

3. Recent activity addressing the topic
   3.1 Government activity
       3.1.1 Local government activity
       3.1.2 Central/federal government activity
   3.2 Non-government activity
   3.3 Appropriateness of action research as a way to approach the topic

4. The Project
   4.1 Aims and objectives
   4.2 Methodology
   4.3 Operation
   4.4 Outcomes

5. Conclusions
   5.1 Lessons of the action research project
   5.2 Implications of the project for policy

6. Recommendations

References/Bibliography

Appendices

Figure 16.2 A model table of contents of a formal research report.

An article in an academic, peer-reviewed journal

An article in an academic, peer-reviewed journal shares two characteristics with a formal, written project report: each organizes your ideas, arguments and information into a clear and coherent whole that comes to a conclusion

- Did you create an outline or plan of what you intended to write?
- Is your message clear and exact?
- Is the most important information at the start of the report?
- Is there any repetition (1) within chapters and (2) between chapters?
- Did you over-generalize?
- Did you use simple words, phrases and sentences?
- Did you use the 'active' (not passive) voice?
- Are the headings in consistent formats?
- Are all the sources you have cited in the report listed in your references or bibliography?
- Are there any sources in your references or bibliography that aren't cited in the report?
- Have you ensured that that each and every reference is in the correct format?
- Did you proof-read the report for errors in a spelling, grammar, syntax and formatting?
- Has someone else read the finished report for you to eliminate ambiguity and maximize clarity?

Figure 16.3   A checklist for writers.

- Do you have a written quote from the printer itemizing the order, including price, binding, bundling (for distribution), payment and delivery date?   ☐
- Do you have a copy of the report to retain and another copy to give the printer?   ☐
- What type/s and colour/s of paper will you use? Have you checked whether your choices affect legibility?   ☐
- Will you supply the printer with the report on paper or on disc? If on disc, is it compatible with the printer's system?   ☐

Figure 16.4   A pre-print checklist.

about your research question; and each communicates particular ideas and information to particular readers or audiences to prompt them to act on it.

A journal article – like a formal report – is a highly structured essay, which describes how and why your project was started; how it was conducted; its results; and the conclusions you drew from its results. It also documents the facts it presents and the sources on which it draws. Generally, it is written in formal, academic language, but nonetheless, you should make it as accessible as possible. You can assume that your readers will have broad knowledge of your field and are used to analysing journal articles such as yours. Your readers will primarily be academics, researchers and students in the early childhood field, but they may also include managers and policy-makers of bureaucratic organizations in the early childhood field. Some may well have detailed knowledge of the topic of your action research project, but virtually none will have your intimate, detailed knowledge of the project, so remember this as you write your article.

How do I prepare a good article for an academic journal?

The similarities between a formal, written project report and an article written for an academic journal mean that much of the advice about producing a formal, written project report also applies to writing an article for a journal. Those similarities also mean that a researcher will often use their formal, written project report as the starting point for a subsequent journal article, rather than starting from scratch. However, readers of an article in an academic journal will expect it to be written in 'academic' language and to display significant scholarship; and they are likely to be less concerned with immediate practical applications to policy in the area. Go through *Figure 16.4 A pre-print checklist*, remembering that not all of its elements will apply to an article in an academic journal.

Why would I write an article and submit it to a journal?

As with a formal project report, you may be required – as a condition of your funding – to submit an article to an academic, peer-reviewed journal. Irrespective of such requirements, an action researcher would want to share the lessons of their project with others so that they can either improve their (professional) social practices or increase justice and equity in their specific circumstances.

A book chapter

A book chapter in an edited collection is another way to share the results of your action research project that is similar to a journal article. An edited collection is a book about a particular topic, in which each chapter is written by a different author (or team of authors). It may be that your chapter will appear in an edited collection intended to appeal primarily to academics and students in the early childhood field. In this case, you should write your chapter in much the same way as you would write an article for an academic journal. Alternatively, your chapter may appear in an edited collection intended to appeal to a broader readership, including not just academics and students but also (for example) managers, policy-makers and practitioners in the early childhood field. In this case, you should concentrate on the outcomes and conclusions and try to make the literature review and discussion of methodology as succinct as possible. Go through *Figure 16.3 A checklist for writers*, remembering that not all of its elements will apply to a chapter in an edited collection.

An article in a specialist magazine

Early childhood – like many fields and occupations – has both its own academic journals (national and international) intended primarily for an academic readership and its own specialist magazines (generally local or national) intended for a broader readership, including practitioners, policy-makers, managers and parents. These specialist magazines are generally commercial concerns, available either by subscription or via newsagents.

An article in a specialist magazine aims to inform readers about your action research project. However, because of the magazine's broad readership, you should describe your project, its outcome and your conclusions clearly and concisely and in the style of an everyday conversation (albeit about a specialist topic!). Avoid writing in a formal (bureaucratic or academic) style, because your readers will be less familiar with this style of writing and probably don't use it themselves. Further, while many readers of a specialist magazine will be familiar with the early childhood field in general (after all, this is why they've bought the magazine), they are unlikely to be familiar with research techniques or with debates and discussions between writers and researchers (those 'professional conversations') that are explored in the literature reviews in more formal publications.

Why would I write an article and submit it to a specialist magazine?

It is unlikely that you will be required – as a condition of your funding – to submit an article to a specialist magazine, so the decision is likely to be all yours. Your reasons for doing so are to enable others to improve their professional practice or to increase justice and equity in their circumstances; and a specialist magazine's readers are either involved directly in the early childhood field, or at least interested in it.

How do I prepare a good magazine article?

Once again, much of the advice about producing a formal, written project report also applies to writing an article for a specialist magazine. However, a magazine's broad readership means that you should work hard to ensure that your article is easy to read and to understand. Ensure that its structure is accessible, that your material is easy to follow and that your writing is clear, concise and easily accessible by a non-specialist reader. Use short, clear sentences; ensure that each paragraph presents one idea or piece of information; and ensure that each paragraph – even each sentence – relates to the topic of your article. Finally, go through *Figure 16.3 A checklist for writers*, remembering that not all of its elements (e.g. those concerning references) will apply to an article in a specialist magazine.

A page on a project website

Action researchers (including those in education) are using websites increasingly to share the lessons of their projects. At the end of this chapter is a list of such websites. A website allows you to bring your story to life by, for example, including graphics, photos and other images. Many existing websites require new material to be submitted in a particular format or according to an existing template, so check whether this is the case *before* you try to upload your material.

Alternatively, you could (as an individual researcher or as a group of researchers) develop your own weblog – your 'blog' – to share your lessons on the web. A blog is a web-based diary or log of issues and ideas that you customize to your needs. To learn more, visit en.wikipedia.org/wiki/Blog. At the end of this chapter is a list of educational blogs.

A formal presentation to a conference

A formal presentation to a conference (often referred to as 'a conference paper' or 'a paper to a conference') resembles a formal, written project report in two ways. Each organizes your information, ideas and arguments into a clear and coherent whole that comes to a conclusion about your research question; and each communicates particular ideas and information to particular readers (or audiences) to prompt them to act on it. Specific audiences for a conference presentation include managers and policy-makers of bureaucratic organizations in the early childhood field, together with researchers, students, teachers, politicians, journalists, your colleagues and the general public.

Why would I make a formal presentation to a conference?

As with a formal, written project report, you may be required – as a condition of your funding – to make a formal presentation to a conference. Action researchers have a further, specific reason to share the lessons of their project. Action researchers for *professional* change aim to improve their chosen (professional) social practices and to increase knowledge about them in order to increase the effectiveness of those practices; and so they would want to share the lessons of their project with others so that they can make equivalent improvements to their (professional) social practices. Action researchers for *social* change aim to improve their chosen social practices and to increase knowledge about them in order to increase justice and equity in their specific ('local') circumstances; and so they would want to share the lessons of their project with others so that they, too, can increase justice and equity in their specific circumstances.

How do I prepare a good conference paper?

Since a formal presentation to a conference is very similar to a formal, written project report, a researcher will often use their formal, written project report as the basis and starting point for a subsequent conference paper, rather than starting from scratch. However, a conference paper differs in important ways from a formal, written project report and so it requires a different approach. The differences derive partly from the fact that a conference paper is presented in person. A presenter can't guarantee that they will be the centre of their audience's attention throughout the presentation. The audience may be distracted by, for example, the temperature and humidity of the room, what other people in the room are doing . . . even by smells of lunch drifting in from an adjacent room! Further, the presenter must make their paper easy to understand, because their audience will only hear them present it once – unlike the reader of a report, who can re-read any parts of it that they can't understand the first time.

To deal with audiences' distractions and to help them to understand the paper, many conference presenters use some form of visual aid, such as overheads or a PowerPoint™ presentation. A visual aid should maintain the audience's attention by reinforcing what a presenter is saying; and it should increase the audience's understanding of a paper's contents by enabling them to see it as well as hear it. A visual aid must be an attractive and informative adjunct to what a presenter says, without distracting audiences from the presenter.

Edward Tufte (2006) has criticized many aspects of the PowerPoint™ software:

- Presenters sometimes use it to guide them, not to enlighten their audience.
- Computer projectors' low resolution leads presenters to present simplistic tables, charts and even text (a PowerPoint™ slide usually contains only about 40 words, i.e. barely eight seconds of reading).
- The program forces ideas into a deep hierarchy of bullet points that encourages simplistic and linear thinking (cf. handouts, which allow readers to relate items as they wish).
- Poorly designed templates and default settings result in poor typography and chart layout.

Another difference between a conference paper and a formal, written project report is that a presenter has only a limited period of time in which to present their material. Most conference presenters are allocated between 15 minutes and an hour to present their paper, which is often considerably less time than it would take to read out a formal project report. Consequently, conference presenters generally exclude or summarize many elements of a formal report, including the references, the literature review, a discussion of the project's methodology and some or all of the detailed evidence (especially if this is an appendix) supporting the conclusions. The amount of material excluded depends on the time allocated to presentation: a 15-minute presentation can do little more than introduce the project, outline the results and draw conclusions; an hour-long presentation can give a far more comprehensive description of a project. However much material you have to exclude from your presentation due to time, you should always have a document that contains every part of the material and you should have copies of this document on hand when you present, so that if someone wishes to know more about an aspect that you've had to exclude, you can give them a copy.

You may have more or less interaction with your audience, again depending on the time allocated to your presentation. The longer the time allocated to it, the more you can allow time for questions and comments from the audience. (The exception is a keynote speech, which isn't usually accompanied by time for audience questions and comments.) Even if your audience is unable to raise comments or questions at the time, individuals may well talk to you afterwards. Once again, you should have copies of your full paper available to give to such people if appropriate.

An informal presentation to colleagues, children or parents

An informal presentation to colleagues, children or parents can take many different forms. For example, in the final session of the *Learning to Learn Engagement through Student Voice* project, participants all gave presentations. Glenda gave them a suggested structure for their presentations, but they chose whether to follow it or not. The outline was as follows:

- Your research question
- Your changing understandings about what student engagement means
- Your most significant learning and what produced this
- Your most meaningful case study of a specific child
- Your most meaningful illustrations of different forms of engagement
- Your current inquiry questions/issues.

Some participants shared their learning through a poster, others used Power-Point presentations that included photos and key moments from their journals. There is no right way to do this. The important thing is to know how long you have for your presentation and what your colleagues hope to learn from you and then to structure your presentation accordingly.

Deciding how best to share the lessons

This chapter has considered various ways in which you can share the lessons of your action research project. They are not mutually exclusive and there is certainly no 'best' way. Use *Figure 16.1 Deciding how best to share the lessons* to assist you to decide which way of disseminating results is most appropriate for your purposes.

Taking Step 16: a case from practice

It can be unnerving and unsettling to share your work with others, even if you've done so before. The best way to gain ideas and confidence is to see how other action researchers have done it. Here are some sources of such inspiration.

Reports

Study the reports of (mainly secondary) teacher action research in New Zealand. They give a flavour of the different ways in which individual teachers can formally report their research. http://www.nzqa.net/ncea/for-schools/actionresearch.html

Articles and chapters

Read *Action Research* and *Educational Action Research*. These journals publish articles by action researchers for *professional* change and action researchers for *social* change.

Action research for **professional** *change*
O'Rourke, M. and Harrison, C. (2004) The introduction of new technologies: new possibilities for early childhood pedagogy, *Australian Journal of Early Childhood*, 29: 11–18.

Action research for **social** *change*
Wilson, A. (2004) Indigenous knowledge recovery is indigenous empowerment, *The American Indian Quarterly*, 28(3–4): 359–72.

CHOICE OF MEDIUM

	PRINT			ONLINE	PRESENTATION	
	A formal, written project report	An article in an academic, peer-reviewed journal	An article in a specialist magazine	A project website	A formal presentation to a conference	An informal presentation to colleagues, children or parents
Whom will I reach through this medium?						
What is my aim in sharing the lessons?						
Can I use this medium well?						
Am I confident to use this medium?						
Are my results, analyses or conclusions in a form that looks good in this medium?						
Do I have sufficient resources to use this medium well?						
Can I meet any deadlines associated with this medium?						
Do I need permission from anyone (e.g. concerning copyright) to use this medium?						

Figure 16.1 Deciding how best to share the lessons

Conference papers

Action research for professional *change*
Meade, A., Ryder, D. and Henroid, S. (2004) Promoting dialogue in early child-hood education centres of innovation, Keynote address to New Zealand Action Research Network Conference, 8 and 9 July 2004, Christchurch. Available at: http://www.minedu.govt.nz/index.cfm?layout=document&documentid= 9850&indexid=8313&indexparentid= 8303

Action research for social *change*
Suda, L. (2006) Building community capacity through student led action research, paper presented to the Learning Communities Conference, Brisbane, 24–27 September. Available at: www.educationfoundation.org.au/downloads/ Liz%20Suda%20Conference%20paper.pdf

Websites

(N.B. These websites primarily host examples of action research for *professional* change.)

Classroom action research
Visit this site to see how other teachers have shared the lessons of their action research projects and review the format that they use. http:// www.madison.k12.wi.us/sod/car/search.cgi

Queens University
Visit this site to see how MEd and BEd have students shared the lessons of their action research projects. http://educ.queensu.ca/~ar/

Further resources: going deeper

In print

Alston, M. and Bowles, W. (1998) *Research for Social Workers*. St. Leonard's, NSW: Allen & Unwin. Chapter 14 'Influencing policy and practice' pp. 261–82.
Anderson, J. and Poole, M. (1997) *Assignment and Thesis Writing*, 3rd edn. Milton, Qld: Jacaranda Wiley.
Blaxter, L., Hughes, C. and Tight, M. (2001) *How to Research*, 2nd edn. Buckingham: Open University Press. Chapter 8. 'Writing up' (pp. 227–52); Chapter 9. 'Finishing off' (pp. 253–76).
Fisher, K. and Phelps, R. (2006) Recipe or performing? Challenging conventions for writing an action research thesis, *Action Research*, 4(2): 143–64.

Greenwood, D., Brydon-Miller, M. and Shafer, C. (2006) Intellectual property and action research, *Action Research*, 4(1): 81–94.

Herr, K. and Anderson, G. (2005) *The Action Research Dissertation: A Guide for Students and Faculty*. Thousand Oaks, CA: Sage Publications.

Online

Badke, W. (2002) Writing research essays in North American academic institutions: a guide for students of all nations. Available at: www.acts.twu.ca/lbr/research_essays.htm

Dick, B. (1999) Qualitative action research: improving the rigour and economy. Available at: http://www.uq.net.au/action_research/arp/rigour2.html

Fox, N. J. (1995) Intertextuality and the writing of social research, *Electronic Journal of Sociology*. 1(2). Available at: www.sociology.org/vol001.002/fox.maintext.html

Blogging resources

Top 100 Education Blogs. Available at: http://www.livemocha.com/pages/resources/education-blog-list

Department of Education and Children's Services, Victoria, Australia. Available at: http://www.education.vic.gov.au/teacher/Global/blogs.htm

References

Alderson, P. and Morrow, V. (2004) *Ethics, Social Research and Consulting with Children and Young People*. Ilford: Barnardos.

Alexander, K. (2007) Searching for equity: how databases can work for you, *CEIEC Members' Briefing*, 6(1). Available at: education-ceiec@unimelb.edu.au

Argyris, C. and Schön, D. (1974) *Theory in Practice: Increasing Professional Effectiveness*. San Francisco: Jossey-Bass.

Argyris, C. and Schön, D. (1978) *Organizational Learning: A Theory of Action Perspective*. Reading, MA: Addison-Wesley.

Arlin, P. (1999) The wise teacher: a developmental model of teaching, *Theory into Practice*, 38(1): 12–17.

Averill, J. (2006) Getting started: initiating critical ethnography and community-based action research in a programme of rural health studies, *International Journal of Qualitative Methods*, 5(2): 1–8.

Bailey, B. (2004) What effect does using e-mail to communicate with staff have on my position as an itinerant teacher of the visually impaired? *Classroom Action Research*. Available at: http://www.madison.k12.wi.us/sod/car/abstracts. cgi?s=502 (Accessed 9 January 2008).

Bartlett, S. and Burton, D. (2006) Practitioner research or descriptions of classroom practice? A discussion of teachers investigating their classrooms, *Educational Action Research*, 14(3): 395–405.

Berge, B.-M. and Ve, H. (2000) *Action Research for Gender Equity*. Buckingham: Open University Press.

Blaxter, L., Hughes, C. and Tight, M. (2001) *How to Research*, 2nd edn. Buckingham: Open University Press.

Bleakley, A. (1999) From reflective practice to holistic reflexivity, *Studies in Higher Education*, 24: 315–30.

Branigan, E. (2003) But how can you prove it? Issues of rigour in action research, *Journal of the HEIA*, 10(3): 37–8.

Brookfield, S. D. (1995) *Becoming a Critically Reflective Teacher*. San Francisco: Jossey-Bass Inc.

Bruce, C. (2007) Inquiry page: learning begins with questions. Available at: http://www.inquiry.uiuc.edu/inquiry/definition.php (Accessed 21 January 2008).

Brydon-Miller, M. and Greenwood, D. (2006) A re-examination of the relationship between action research and human subjects review processes, *Action Research*, 4(1): 117–28.

Campbell, S. (2001) The description and definition of a justice disposition in young children, unpublished PhD thesis, the University of Melbourne.

Campbell, S., Saitta S. and Smith, K. (1999) Bungee jumping in the classroom: action research in early childhood. Paper presented to the Australian Early Childhood Conference, Looking In, Looking Forward, Looking Beyond, Darwin, 14–17 July.

Carr, W. and Kemmis, S. (1986) *Becoming Critical: Education, Knowledge and Action Research*. Lewes: Falmer.

CEIEC (2006) *A Report to the City of Melbourne*. Melbourne: Centre for Equity and Innovation in Early Childhood, the University of Melbourne.

Charles, C. (1998) *Introduction to Educational Research*, 3rd edn. New York: Longman.

Cherry, N. (1999) *Action Research: A Pathway to Action, Knowledge and Learning*. Melbourne: RMIT Publishers.

Coady, M. (2001) Ethics in early childhood research, in G. Mac Naughton, I. Siraj-Blatchford and S. Rolfe (eds), *Doing Early Childhood Research: International Perspectives on Theory and Research*, Sydney: Allen and Unwin, pp. 64–74.

Cochran-Smith, M. and Lytle, S. (1993) *Inside/Outside: Teacher Research and Knowledge*. New York: Teachers College Press.

Coghlan, D. and Brannick, T. (2004) *Doing Action Research in Your Own Organization*, 2nd edn. Thousand Oaks, CA: Sage Publications.

Cornwall, A. and Jewkes, R. (1995) What is participatory research? *Social Science and Medicine*, 41(12): 1667–76.

Crane, P. (2004) Rigour or rigor mortis? The small 'r' approach to research. Paper presented to the conference, National Action Research Training for Reconnect and Home Advice, Sydney, 10–12 November.

Cranton, P. (1996) *Professional Development as Transformative Learning: New Perspectives for Teachers of Adults*. San Francisco: Jossey-Bass Inc.

Crotty, M. (1998) *The Foundations of Social Research*. London: Sage.

Davies, B. (1994) *Poststructuralist Theory and Classroom Practice*. Geelong: Deakin University Press.

Davis, K. (2004) Approaches to teaching young children about indigenous Australians, unpublished PhD thesis, the University of Melbourne.

Davis, K., Mac Naughton, G. and Smith, K. (2007) Researching with children: the challenges and possibilities for building 'child friendly' research, in A. Hatch (ed.) *Handbook on Qualitative Research in Early Childhood*. London: Routledge, pp. 167–84.

Davis, K., Mac Naughton, G. and Smith, K. (2005) A rhizoanalysis of preschool children's constructions of cultural and 'racial' diversity, paper presented at 13th Reconceptualizing Early Childhood Education Conference: Research, Theory And Practice, University of Wisconsin, Madison, WI, 16–20 October.

Department of Education (2004) *Research into Action*. Hobart, Tasmania: Department of Education.

Detardo-Bora, K. A. (2004) Action research in a world of positivist-oriented review boards, *Action Research*, 2: 237–53.

Dick, B. (1999a) Qualitative action research: improving the rigour and economy. Available at: http://www.uq.net.au/action_research/arp/rigour2.html (Accessed 27 February 2008).

Dick, B. (1999b) Sources of rigour in action research: addressing the issues of trustworthiness and credibility, paper presented to the Association for Qualitative Research conference, Melbourne, 6–10 July.

Diebling, K., Mackman, L. and Myers, K. (2006) Putting the pieces together. Available at: http://www.madison.k12.wi.us/sod/car/search.cgi

Eikeland, O. (2006) Condescending ethics and action research: extended review article, *Action Research*, 4: 37–47.

Farrell, A. (2005). Ethics and research with children, in A. Farrell (ed.) *Ethical Research with Children*. Milton Keynes: Open University Press, pp. 1–14.

Fay, B. (1987) *Critical Social Science: Liberation and its Limits*. London: Polity Press.

Feldman, A. (2007) Validity and quality in action research, *Educational Action Research*, 15(1): 21–32.

Fleming, P. (2002) Lines of flight, *Ephemera*, 2(4): 193–208.

Foucault, M. (1977) Truth and power, in C. Gordon (ed.) *Michel Foucault: Power/Knowledge: Selected Interviews and Other Writings 1972–1977*. Sussex: The Harvester Press, pp. 109–33.

Foucault, M. (1985) *The Use of Pleasure: A History of Sexuality*, Vol. 1. London: Penguin.

Foucault, M. (1997) The ethics of the concern for self as a practice of freedom. Trans. R Hurley and others. In P. Rabinow (ed.) *Michel Foucault: Ethics, Subjectivity and Truth. The Essential Works of Michel Foucault, 1954–1984*, Vol. 1. London: The Penguin Press, pp. 281–301.

Foucault, M. (2001) Fearless speech, Los Angeles, *Semiotext(e)*, 9.

Freire, P. (1996) *Pedagogy of the Oppressed*. London: Penguin Books.

Gaffeney, G. (1999) Affinity diagramming, information and design. Usability Techniques Series. Available at: http:www.infodesign.com

Giroux, H. (1991) Modernism, postmodernism and feminism: rethinking the boundaries of educational discourse, in H. A. Giroux (ed.) *Postmodernism, Feminism and Cultural Politics: Redrawing Educational Boundaries*. New York: State University of New York Press, pp. 1–59.

Gore, J. (1993) *The Struggle for Pedagogies: Critical and Feminist Discourses as Regimes of Truth*. New York: Routledge.

Grundy, S. (1987) *Curriculum: Product or Praxis?* London: The Falmer Press.

Hamelink, C. J. (2000) Mass media performance: do people matter? In K. Kersten and W. E. Biernatzki (eds) *Value and Communication: Critical Humanistic Perspectives*. Cresskill, NJ: Hampton Press, Inc. pp. 139–63.

Hammersley, M. (1992) *What's Wrong with Ethnography?* London: Routledge.

Handy, C. (1986) *Understanding Organizations*, 3rd edn. Harmondsworth: Penguin Books.

Hart, C. (2001) *Doing a Literature Search: A Comprehensive Guide for the Social Sciences.* Thousand Oaks, CA: Sage Publications.

Heikkinen, H. L. T., Huttunen, R. and Syrjala, L. (2006) Action research as narrative: five principles for validation, *Educational Action Research*, 15(1): 5–19.

Hilson, A. I. (2006) And they shall be known by their deeds: ethics and politics in action research, *Action Research*, 4(1): 23–36.

Hughes, P. and Mac Naughton, G. (1999) *Communication in Early Childhood Services: A Practical Guide*. Melbourne: RMIT Press.

Kay, J. (2004) *Good Practice in the Early Years*. London and New York: Continuum International Publishing Group.

Kemmis, S. (1993) Action research and social movements: a challenge for policy research, *Education Policy Analysis Archives*, 1(1). Available at: http://epaa. asu.edu/epaa/v1n1.html (Accessed 1 November 2007).

Kemmis, S. (2007) Participatory action research and the public sphere, *Educational Action Research*, 14(4): 459–76.

Kemmis, S. and McTaggart, R. (eds) (1988) *The Action Research Planner*, 3rd edn. Victoria: Deakin University Press.

Khanlou, N. and Peter, E. (2005) Participatory action research: considerations for ethical review, *Social Science Medicine*, 60(10): 2333–40.

Killion, J. P. and Todnem, R. (1991) A process for personal theory-building, *Educational Leadership*, 48(6): 14–16.

King, J. and Lonnquist, P. (1992) A review of writing on action research (1944–Present). ED355664, ERIC Digest.

Kopp, S. (2005) Educating for 21st century thinking and learning. Education that Transforms the Intellect Accountability, Leadership and Organizational Development Challenges, Workshop presentation. Available at: http://www.marshall.edu/president/presentation/faculty/FACULTY%20Critical%20Thinking.pps.

Lather, P. A. (1991) *Getting Smart: Feminist Research and Pedagogy with/in the Postmodern*. London: Routledge.

Lewin, K. (1946) Action research and minority problems, *Journal of Social Issues*, 2: 34–46.

Lundy, P. and McGovern, M. (2006) The ethics of silence: action research, community 'truth-telling' and post-conflict transition in the North of Ireland, *Action Research*, 4: 49–64.

MacIsaac, D. (1996) The critical theory of Jürgen Habermas. Available at: http://www.physics.nau.edu/- danmac (Accessed 1 February 2008).

Mac Naughton, G. (2000) *Rethinking Gender in Early Childhood Education*. Sydney: Allen and Unwin.

Mac Naughton, G. (2005) *Doing Foucault in Early Childhood*. New York: Routledge.

Mac Naughton, G., Hughes, P. and Smith, K. (2007) Rethinking approaches to working with children who challenge: action learning for emancipatory practice, *International Journal of Early Childhood*, 39(1): 39–57.

Mac Naughton, G., Rolfe, S. and Siraj-Blatchford, I. (eds) (2001) *Doing Early Childhood Research: International Perspectives on Theory and Practice*. Sydney: Allen and Unwin.

Mac Naughton, G. and Smith, K. (2005) Exploring ethics and difference: the choices and challenges of researching with children, in A. Farrell (ed.) *Exploring Ethical Research with Children*. Buckingham: Open University Press, pp. 112–13.

Mac Naughton, G., Smith, K. and Davis, K. (2008) Working and reworking children's performance of 'Whiteness' in early childhood education, in M. O'Loughlin and R. Johnson (eds) *Working the Space In Between: Pedagogical Possibilities in Rethinking Children's Subjectivity*. New York: SUNY Press.

Mansfield, N. (2000) *Subjectivity: Theories of the Self from Freud to Haraway*. Sydney: Allen and Unwin.

Marshall, C. and Rossman, G.B. (2006) *Designing Qualitative Research*, 4th edn. Thousand Oaks, CA: Sage.

Maxwell, J. A. (2005) *Qualitative Research Design: An Interactive Approach*, 2nd edn. London: Sage.

Mayring, P. (2000) Qualitative content analysis, *Forum: Qualitative Research*, 1(2). Available at: http://www.qualitative-research.net/fqs-texte/2-00/2-00mayring-e.htm (Accessed 19 April 2004).

McTaggart, R. (1992) Study a graduate course in participatory action research: an initiative in interactive global pedagogy. Posted from rmct@deakin.oz.au to list EDAD-L <EDAD-L@wvnvm.bitnet> 2 Oct 1992.

Meade, A., Ryder, D. and Henroid, S. (2004) Promoting dialogue in early childhood education centres of innovation. Keynote Address to New Zealand Action Research Network Conference, Christchurch, 8–9 July.

Mezirow, J. (1990) *Fostering Critical Reflection in Adulthood: A Guide to Transformative and Emancipatory Learning*. San Francisco: Jossey-Bass.

O'Brien, R. (2001) An overview of the methodological approach of action research, in R. Richardson (ed.) *Theory and Practice of Action Research*. João Pessoa, Brazil: Universidade Federal da Paraíba. (English version) Available at: http://www.web.ca/~robrien/papers/arfinal.html (Accessed 2 February 2007).

Olcay, M. (2007) Exploring the challenges and possibilities for educators in honouring children's voices in early childhood curricula, unpublished Masters thesis, the University of Melbourne.

Peters, J. M. (1999) The DATA-DATA model, paper presented to the International Human Science Research Conference, Sheffield, 20–22 July.

Rabinow, P. (ed.) (1997) *Ethics*. New York: The New Press. (Quoting Foucault, M. (1984) 'The ethics of the concern of the self as a practice of freedom'. Interview published in *Concordia: Revisita internacional de filosophia*. 6. [July–December] pp. 96–116.)

Revans, R. (1982) *The Origins and Growth of Action Learning*. London: Chartwell-Bratt.

Riel, M. (2007) Understanding action research. Center for Collaborative Action Research. Available at: http://cadres.pepperdine.edu/ccar/define.html (Accessed 1 February 2008).

Robertson, J. (2000) The three Rs of action research methodology: reciprocity, reflexivity and reflection-on-reality, *Educational Action Research*, (2): 307–26.

Schmuck, R. (2006) *Practical Action Research for Change*. Thousand Oaks, CA: Corwin Press.

Scriven, M. and Paul. R. (1996) Defining critical thinking: a draft statement for the National, Council for Excellence in Critical Thinking. Available at: http://www.criticalthinking.org/university/univclass/Defining.html (Accessed 3 February 2008).

Silverman, D. (1993) *Interpreting Qualitative Data*. Thousand Oaks, CA: Sage Publications.

Smith, D. and Lovat, T. (1990) *Curriculum: Action on Reflection*. Sydney: Social Science Press.

Smith, K. (2004) Reconceptualising observation in early childhood settings, unpublished PhD thesis, the University of Melbourne.

Smith, R. (2001) Equality as a part of algebra: How far can one kindergarten class go? Available at: http://www.madison.k12.wi.us/sod/car/search.cgi (Accessed 1 February 2008).

Sommers, W., Montie, J., York-Barr, J. and Ghere, G. (2005) *Reflective Practice to Improve Schools: An Action Guide for Educators*. Thousand Oaks, CA: Corwin Press.

Swepson, P. (2000) Reconciling action research and science, paper presented to the Action Research World Congress, Ballarat, 5–9 September.

Taylor, L. (2007) Reflective practice as a process of change, unpublished PhD thesis, the University of Melbourne.

Tufte, E. R. (2006) *The Cognitive Style of PowerPoint*, 2nd edn. Cheshire, CT: Graphics Press.

Weems, L. (2006) Unsettling politics, locating ethics: representations of reciprocity in postpositivist inquiry, *Qualitative Inquiry*, 12(5): 994–1011.

Winter, R. (1989) *Learning from Experience*. London: Falmer.

Winter, R. and Munn-Giddings, C. (2001) *A Handbook for Action Research in Health and Social Care*. London: Routledge.

Yost, D, Sentner, S. and Forlenza-Bailey, A. (2000) An examination of the construct of critical reflection: implications for teacher education programming in the 21st century, *Journal of Teacher Education*, 51: 39–49.

Zeichner, K. (2001) Educational action research, in P. Reason and H. Bradbury (eds) *Handbook of Action Research: Participative Inquiry and Practice*. Thousand Oaks, CA: Sage, pp. 273–83.

Zeni, J. (2005) A guide to ethical issues in action research, in K. Sheehy, M. Hind, J. Rix and K. Simmons (eds) *Ethics and Research in Inclusive Education: Values into Practice*. London: Routledge Falmer, pp. 205–14.

Author Index

Subject Index